中国的世界遗产
CHINA'S
WORLD HERITAGES

《中国的世界遗产》编写组 编

北京语言大学出版社
BEIJING LANGUAGE AND CULTURE
UNIVERSITY PRESS

图书在版编目（CIP）数据

中国的世界遗产：汉、英 /《中国的世界遗产》编写组编.－北京：北京语言大学出版社，2008.10
ISBN 978-7-5619-2191-3

Ⅰ.中… Ⅱ.中… Ⅲ.①名胜古迹－简介－中国－汉、英②自然保护区－简介－中国－汉、英 Ⅳ.K928.7 S759.992

中国版本图书馆CIP数据核字(2008)第150297号

书　　名	中国的世界遗产	
项目执行	苗　强	
编写者	陈垣铭　江边　陆平	
英文翻译	Matthew Trueman　李　碧	
责任编辑	陈维昌　吴小芬　徐　雁	
英文编缉	侯晓娟　武思敏	
平面设计	闫志杰　张　雷	
版式设计	北京鑫联必升文化发展有限公司	
责任印制	汪学发	

出版发行　北京语言大学出版社
社　　址　北京市海淀区学院路15号　邮政编码：100083
网　　址　www.blcup.com
电　　话　编辑部 010-8230 3647
　　　　　发行部 010-8230 3648/3591/3651/3080
　　　　　读者服务部 010-8230 3653/3908
　　　　　网上订购电话 010-8230 3668
　　　　　客户服务信箱 service@blcup.net
印　　刷　北京新丰印刷厂
经　　销　全国新华书店
版　　次　2008年10月第1版　2008年10月第1次印刷
开　　本　787毫米×1092毫米　1/16　印张：13.25
字　　数　390千字　印数：1—2000册
书　　号　ISBN 978-7-5619-2191-3/H.08180
　　　　　06500

部分图片提供：时代图库
凡有印装质量问题，本社负责调换。电话：010-8230 3590

序言

遍赏中国遗产盛景
感受华夏文明精粹

  中国是世界上遗产资源最丰富的国家之一。自1985年中国加入《保护世界文化和自然遗产公约》以来，中国的遗产总数已经达到37项，数量总额名列世界第三位。中国的37处世界遗产不仅属于中国，而且属于全世界。

  《中国的世界遗产》以中国的文物古迹和自然景观被列入《世界遗产名录》的时间为线索，通过大量精美的图片和流畅生动的文字，向世人展现了中国的壮丽河山和中华民族的文明遗迹。

  明清故宫，天坛，明清皇家陵寝等帝王宫阙陵墓标志着古代社会权力的至高无上；莫高窟，孔庙、孔府、孔林，龙门石窟，青城山等文化景观集合了中国的佛、道、儒等文化艺术精华；颐和园，承德避暑山庄，苏州园林等园林景观体现了典型的东方文化和审美观念；泰山，庐山，黄山，峨眉山，九寨沟，黄龙等山水奇观蕴含了"天人合一"的思想文化……大自然的沧海桑田和几千年的中华文明，为我们铺开了世界遗产的巨幅精美画卷。

  希望《中国的世界遗产》能带领您走进中国人的精神世界，深入中国人的心灵家园！

北京语言大学出版社总编辑：戚德祥

Preface

Admire China's Spectacular World Heritages
Appreciate the Essence of Chinese Civilization

China is one of the countries that have the richest world heritage resources. Since it acceded to the Convention Concerning the Protection of the World Cultural and Natural Heritage in 1985, China has altogether 37 inscribed heritage sites, ranking the third in the world in terms of total amount of the world heritages. China's 37 world heritages belong not only to China, but also to the whole world.

When these China's cultural relics and natural landscapes were inscribed to the World Heritage List threads this product. With a wealth of exquisite illustrations and in fluent and vivid language, *China's World Heritages* presents China's magnificent and beautiful mountains and rivers as well as cultural relics.

The imperial palaces and tombs such as the Imperial Palaces of the Ming and Qing dynasties in Beijing, the Temple of Heaven, the Imperial Tombs of the Ming and Qing Dynasties symbolize the supreme power of ancient society; the cultural landscapes such as Mogao Caves, the Kong Family Mansion, Cemetery and Temple of Confucius, Longmen Grottoes, Mount Qingcheng distill the cultural and artistic essence of Buddhism, Taoism and Confucianism; the Summer Palace, the Mountain Resort of Chengde and the Classical Gardens of Suzhou embody the typical oriental culture and aesthetic values; the landscape wonders such as Mount Taishan, Lushan National Park, Mount Huangshan, Mount Emei, Jiuzhaigou Valley, Huanglong Scenic and Historic Interest Area reflect the concept of harmony between man and nature. The vicissitudes of nature and the Chinese civilization with a history of thousands of years unfold a great and delicate scroll painting of the world heritages for us.

We hope that China's World Heritages can guide you to explore the inner world of the Chinese people.

戚法祥

Editor-in-chief
Beijing Language
and Culture University Press

世界遗产简介

世界遗产，特指被联合国教科文组织和世界遗产委员会确认的人类罕见且目前无法替代的财富，是全人类公认的具有突出意义和普遍价值的文物古迹及自然景观。具体可分为文化遗产、自然遗产、文化与自然遗产（即双重遗产）和文化景观等。

1972年，联合国教科文组织第17届世界遗产大会在法国巴黎通过了《保护世界文化和自然遗产公约》（即《世界遗产公约》）。根据该公约，设立了世界遗产委员会和世界遗产基金。《世界遗产公约》将世界范围内被认为具有突出和普遍价值的文物古迹和自然景观列入《世界遗产名录》，作为全人类的共同遗产加以保护，即使在战争中也不能成为军事攻击的目标，以确保遗产的价值能永续长存。

根据《世界遗产公约》，世界遗产具有明确的定义和供会员国提名及遗产委员会审批遵循的标准。

凡提名列入《世界遗产名录》的文化遗产项目，必须符合下列一项或几项标准方可获得批准。

I. 代表一种人类创造性的天才杰作；

II. 能体现在一定时期内或世界某一文化区域内，人类在建筑、技术、纪念物艺术、城镇规划或景观设计方面的价值的发展变化；

III. 能为一种现存的或已消逝的文明或文化传统提供一种独特的至少是特殊的见证；

IV. 可作为一种建筑物或建筑群或技术体系或景观的杰出范例，展示出人类历史上一个（或几个）重要阶段；

V. 可作为传统的人类居住地或土地使用或海洋使用的杰出范例，代表一种(或几种)文化，或人与环境之间的互动，尤其在不可逆转之变化的影响下变得易于损坏；

VI. 与具特殊普遍意义的事件或现行传统或思想或信仰或文学艺术作品有直接或实质的联系。（委员会认为只有在此项标准与其他标准一起作用时，此款才能成为列入《世界遗产名录》的理由。）

凡提名列入《世界遗产名录》的自然遗产项目，必须符合下列一项或几项标准方可获得批准。

I. 代表地球演化的各主要发展阶段的典型范例，包括生命的记载、地形发展中主要的地质演变过程或具有主要的地貌或地形特征；

II. 代表陆地、淡水、沿海和海上生态系统植物和动物群演变及发展中重要过程的典型范例；

III. 包括绝妙或重要的自然美现象和地区；

IV. 具有最重要的保护生物多样性的自然栖息地，包括那些具有世界重大科学价值的濒危物种。

本书中各世界遗产项目的"收录理由"即为《世界遗产公约》中相应的评选标准。

截至2008年10月，全世界被列入《世界遗产名录》的项目共有878项。其中文化遗产679项，自然遗产174项，文化和自然双遗产25项，这些遗产分布在145个国家。

自1987年世界遗产委员会第11届会议批准中国的故宫等6处遗产列入《世界遗产名录》起，截至2008年7月底，中国已有37处文化遗址和自然景观列入《世界遗产名录》，所有的世界遗产数仅次于西班牙和意大利。

目前中国的世界遗产有：

文化遗产

长城，莫高窟，明清故宫，秦始皇陵及兵马俑，周口店"北京人"遗址，承德避暑山庄及周围寺庙，孔庙、孔府、孔林，武当山古建筑群，拉萨布达拉宫和大昭寺，丽江古城，平遥古城，苏州古典园林，颐和园，天坛，明清皇家陵寝，龙门石窟，大足石刻，青城山—都江堰，皖南古村落——西递、宏村，云冈石窟，高句丽王城、王陵及贵族墓葬，澳门历史城区，殷墟，开平碉楼与村落，福建土楼共25项。

自然遗产

武陵源风景名胜区，九寨沟风景名胜区，黄龙风景名胜区，云南"三江并流"保护区，四川大熊猫栖息地，中国南方喀斯特，三清山共7项。

文化景观

庐山1项。

文化和自然双遗产

泰山，黄山，武夷山，峨眉山—乐山大佛共4项。

A Brief Introduction to World Heritages

World heritages refer to the rare and currently irreplaceable human assets confirmed by UNESCO World Heritage Committee. As the universally recognized cultural relics and natural landscapes of exceptional significance and value, world heritages can be classified into cultural heritage, natural heritage, cultural and natural heritage (i.e. dual heritage) and cultural landscape etc.

In 1972, at the 17th session of the UNESCO World Heritage Committee in Paris of France, *Convention Concerning the Protection of the World Cultural and Natural Heritage* (i.e. *the World Heritage Convention*) was approved. World Heritage Committee and World Heritage Fund were established based on this convention. It allows the universally recognized cultural relics and natural landscapes of exceptional significance and value to be inscribed to World Heritage List and be protected as human common heritages. Even in wartime, these heritages cannot be the target of military attack, so as to keep their values forever.

According to *the World Heritage Convention*, world heritage has a clear definition and criteria for member states to nominate heritage items and World Heritage Committee to examine, approve and follow.

To be approved, the nominated cultural heritage items must meet one or several of the following criteria:

I. to represent a masterpiece of human creative genius;

II. to exhibit an important interchange of human values, over a span of time or within a cultural area of the world, on developments in architecture or technology, monumental arts, town-planning or landscape design;

III. to bear a unique or at least exceptional testimony to a cultural tradition or to a civilization which is living or which has disappeared;

IV. to be an outstanding example of a type of building, architectural or technological ensemble or landscape which illustrates (a) significant stage(s) in human history;

V. to be an outstanding example of a traditional human settlement, land-use, or sea-use which is representative of a culture (or cultures), or human interaction with the environment especially when it has become vulnerable under the impact of irreversible change;

VI. to be directly or tangibly associated with events or living traditions, with ideas, or with beliefs, with artistic and literary works of outstanding universal significance. (The Committee considers that this criterion should preferably be used in conjunction with other criteria).

To be inscribed to World Heritage List, the nominated natural heritage items must meet one or several of the following criteria:

I. to be outstanding examples representing major stages of earth's history, including the record of life, significant on-going geological processes in the development of landforms, or significant geomorphic or physiographic features;

II. to be outstanding examples representing significant on-going ecological and biological processes in the evolution and development of terrestrial, fresh water, coastal and marine ecosystems and communities of plants and animals;

III. to contain superlative natural phenomena or areas of exceptional natural beauty and aesthetic importance;

IV. to contain the most important and significant natural habitats for in-situ conservation of biological diversity, including those containing threatened species of outstanding universal value from the point of view of science or conservation.

The world heritage items included in this book are inscribed to the UNESCO World Heritage List based on the criteria described in *the World Heritage Convention*.

As of October 2008, a total of 878 items around the world have been included in World Heritage List, among which 679 were cultural heritages and 174 were natural heritages, and 25 items were cultural and natural heritages. These heritages were scattered in 145 countries. Since China's six heritages (such as the Chinese Imperial Palaces) were included at the 11th session of the UNESCO World Heritage Committee in 1987, as of the end of July, 2008, 37 Chinese cultural heritage sites and natural landscapes have been inscribed to World Heritage List, second only to Spain and Italy in terms of total amount.

At present, China's world heritages include:
25 cultural heritages:
The Great Wall, Mogao Caves, Imperial Palaces of the Ming and Qing Dynasties in Beijing, Mausoleum of the First Qin Emperor, Peking Man Site at Zhoukoudian, Mountain Resort and its Outlying Temples of Chengde, Temple, Family Mansion and Cemetery of Confucius, Ancient Building Complex in the Wudang Mountains, Historic Ensemble of the Potala Palace of Lhasa, Old Town of Lijiang, Ancient City of Pingyao, Classical Gardens of Suzhou, Summer Palace, Temple of Heaven, Imperial Tombs of the Ming and Qing Dynasties, Longmen Grottoes, Dazu Rock Carvings, Mount Qingcheng and the Dujiangyan Irrigation System, Ancient Villages in Southern Anhui—Xidi and Hongcun, Yungang Grottoes, Capital Cities and Tombs of the Ancient Koguryo Kingdom, Historic Center of Macao, Yin Xu, Kaiping Diaolou and Villages, and Fujian Tulou.

7 natural heritages:
Wulingyuan Scenic and Historic Interest Area, Jiuzhaigou Valley Scenic and Historic Interest Area, Huanglong Scenic and Historic Interest Area, Three Parallel Rivers of Yunnan Protected Areas, Sichuan Giant Panda Sanctuaries, South China Karst and Mount Sanqing National Park

1 cultural landscape: Lushan National Park
4 cultural and natural heritages:
Mount Taishan, Mount Huangshan, Mount Wuyi, Mount Emei and Leshan Giant Buddha

目录 Contents

序言 Preface
世界遗产简介 A Brief Introduction to World Heritages

- 02 /〇一 长城 The Great Wall
- 07 /〇二 明清故宫 Imperial Palaces of the Ming and Qing Dynasties in Beijing
- 12 /〇三 莫高窟 Mogao Caves
- 17 /〇四 秦始皇陵及兵马俑 Mausoleum of the First Qin Emperor
- 22 /〇五 周口店"北京人"遗址 Peking Man Site at Zhoukoudian
- 27 /〇六 泰山 Mount Taishan
- 33 /〇七 黄山 Mount Huangshan
- 38 /〇八 九寨沟风景名胜区 Jiuzhaigou Valley Scenic and Historic Interest Area
- 44 /〇九 黄龙风景名胜区 Huanglong Scenic and Historic Interest Area
- 50 /一〇 武陵源风景名胜区 Wulingyuan Scenic and Historic Interest Area
- 55 /一一 承德避暑山庄及周围寺庙 Mountain Resort and its Outlying Temples, Chengde
- 60 /一二 孔庙、孔府、孔林 Temple and Cemetery of Confucius and the Kong Family Mansion
- 66 /一三 拉萨布达拉宫和大昭寺 Historic Ensemble of the Potala Palace, Lhasa
- 71 /一四 武当山古建筑群 Ancient Building Complex in the Wudang Mountains
- 76 /一五 庐山 Lushan National Park
- 81 /一六 峨眉山—乐山大佛 Mount Emei and Leshan Giant Buddha
- 87 /一七 丽江古城 Old Town of Lijiang
- 93 /一八 平遥古城 Ancient City of Pingyao
- 98 /一九 苏州古典园林 Classical Gardens of Suzhou
- 104 /二〇 颐和园 Summer Palace
- 110 /二一 天坛 Temple of Heaven
- 116 /二二 武夷山 Mount Wuyi

121 /二三 大足石刻 Dazu Rock Carvings

126 /二四 明清皇家陵寝 Imperial Tombs of the Ming and Qing Dynasties

132 /二五 龙门石窟 Longmen Grottoes

137 /二六 青城山——都江堰 Mount Qingcheng and the Dujiangyan Irrigation System

142 /二七 皖南古村落——西递、宏村 Ancient Villages in Southern Anhui
　　　　　　　　　　　　　　　　　　—Xidi and Hongcun

148 /二八 云冈石窟 Yungang Grottoes

153 /二九 云南"三江并流"保护区 Three Parallel Rivers of Yunnan Protected Areas

158 /三〇 高句丽王城、王陵及贵族墓葬 Capital Cities and Tombs of the
　　　　　　　　　　　　　　　　　　Ancient Koguryo Kingdom

163 /三一 澳门历史城区 Historic Center of Macao

169 /三二 殷墟 Yin Xu

175 /三三 四川大熊猫栖息地 Sichuan Giant Panda Sanctuaries

180 /三四 开平碉楼与村落 Kaiping Diaolou and Villages

186 /三五 中国南方喀斯特 South China Karst

191 /三六 福建土楼 Fujian Tulou

197 /三七 三清山 Mount Sanqingshan National Park

长城
The Great Wall

约公元前220年，一统天下的秦始皇，将修建于早些时候的一些断续的防御工事连接成一个完整的防御系统，用以抵抗来自北方的侵略。在明代（公元1368—1644年），又继续加以修筑，使长城成为世界上最长的军事设施。它在文化艺术上的价值，足以与其在历史和战略上的重要性相媲美。

世界遗产委员会评价

长城是世界上最长的古代军事工程，与罗马斗兽场、比萨斜塔等并列为中古世界七大奇迹之一。长城位于中国北部，横贯河北、北京、内蒙古、山西、陕西、宁夏、甘肃等省区，全长6,700公里，约13,300华里，因此也被称为"万里长城"。1987年，长城被联合国教科文组织列入《世界文化遗产名录》。

In 220 B.C., under Qin Shi Huang, sections of earlier fortifications were joined together to form a united defence system against invasions from the north. Construction continued up to the Ming dynasty (1368–1644), when the Great Wall became the world's largest military structure. Its historic and strategic importance is matched only by its architectural significance.

The Great Wall is the world's longest ancient military project. Together with the Roman Colosseum and the Leaning Tower of Pisa etc, it is listed as one of the Seven Wonders of the World. The Great Wall is situated in northern China, stretching across many provinces and autonomous regions including Hebei, Beijing, Inner Mongolia, Shanxi, Shaanxi, Ningxia and Gansu, spanning a length of 6,700 kilometers or 13,300 *huali* (Chinese miles). Hence it is also called *Wanli Changcheng* (the Great Wall of Ten Thousand Miles). In 1987, the Great Wall was included in the UNESCO World Heritage List.

The most ancient section of the Great Wall of China was built in China in the 7th century BC during the Spring and Autumn Period. As the feudal lords of different kingdoms fought against each other and contended for dominance, the Great Walls were constructed on their respective borders. These walls were built intermittently, in varying directions and lengths, but were not very effective. In 220 BC, in

小贴士 世界中古七大奇迹 意大利罗马大斗兽场、利比亚亚历山大地下陵墓、中国万里长城、英国巨石阵、中国大报恩寺琉璃宝塔、意大利比萨斜塔、土耳其索菲亚大教堂。

收录时间 Date of inscription：1987
遗产类别 Heritage category：文化遗产 C
收录理由 Criteria：C(I)(II)(III)(IV)(VI)

中国最古老的长城始建于公元前7世纪春秋战国时期，各诸侯国为了互相争霸、互相防守，在各自的边境上筑起了长城。这些城墙断断续续、方向各异、长度较短、功效不大。公元前220年，为了防止北方游牧民族进入中原，秦始皇派遣士兵征用了无数老百姓把各诸侯国的旧城墙连缀起来，还增筑扩修了很多城墙。一条几乎横贯中国北部地区的长城矗立起来了。此后，各个朝代对长城都有所增筑。我们今天看到的是明

order to prevent the northern nomads from entering the Central Plains, Qin Shi Huang sent out soldiers and conscripted countless commoners to connect the old walls that were built by the feudal lords, and to construct and repair many city walls. The Great Wall that almost fully traversed across China's northern region was thus built.Thereafter, construction of the Great Wall was continued by every succeeding dynasty. What we see today has been preserved from the Ming Dynasty—from Shanhaiguan in the east to Jiayuguan in the west—spanning a length of 5,130 kilometers.

The "Ming" Great Wall around Beijing is a magnificent sight, meandering from Shanhaiguan to enter the Beijing city boundary at the vicinity of Jiangjunguan at Pinggu County. With a total length of 629 kilometers, it encircles the Beijing plains from east to west along the northern mountain areas, and became the most stable defence of the ancient Beijing city. Some sections of the Ming Great Wall around Beijing have now become tourist spots famous both in China and around the world. The Badaling Great Wall was China's earliest protected restoration; it is

TIPS Seven wonders of the world during the Middle Ages Seven wonders of the world during the Middle Ages refer to the Colosseum in Rome, Italy, Alexandria Underground Mausoleum in Libya, the Great Wall of China, the Stonehenge in England, the Glazed Pagoda in the Great Baoen Temple in China, the Leaning Tower of Pisa in Italy, and Hagia Sophia Church in Turkey.

小贴士 万里长城 据统计，如果把各个时代修筑的长城加起来，总长度将超过5万公里；如果用修建长城的砖石土方筑一道1米厚、5米高的大墙，这道墙可以环绕地球一周有余。

代保存下来的长城。明长城东起山海关，西到嘉峪关，全长5,130公里。

　　北京周围的明长城雄伟壮观，从山海关蜿蜒而来，在平谷区将军关附近进入北京市界，全长629公里，从东到西沿北部山区呈半环形状环抱着北京平原，成为古代北京城最稳固的守卫者。现在，北京周边明长城的一些段落已成为驰名中外的旅游胜地。八达岭长城是中国保护性修复最早、最好的一段长城，也是观赏长城的理想之地。城墙高7米、宽4米，沿着山脊绵延起伏，气势令人震撼。居庸关长城蜿蜒曲折，在东西两边的山巅上汇合，如同从南北伸出的两只巨手，环抱着山坳里的军事指挥部。

黄花城长城本来是顺着山脊修建的，后来因为修建水库，将三段城墙淹在了水下，因此出现了水下长城的奇特景观。慕田峪长城的风景特别迷人，人们常说"万里长城慕田峪独秀"。这里气候相对温暖湿润，青山翠绿。箭扣长城的走势具有艺术般的变化和音乐的韵律感。登临绝壁，是一处顶部相对平坦的山峰，三道长城分别从东、北、西南三个方向朝这里汇聚，结成一个巨大的花结，这就是有名的"长城北

the best section of the Great Wall as well as an ideal place to enjoy the view. The city wall measures seven meters high and four meters wide, and winds up and down along the mountain ridges with overwhelming force. The Juyongguan Great Wall zigzags and converges at the mountaintops from the East to the West on both sides, like two giant hands extending from the North and South, holding the military headquarters in the mountains. Huanghuacheng Great Wall was originally built along the mountain ridges, but due to later construction of the reservoirs, three sections of the wall were submerged under water, resulting in a strange underwater landscape. The scenery at Mutianyu Great Wall is particularly charming. People often say, *Wanli Changcheng Mutianyu du xiu* (Mutianyu is the beauty of the Great Wall). The weather is relatively warm and moist, while the mountains are emerald green. It seems the ambiance of the Jiankou Great Wall changes artistically like the rhythm of music. Mounting these cliffs, you will reach a relatively flat summit, where three sections of the Great Wall coming from the East, North, and Southwest converge here to form a flower knot—the famous *Changcheng Beijing Jie* (Beijing Great Wall Knot). The Simatai Great Wall is situated at the northeast suburbs of Beijing; it is the most precipitous, and the only section in China that has retained the original appearance of the ancient Great Wall from the Ming Dynasty. This is a *tianti* (heavenly ladder), reaching 100 meters high and with an inclination of 85 degrees, almost perpendicular to the ground. At the top of the tianti is a *tianqiao* (heavenly bridge), which is less than 100 meters long, only 40 centimeters wide, and has cliffs on both sides. Wangjing Lou is an important part of the landscape of Simatai Great Wall. It is a *dilou* (enemy tower), and commands the greatest height of this section at 986 meters above sea level. In good

小贴士 八达岭名字的由来 有多种说法，其中比较令人信服的一种说法是：八达岭处于居庸关的北口，南通南口、北京、昌平，北通延庆，西通沙城、宣化、张家口、大同，可谓四通八达，故名八达岭。

TIPS **Ten-thousand-li Great Wall** According to statistics, if we sum up the lengths of all the walls built in different times, the total length of the Great Wall would be more than 50,000 kilometers. If we build a wall of 1 meter thick and 5 meters high with the bricks and earth used in the Great Wall, this wall would be long enough to circle around the earth.

京结"。司马台长城位于北京东北郊，是长城中最为险峻的段落，也是中国唯一一段保留明代原貌的古长城。天梯高达百米，倾斜度为85度，几乎是垂直于地面的。天梯的顶端便是天桥，长不足百米，宽仅40厘米，两侧是悬崖绝壁。望京楼是司马台长城的重要景观，是一座敌楼，也是这段长城的制高点，海拔986米。遇上晴朗天气，夜间登上此楼可以望见北京城的灯火，当地称之为"望京楼"。

长城依山借势、高大坚固，防御体系完备。据专家介绍，明代的工匠把自然石头加工成条石，用石灰掺着糯米熬成的黏汁作为胶结条石的材料。砌筑的城砖每层并不是平行的，而是像狗的牙齿一样交错咬合，以此增加内部的拉力。在重点防御的长城段落，垒砌好条石后，还要用大量的青砖包砌在城墙的内外壁。城墙顶部的外

weather, you can see the lights of metropolitan Beijing when you get on this tower at night; the locals thus call it *Wangjing Lou* (the Beijing Watchtower).

The Great Wall relies on the mountains and takes advantage of the terrain; large and tall, firm and strong, it is a complete defense system. According to experts, the craftsmen in Ming Dynasty had utilized natural stone and processed them into *tiaoshi* (rock strips); then they mixed mortar with glutinous rice and cooked them into a kind of sticky juice that was used as the material to glue the *tiaoshi*. The wall bricks laid and constructed at each floor were not parallel; rather, like the bite of a dog's teeth, they were staggered and interlocking, thereby increasing internal tension. In key defense sections of the Great Wall, after having built up the *tiaoshi*, large volumes of green bricks were also constructed in the interior and exterior walls. At the outside on top of the walls, many continuous bumpy teeth-shaped short walls were built. The outside of these short walls were shrinking, but the insides were wide open. This

TIPS **The origin of the name of Badaling** There are many versions about the name of Badaling Great Wall. One convincing story is that Badaling Great Wall is located at the north gateway of Juyongguan, leading southward to Nankou, Beijing, Changping, northward to Yanqing, and westward to Shacheng, Xuanhua, Zhangjiakou and Datong, providing easy access to all directions, hence the name Badaling.

侧，建有许多连续凹凸的齿形矮墙。这些矮墙的外面是收缩的，但内部却是敞开的。这样不但可以保证防守者有着良好的视线，还可以有效地躲避墙外敌人的射击。这种高出城墙之上有两层或三层的敌楼，两面都没有门，仿佛是一个独立封闭的堡垒，既可以住人，也可以储藏兵器。除了城墙和敌楼外，还有关城、墩堡、营城、镇城烽火台等多种防御工程。

今天，无数的中外游客来到长城，在气喘吁吁的攀登中体验着横亘古今的人类文明以及源源不断的生命活力。中国人爱说："不到长城非好汉"，您要不要试试？

not only ensured that the defenders would have a good line of sight, but could also effectively evade the enemy's shots. This type of *dilou* would be two or three floors higher than the walls, with no doors on either side, as if it were an independently sealed fortress that could accommodate people as well as store weapons. Besides the walls and dilou, there were also *guancheng* (the center of the Huangyaguan section of the Huangyaguan Great Wall), *dunbao* (beacon towers constructed by Emperor Qianlong in 1782), *yingcheng* (another name for *guancheng*), *zhencheng fenghuotai* (military beacon towers) and many other defensive projects.

Today, countless Chinese and foreign tourists come to the Great Wall and, while gasping for breath on their climb, they can experience the journey of ancient and present human civilization and the endless vitality of life. Chinese people love to say, "He who has never been to the Great Wall is not a true man!" Would you like to give it a try?

收录时间 Date of inscription：1987；2004
遗产类别 Heritage category：文化遗产 C
收录理由 Criteria：C(I)(II)(III)(IV)

明清故宫
Imperial Palaces of the Ming and Qing Dynasties in Beijing

　　紫禁城是中国五个多世纪以来的最高权力中心，它以园林景观和容纳了家具及工艺品的近万间的庞大建筑群，成为明清时代中国文明无价的历史见证。

世界遗产委员会评价

　　北京故宫又称"紫禁城"，屹立于中国北京的市中心，是中国明清时期的皇宫，现辟为"故宫博物院"。故宫是中国现存最大、最完整的皇宫建筑群，于1987年被联合国教科文组织列入《世界文化遗产名录》。

　　故宫南北长961米，东西宽753米，占地72万多平方米。四周10米高城墙约3,400米，墙外环绕52米宽的护城河。故宫始建于公元1406年，历时14年建成。1420年，明成祖朱棣迁都于此。自此，先后有明朝14位皇帝、清朝10位皇帝，共24位皇帝在这里统治中国长达500年之久。

Seat of supreme power for over five centuries (1416-1911), the Forbidden City in Beijing, with its landscaped gardens and many buildings (whose nearly 10,000 rooms contain furniture and works of art), constitutes a priceless testimony to Chinese civilization during the Ming and Qing dynasties. The Imperial Palace of the Qing Dynasty in Shenyang consists of 114 buildings constructed between 1625 26 and 1783. It contains an important library and testifies to the foundation of the last dynasty that ruled China, before it expanded its power to the center of the country and moved the capital to Beijing. This palace then became auxiliary to the Imperial Palaces in Beijing. This remarkable architectural edifice offers important historical testimony to the history of the Qing Dynasty and to the cultural traditions of the Manchu and other tribes in the north of China.

Beijing's Imperial Palace is also known as the "Forbidden City". Situated in the city center of Beijing, China, it was the imperial palace during the Ming and Qing

小贴士 紫禁城 故宫之所以又称"紫禁城",与中国古代哲学、天文学和神话传说有关。紫禁城取紫微星居于天地中心之意,表示这里是世界的中心。另外皇宫戒备森严,又是禁地,所以称为"紫禁城"。

故宫有殿宇宫室近万间,有"殿宇之海"之称。宫殿是沿着一条贯通南北的中轴线排列,左右对称。这些宫殿以乾清门为界分为两大部分,南面为前朝,北面是内廷。

前朝又称外朝,是皇帝处理政务、举行各种仪式、大典的部分,内廷是皇帝生活和处理日常政务活动的区域。太和、中和、保和三大殿是前朝的中心,都建在汉白玉砌成的8米高的台阶上,远观如神话中的琼楼玉宇。

故宫里首屈一指的就是太和殿,俗称"金銮殿",占地2,300多平方米,是中国现存古建

dynasties, and has now become the Palace Museum. The Forbidden City is the largest and most complete existing imperial palace architectural complex in China, and was registered on the UNESCO World Heritage List in 1987.

The Forbidden City is 961 meters long from north to south, 753 meters wide east to west, and covers an area of over 720,000 square meters. All around the city is a 10-meter-high wall which is about 3,400 meters in length, and an exterior wall surrounded by a 52-meter-wide moat. The Forbidden City was founded in 1406 AD and took 14 years to construct. In 1420 AD, the Ming Emperor Zhu Di relocated the capital to Beijing. Since then, a succession of 14 emperors of the Ming Dynasty and 10 emperors of the Qing Dynasty—24 emperors in total—ruled China at this spot for some 500 years.

The Forbidden City contains nearly 10,000 buildings and is thus also known as *Dianyuzhihai* ("sea of palaces and halls"). The Imperial Palace is based on a symmetrical north-south axis. Using Qianqingmen as the boundary, the Palace is divided into two large parts, with the southern

小贴士 数字"九" 在中国传统文化中,数字"九"除了表示数量,还有"最高、最多、最久"的文化含义。数字"九"在皇家建筑或装饰物上经常被运用,以此象征至高无上的皇权。例如,北京故宫的房子总数据说是九千九百九十九间,皇宫三大殿的总高度是九丈九尺。

> **TIPS** **The Forbidden City** The Imperial Palace was also called "the Purple Forbidden City", which is closely related with ancient Chinese philosophy, astronomy, myths and legends. The so-called "Purple Forbidden City" was named after the Ziwei Star, which was situated in the center of Heaven and Earth. As the royal palace was heavily guarded on all sides and not everyone was allowed to enter, the palace was called the Purple Forbidden City.

筑中最大的宫殿。太和殿下面的台阶有三层，下层台阶21级，中上层各9级。皇帝的宝座——一把雕龙镏金大椅——高搁于7层阶梯的台上。明清曾有24位皇帝在此登基，宣布即位诏书。太和殿的广场空旷宁静。台阶东西两侧有铜制的仙鹤、龟。身着朝服的文武百官在乐声中行礼，更显示了高坐在金銮殿龙椅上的天子威严。故宫宫殿多为木质结构，这些能够蓄水防火的大缸就显得极为必要了。这样的大缸故宫里有300多个，缸下

可烧炭加温。屋脊上的装饰物据说可以避邪，装饰越多，等级越高。太和殿是中国唯一有10个装饰物的建筑。

乾清宫、交泰殿、坤宁宫是内廷的中心，是皇帝生活和处理日常政务活动的区域。两侧的东西六宫是嫔妃的住所。明代和清初的300年里，皇帝们就住在乾清宫及其配殿里。如果不是三品以上官员，或是皇帝身边的高级侍卫、随从，

section called *qianchao* (the outer court), and the northern section named *neiting* (the inner court).

The outer court was where the emperors would deal with court affairs and hold various ceremonies. The inner court was the area where the emperors lived and handled routine official activities. Taihe, Zhonghe and Baohe are the three main large halls which are the heart of the outer court. Each of them is built on an 8-meter-high white marble terrace; from a distance, they look like fine jade buildings from fairytales.

The best building in the Forbidden City is *Taihedian* (the Hall of Supreme Harmony), commonly known as *Jinluandian* (the Golden Carriage Palace), covering over 2,300 square meters; it is also the largest palace of China's extant ancient buildings. The terrace below Taihedian has three tiers: the lowest tier has a flight of 21 steps, and the upper and middle tiers have a flight of 9 steps each. The emperor's golden throne, decorated with carved dragons, was laid down on a 7-tier-high platform. 24 emperors from the Ming and Qing dynasties ascended to this throne and announced their enthronement decrees at this Hall. The Square at Taihedian is spacious and serene. On the east and west sides of the platform stand a bronze crane and bronze tortoise. Dressed in court attire, the civil and military officials would observe court manners under musical accompaniment, demonstrating the prestige and dignity of the "son of heaven" (i.e., the emperor) sitting high on his golden dragon throne. The buildings in the Forbidden City are mainly wooden structures; the use of a *dagang* (large jar), which could store water and prevent fires, was thus essential. The Forbidden City has over 300 *dagangs* which could be heated by burning coal underneath. Statuettes on the roof are said to ward off evil—a greater number

> **TIPS** **The number "nine"** In traditional Chinese culture, the number "nine" also means "supreme", "most" or "longest". It was frequently employed in royal architectures and decorations to symbolize the supreme imperial power. For example, it is said there are altogether 9999 rooms in the Forbidden City, and the total height of the three main halls in it is 9 zhang and 9 chi. (zhang, a unit of length, equal to 3 1/3 meters, and ten chi equal to one zhang.)

小贴士　吻兽　屋脊上的装饰物叫吻兽。数字"十"在中国传统文化中象征完美、圆满。太和殿是等级最高的建筑，吻兽有十个，其他皇家建筑吻兽至多为九个。

几乎没有人会贸然出现在这里。自清朝雍正皇帝以后，乾清宫前面的广场成为皇帝们每天办公议事的场所，被称为"御门听政"。皇帝们虔诚地相信，在露天听政可以将他们贤明勤政的心意传达给上天，上天会因此而保佑皇帝们的江山社稷。清代雍正皇帝的寝室在乾清宫西侧养心殿，其后殿是现在能够看到的唯一一处中国皇帝的卧室，朴素程度和狭小空间已超出了我们的想象，这里也是第一个装上玻璃的宫殿。侍奉皇室家族的宫女太监们居住在各区域低矮的小耳房里。

皇帝是故宫里唯一的主人，皇帝的权威在这里处处得到体现。中国人在上古时代创造了龙的图腾，把龙视为力量、神奇和威武的化身。汉代以后，龙成为皇帝的象征，龙的图案和纹饰开始为皇帝所专用，仅太和殿各种龙雕龙饰就多达13,844条。红墙和黄瓦是皇宫不变的主题。中国古人认为，黄色代表着土，土居中央，以示天子位于中央，统治四方。而红色自古就是中国人喜爱的吉祥色，代表着幸福、美满、红火。明黄色是皇室专用色，如果大臣或者百姓们使用了这种颜色，就会被视为犯上作乱。从正阳门到皇帝宝座之间距离长达1,700

of statuettes indicate a higher status of the building. Taihedian was the only building in China fitted with 10 of statuettes.

Qianqinggong, Jiaotaidian and Kunninggong—constituting the heart of the inner court—were where emperors lived and handled routine official activities. The six palaces on the east and west sides were the living quarters of the imperial ladies and concubines. In the 300 years from the Ming Dynasty to the early Qing Dynasty, the emperors lived in Qianqinggong (the Palace of Heavenly Purity) and the side halls. Only civil officials with a rank higher than of the third rank, senior attending guards or attendants close to the emperors could enter. Since the reign of the Qing Emperor Yongzheng, the square in front of Qianqinggong became the place for emperors to conduct their everyday official business, and was called *yumentingzheng* (an imperial door used for hearing affairs). The emperors sincerely believed that working outdoors could convey their virtues of clarity and diligence to Heaven, which would therefore bless their kingdom. The Qing Emperor Yongzheng's bedroom was located at Yangxindian, on the west side of Qianqinggong. This is the only Chinese emperor's bedroom that can be seen today, the degree of simplicity in the narrow quarters is beyond one's imagination! This was also the first palace installed with glass; The palace maids and eunuchs serving the royal household lived in the small rooms nearby.

The emperor was the sole master of the Forbidden City and his authority could be exemplified everywhere. In ancient times, the Chinese people created the dragon totem, and the dragon was perceived as symbolizing strength and embodying magic and power. After the Han Dynasty, dragons had become the symbol of the emperor. Its designs and ornaments began to be dedicated for use by the

小贴士　門　午门以及故宫其他各门匾中的"門"字末笔直下至底，没有向上的勾脚。相传"門"字末笔勾脚带火笔，不写以免招致火灾。

TIPS **Wenshou** It refers to the decorative sculptures of animal on the roof ridges. The number "ten" in Chinese culture symbolizes perfect and harmony. Taihedian ranks as the top building in the Forbidden City, so there are 10 Wenshou sculptures on its roof ridge, while there are only 9 sculptures on the ridges of the other imperial buildings.

emperor. At just Taihedian only, a display of as many as 13,844 various kinds of dragon carvings and ornaments exist. Red walls and yellow tiles are unchanging themes of the palaces. Ancient Chinese people believed that yellow represents the Earth which resides at the center, thereby showing that the Son of Heaven (the emperor) is situated in the middle, ruling over the four corners (the kingdom). Since ancient times, red has been an auspicious color adored by the Chinese people, representing happiness, bliss, and prosperity. The use of bright yellow was strictly reserved for royalty; if ministers or commoners were to use this color, it would have been regarded as disrespecting the emperor or planning a revolt. The distance from the Zhengyang Gate to the emperor's throne is almost 1,700 meters, a walking time of nearly 20 minutes. Although this course serves no practical function, five gates were erected for the purpose of cutting the space and creating a visual obstruction of sight that could trigger psychological anxiety and fear of kings, dukes and senior ministers. Divinity of the emperor was thus effectively upheld and highlighted by the complex overlapping architecture.

At present, the Forbidden City has a collection of over one million pieces of ancient art treasures, accounting for one-sixth of the total number of Chinese artifacts. It has therefore become the museum with the biggest collection of Chinese artifacts, as well as a world-renowned ancient cultural and arts museum.

As visitors stroll through the Palace and great halls and enjoy the art treasures available to see, they may imagine the rich history and countless stories that have unfolded here.

米，步行需要近二十分钟。在这段没有实际功能的路程上设置了五道门，这种独特的空间分割设计造成了视线的不畅，从而引发了王公大臣们心理的焦虑与恐惧，皇帝的神圣被复杂重叠的建筑有效地营造和烘托出来。

现在，故宫收藏着一百多万件古代艺术珍品，占中国文物总数的1/6，成为中国收藏文物最丰富的博物馆，也是世界著名的古代文化艺术博物馆。

穿行于一道道宫墙和大殿之间，游人们在欣赏这些艺术珍品的同时，也在猜想着曾经发生在这里的无数故事。

TIPS **Men** When examining the Chinese character "門" inscribed on the horizontal tablet placed above each gate of the Forbidden City, there's no hook in the last stroke, which is different from the usual one. This is because people believed that the hook in the last stroke of the character "門" was a symbol of "fire". By omitting the hook, there would be no fire accident in the palace.

莫高窟
Mogao Caves

莫高窟地处丝绸之路的一个战略要点，它不仅是东西方贸易的中转站，同时也是宗教、文化和知识的交汇处。莫高窟的492个大小石窟和洞穴庙宇，以其雕像和壁画闻名于世，展示了延续千年的佛教艺术。

世界遗产委员会评价

Situated at a strategic point along the Silk Route, at the crossroads of trade as well as religious, cultural and intellectual influences, the 492 cells and cave sanctuaries in Mogao are famous for their statues and wall paintings, spanning 1,000 years of Buddhist art.

长长的栈道将大大小小的石窟曲折相连，洞窟中端坐着庄严慈祥的佛像，四壁上布满了精美华丽的壁画，构造出一个无比绚烂的艺术殿堂和文化长廊。

这就是敦煌莫高窟，位于中国敦煌市东南25公里处的鸣沙山上。它是世界上现存规模最大、内容最宏富，也是保留最完整的佛教艺术宝库。

A long and zigzagging plank road alongside the cliffs connects grottoes of all sizes; statues of the sacred and amiable Buddha sit in the grottoes; and exquisite frescos are spread over the walls. The result is an incomparably gorgeous art palace and a cultural corridor.

These are the Dunhuang Mogao Grottoes, situated on Mount Mingsha, 25 kilometers away from Dunhuang City in China. They comprise the largest, best-preserved and richest treasury of Buddhist art in the world.

The Mogao Caves are a system of large cave temples combining architecture, carving and painting. From south to north, the Mogao Caves extend for over 1,600 meters. The Mogao Caves are divided into five levels, with the highest caves up to 50 meters. There

小贴士 "莫高窟"名称的含义 据研究，莫高窟一词的含义有二。一说为，"莫"是"不可能"、"没有"的意思，莫高窟就是说没有人的修为比建造者更高了。二说即盛赞莫高窟水平极高，没有水平更高的石窟了。

| 收录时间 Date of inscription：1987 |
| 遗产类别 Heritage category：文化遗产 C |
| 收录理由 Criteria：C(I)(II)(III)(IV)(V)(VI) |

莫高窟是集建筑、雕塑和绘画于一体的大型石窟寺。石窟南北长1,600余米，上下共五层，最高处达50米。现存洞窟492个，壁画45,000余平方米，彩塑2,415身，飞天塑像4,000余身。莫高窟是中华文化艺术史上的瑰宝，也是古代东方文化艺术的灿烂明珠。

1987年12月，甘肃敦煌莫高窟被列入《世界遗产名录》。

公元前139年和公元前119年，张骞两次出使西域，打通了横贯亚洲大陆、沟通中西文化经济交流的"丝绸之路"。敦煌，地处"丝绸之路"交通枢纽，东来西往的文化都在此交汇，极大地

are currently 492 caves, more than 45,000 square meters of frescos, 2,415 painted sculptures and over 4,000 flying Apsaras in existence. The Mogao Caves are the treasure of Chinese culture and art history and the bright pearl of the ancient Eastern cultural arts.

In December 1987, the Dunhuang Mogao Caves were inscribed to the UNESCO World Heritage List.

In 139 BC and again in 119 BC, Zhang Qian (a minister of the Western Han Dynasty) was sent on a diplomatic mission to the Western Regions. He opened up the Silk Road—which transverses the Asian Continent and activated cultural and economic exchange between China and the West. Dunhuang, as the transport hub on the Silk Road, accumulated the cultures of the West and the East and became prosperous accordingly. "Dun" means "large" while "huang" means "prosperous."

The word "mogao" means "extrication", indicating people's limitless respect for, and yearning towards, the Buddhist world. Construction of the Mogao Caves began in 366 AD. A buddhist monk, Le Zun, came here and had a vision of a thousand Buddhas, inspiring construction of the caves he envisioned. He built the first Buddha cave on the cliff. In the Sui Dynasty and the early Tang Dynasty, construction of the Mogao Caves reached a height of power and splendor. Later, the Mogao Caves continued to be built until the Yuan Dynasty. Since the Yuan Dynasty, the Mogao cave were gradually neglected and faded from people's awareness.

The caves, as the carrier of Buddhist sculptures and frescos, are constructions of solid space. The largest cave has an area of about 300 square meters and a width of about 13 meters; the smallest grotto is too small to allow a person to enter. There are various types of caves. Of the caves excavated in the

TIPS **The meanings of Mogao Caves** There are two explanations for the name of Mogao Caves. One holds that "mo" means "no" or "impossible" in Chinese. Thus "mogao" means no one was better than the cave builder in practicing Buddhism. Another explanation is that the artistic level of Mogao Caves was then considered the highest and there were no other surpass them.

小贴士 石窟的建造 敦煌石窟的营造者大致分为三类：窟主（即石窟的主人）、施主（出钱出力帮助窟主建窟的人）和工匠（石窟营造的具体操作者）。工匠按照实际需要可分为石匠（打窟人）、泥匠、塑匠、木匠等。

促进了它的繁华。"敦"意为"大"，"煌"意为"盛"。

"莫高"一词的意思是解脱，更是出于对佛国世界的无限崇敬和向往。石窟的开凿始于公元366年。一位法名乐尊的僧人云游到此，因看到三危山金光万道，状若千佛，感悟到这里是佛地，便在崖壁上凿建了第一个佛窟。到了隋和唐代前期，莫高窟的开凿进入鼎盛时期。以后经过历代的修建，至元代基本结束，逐渐冷落荒废，鲜为人知。

石窟是佛像和壁画的载体，本身就是具有立体空间的建筑。莫高窟面积最大的石窟将近300平方米，宽约13米，而最小的石窟却小得连人也不能进入。石窟的建造形式多种多样，前期开凿的洞窟多在中央有一个方柱，在柱子的上面开龛，龛内塑像，这叫"中央塔柱窟"。这一外来形式的窟型，反映了古代艺术家在接受外来艺术的同时，对它加以消化、吸收，使之成为中国的民族形式。正是这种对外来文化的持续吸收与发展，才最终成就了敦煌长久的生命力。

莫高窟因为佛像众多，也被称为"千佛洞"。各窟佛像大小差异很大，最小的只有几十厘米，而高大的佛像则气势恢弘。早期的泥塑作品还留有印度艺术的痕迹。随着时代的变迁，泥

early period, most have a square column in the middle; on the column, there are niches; and in the niches are sculptures. Therefore, these caves are known as "central column caves." They represent a cave type from outside of China and indicate that, while accepting foreign arts, the ancient Chinese artisans consumed and absorbed them, ultimately creating China's own national style. It was precisely the continuous absorption and development of foreign arts that instilled the Dunhuang Mogao Caves with its vital life force.

The Mogao Caves, due to their numerous Buddhist sculptures, are also known as the "Caves of the Thousand Buddhas." These Buddhist sculptures vary greatly from one another in size. The smallest is only several tens of centimeters high while the largest is grand and vigorous. The early clay sculptures still show traces of Indian art. With the passage of time, the clay sculptures came to increasingly resemble the Chinese people, with an artistic style trending toward the graceful and luxurious. This is especially true of the Tang Dynasty painted sculptures, which reflect a peak of artistic excellence. The Buddhist statues of the Tang Dynasty are realistic, vivid and stylish, representing the supreme elegance of the flourishing Tang Dynasty.

The most magnificent and colorful view of the Mogao Caves is the frescos found in the caves. These frescos are splendid and colorful. Various architectural paintings, landscape paintings and flower patterns—which record sutra stories, mountain scenes, pavilions, flying Buddhist images and the scenes of working labors—reproduce the folk customs and historical development from the Sixteen States to the Qing Dynasty over a period of 1,500 years. For this reason, scholars refer to the frescos in the Mogao Caves as a "library on the wall." Among all the frescos, those created during the glorious Tang Dynasty are the most magnificent and colorful. The most prevalent

小贴士 敦煌 中国著名学者季羡林曾说：世界上历史影响最具深远的四大文明体系——中国文化、印度文化、希腊文化和伊斯兰文化，有两个最集中的交汇地：一个是西域，也就是今天的中国新疆；另一个就是敦煌。

TIPS **The construction of grottoes** The builders of the caves in Dunhuang fall into three kinds: the owners of the caves, the sponsors of the caves and the craftsmen of the caves. According to the actual, the craftsmen can also be divided into stonemasons, brick layers, engravers, carpenters, etc.

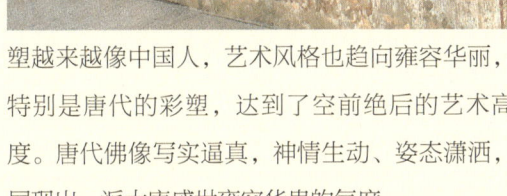

塑越来越像中国人，艺术风格也趋向雍容华丽，特别是唐代的彩塑，达到了空前绝后的艺术高度。唐代佛像写实逼真，神情生动、姿态潇洒，展现出一派大唐盛世雍容华贵的气度。

莫高窟最瑰丽多彩的图景是石窟中的壁画。石窟壁画富丽多彩，各种各样的佛经故事、山川景物、亭台楼阁等建筑画、山水画、花卉图案、飞天佛像，以及当时劳动人民进行生产的各种场面等，是十六国至清代一千五百多年的民俗风貌和历史变迁的艺术再现。因此学者将敦煌壁画称做"墙壁上的图书馆"。所有壁画中，尤其以盛唐时期的壁画最为富丽华美。壁画中最广泛的题材是尊像画，即人们供奉的佛、菩萨、天王等等，即使是相同的题材也没有完全相同的表现。所谓"一佛千面"，表现出画师高度自由的创作心态和变化无穷的高超技法。这种创造的丰富性，使得莫高窟变成永远为后人所敬仰的艺术宝库。

subjects for the frescos are depictions of Buddhas, Bodhisattvas and heavenly kings worshiped by the people. However, even if two frescos share the same subject, their appearances are never exactly the same. The so-called "one Buddha, thousand looks" indicates the free style and limitless expertise of the painters. It is this creative abundance that has made the Mogao Caves an art treasure house revered through the ages.

From these numerous frescos, we can see that the ancient Chinese artists added to the foundation of their own domestic art by absorbing the advantages of the arts of other civilizations, including ancient Iran, India and Greece, indicating the developed and open civilization of the Chinese people.

After the 16th century AD, with the gradual decline of the Silk Road, Dunhuang became silent. Dunhuang is located in the deserts, with little human habitation and dry weather, so the painted sculptures and frescos retained an excellent condition. However,

TIPS Dunhuang Ji Xianlin, a famous Chinese scholar, once said that the four greatest and most influential civilizations in the world's history—Chinese Civilization, Hindu Civilization, Greek Civilization and Islam Civilization—blend and communicate best in two areas: one is the Western Regions, which refers to present-day Xinjiang of China and the other is Dunhuang.

在大量的壁画艺术中还可发现，古代艺术家们在民族化的基础上，吸取了伊朗、印度、希腊等国古代艺术之长，这是中华民族发达文明的象征。

公元16世纪后，随着丝绸之路的逐步衰落，敦煌悄然沉寂。这里地处沙漠，人烟稀少、气候干燥，也正因为如此，敦煌的彩塑和壁画得以比较完好地保存。但是，数百年的风沙，几乎掩埋了曾经香火鼎盛的石窟，莫高窟最终淡出了历史的视线。直到1900年，在莫高窟偶然发现了"藏经洞"，洞里藏有从公元4世纪到14世纪的历代文物五六万件。这是20世纪初中国考古学上的一次重大发现，震惊了世界，莫高窟重新吸引了世界的目光。此后又由此发展出著名的"敦煌学"。

沙漠是生命望而却步的地方，但是我们希望这个全人类的艺术宝库和文明殿堂将在大漠中生生不息，放射出永恒的佛光。

the wind and sands of several hundreds of years almost buried these grottoes that used to possess such power and splendor. The Mogao Caves finally faded from history and it was not until 1900 that the "Scripture-storing Cave" was accidentally discovered. In the cave were found 50,000 to 60,000 cultural relics of past dynasties from the 4th to the 14th centuries. This was an important discovery for Chinese archaeology in the early 20th century that astonished the world, and the Mogao Caves again drew attention from around the globe. Later, based on the Mogao Caves, the renowned scholarly pursuit known as "Dunhuang Studies" came into being.

In general, deserts tend to be barren and devoid of life. However, it is our hope that this palace of human civilization and global treasury of art can achieve immortality in the desert and emanate eternal Buddhist light.

收录时间 Date of inscription：1987
遗产类别 Heritage category：文化遗产 C
收录理由 Criteria：C(I)(III)(IV)(VI)

秦始皇陵及兵马俑
Mausoleum of the First Qin Emperor

　　毫无疑问，如果不是1974年被发现，这座考古遗址上的成千件陶俑将依旧沉睡于地下。秦始皇，这个第一个统一中国的皇帝，殁于公元前210年，葬于陵墓的中心。在他陵墓的周围环绕着那些著名的陶俑。结构复杂的秦始皇陵是仿照其生前的都城——咸阳的格局而设计建造的。那些略小于人形的陶俑形态各异，连同他们的战马、战车和武器，成为现实主义的完美杰作，同时也保留了极高的历史价值。

世界遗产委员会评价

　　这些和真人一样大小的陶制塑像曾经在地下沉睡了将近二十二个世纪。当他们重新站立在阳光下的时候，你会发现，他们神态各异、气宇轩昂。这些就是从中国历史上第一个皇帝秦始皇陵墓中出土的兵马俑。

　　在中国陕西省临潼县城以东5公里处的骊山北麓，有一座55米高的土丘，那位雄才大略的始皇帝就埋葬在

No doubt thousands of statues still remain to be unearthed at this archeological site, which was not discovered until 1974. Qin (210 B.C.), the first unifier of China, is buried, surrounded by the famous terracotta warriors, at the centre of a complex designed to mirror the urban plan of the capital, Xianyang. The small figures are all different; with their horses, chariots and weapons, they are masterpieces of realism and also of great historical interest.

These life-sized ceramic statues once slept beneath the earth's surface for nearly 22 centuries. Now that they are standing once again under the sunlight, you will discover that, although they share in common an impressive bearing, each statue has its own unique expression. These are the Terracotta Warriors, excavated near the Mausoleum of Qin Shi Huang, the first emperor of China.

小贴士 始皇帝 公元前221年，秦王嬴政统一天下后，自称"始皇帝"，宣布子孙称二世、三世，以至万世，幻想秦王朝的统治能够一直延续下去。此后"皇帝"成为历代中国封建君主的称号。

下面。秦始皇陵建于公元前246年至公元前208年，由72万工匠花费了39年才建成。土丘上原来是庞大的宫殿群，而地下也是一座宏伟的宫殿。据说，秦始皇用大量的水银模仿了帝国疆域内的江河湖海，象征着自己所征服的世界。

1974年2月，在秦始皇陵墓东侧1.5公里的地方，几个打井的农民无意中挖出了几个真人大小的陶制人头像，秦始皇陵墓的陪葬坑被发现了，这被称为20世纪最伟大的考古发现之一，一个震惊世界的考古发掘由此开始。

相继发掘的三个大型的陪葬坑分别被命名为一号、二号、三号兵马俑坑，呈"品"字形分布，总面积达22,000多平方米。坑内有8,000

余尊真人真马大小的陶制兵马俑。和秦始皇陵的原始状态保存不同，这几个陪葬坑上面建有保护大厅，现已变成了中国最大的古代军事博物馆。这些兵马俑是博物馆几代工作人员，历时三十多年，从无数残片中寻找对比，将属于同一尊兵马俑的陶片粘在一起，才使沉睡2,200多年的兵马俑复活了。

At the north foot of Mount Li, located five kilometers east of Lintong County in China's Shaanxi Province, there is a 55-meter-high mound. Qin Shi Huang, the talented and far-sighted emporer is buried beneath its surface. The Mausoleum of Qin Shi Huang was constructed from 246 to 208 BC; 720,000 laborers spent 39 years to build it. Countless palaces formerly stood on the burial mound and a magnificent palace was built below ground. It is said that Qin Shi Huang used a large amount of mercury to imitate the rivers, lakes and seas of his empire, symbolizing the world that he had conquered.

In February 1974, 1.5 kilometers from the east end of the Mausoleum of Qin Shi Huang, a few farmers, while digging a well, accidentally dug up several life-sized ceramic statue heads. This led to the discovery of an accompanying burial pit of the Mausoleum of Qin Shi Huang, deemed one of the greatest archaeological discoveries of the 20th century. After this discovery was made, a massive archaeological excavation that shocked the world was initiated.

Three large-scale accompanying burial pits were sequentially excavated, and named Terracotta Army Pit One, Two and Three, respectively. Distributed in a triangular layout, the pits cover a total area of over 22,000 square meters. Inside the pits are more than 8,000 life-sized terracotta figures of humans and horses. Whereas the Mausoleum of Qin Shi Huang was preserved in its original state, a protection hall was built on these accompanying burial pits. Today, they have been converted into China's largest ancient military museum. Museum workers spent over 30 years to find and place countless broken fragments of these terracotta warriors. Only after the ceramic fragments were carefully put back to the statues to

小贴士 《史记》是中国历史上第一部纪传体通史，作者是西汉时期的司马迁。全书共一百三十篇，记事时间始于传说中的黄帝时期，一直到汉武帝元狩元年，叙述了中国古代三千年左右的历史。该书中的《秦始皇本纪》以编年记事的形式，记载了秦始皇及秦二世一生的主要活动和所发生的重大事件。

TIPS *The first emperor* Ying Zheng, the King of Qin, united China for the first time in Chinese history in 221 B.C. He gave himself the title "Shihuangdi", which means the first emperor. He declared that his descendants be entitled the second, the third, and so on, with the hope that the reign of the Qin Dynasty could continue forever. Since then, the title "Emperor" was used to address the feudal monarch in China.

秦始皇陵及兵马俑

从各坑形制结构和兵马俑装备来看，一号坑最大，有6,000多尊陶人陶马，主要是步兵和战车，井然有序地排列成环形方阵；二号坑还没有复原，经探测发现，主要是骑兵和战车，加上步兵和弩兵，四个兵种混编成一个大型混合部队；三号坑最小，似乎是整个军团的指挥部。秦始皇曾拥有当时世界上人数最多的军队，这个兵马俑陪葬军团显然是秦始皇按照自己军队的原样制作的。

兵俑身材魁梧、姿态端正、长相各异、威风凛凛。在当时条件下，雕塑能取得这么高的成就，在世界上都是极为罕见的。兵俑的发式、装束完全是按照军中爵位等级划分的。梳椎髻、穿便装的弩兵叫公士，爵位最低；身穿铠甲、戴着圆帽的步兵叫做上造，级别要高一级。公士和上造构成了秦军的主体。双手按剑、气势威严的军官俑是都尉，他是这个阵列中的最高指挥官。军官俑帽子形状十分独

which they belonged were these terracotta warriors, who had lain dormant for over 2,200 years, finally brought back to life.

Judging from the shape and structure of each pit as well as the equipment and accessories found in each one, Pit One is the largest. It contains over 6,000 terracotta warriors and horses, mainly infantrymen and war chariots, neatly arranged in a square-shaped formation. Although Pit Two has not been fully restored, surveying work indicates that it consists mainly of cavalrymen and war chariots, as well as infantry and archers; these four types of units were amalgamated into a large-scale mixed force. Pit Three is the smallest and seems to be the command post for the entire legion. Qin Shi Huang once had the largest army in the world; this accompanying burial legion of terracotta warriors was clearly made according to the original appearance of Qin Shi Huang's own army.

Behold the majestic-looking terracotta warriors, each with unique feature, grand stature and upright posture. Such an impressive sculptural achievement was a rare feat in the world under the conditions of the time. The hairstyle and attire of the different terracotta warriors correspond with their military rank. The archers, who wear everyday clothes and have their hair tied in knots, are called *gongshi*; they have the lowest rank. The infantrymen, who wear loricae and round caps, are known as *shangzao* and rank just above the *gongshi*. The *gongshi* and *shangzao* formed the main body of the Qin army. The statue of the mighty and dignified military officer, with his hands placed over his sword, represents the *duwei*; he is the highest commander in this battalion. His hat has a very unique shape and the loricae that he wears is the most exquisite of all the ceramic statues; the front and back of his upper garment has a floral

TIPS *The Records of the Historian* by Sima Qian in the Western Han Dynasty is the first historical record presented in a series of biographies. This book contains altogether 130 pieces, recording a history of 3000 years in ancient China from the period of the legendary Huang Di to the first year of Emperor Wu Di of the Han Dynasty. The Biography of the First Qin Emperor was written in the form of a chronicle listing the major events during the reign of Qin shihuang and his successor Qinershi, the Second Qin Emperor.

特，所穿铠甲是所有陶俑中最为精致的，前胸和后背都有花结。这些花结类似于现代军官的肩章。据此推断，秦军已经建立了比较完备的军衔体系，组织管理已经很接近今天的军队了。

秦军的装备非常精良。兵马俑坑共出土了四万多件各式各样的青铜兵器。这些兵器是由铜和锡搭配冶炼出来的，非常坚固，而且规格都完全一致。由此看出，那时候的秦国已经实现了兵器的标准化生产。秦弩杀伤力非常强大，有效射程达到300米，有效杀伤距离达到150米，是普通弓箭的三倍。秦弩安装了精巧的发射扳机和瞄准工具，这使它成为古代战场上最为精准的远程武器。坑内战马昂首嘶鸣，栩栩如生，高度都是133厘米，令人称奇。

秦军不仅兵器先进，阵列组合和兵种协同作战的部署也是非常严密的。兵马俑坑中有一支纯粹由64辆战车组成的部队，后面没有跟随步兵，这支独立战车部队的攻击速度相当于骑兵。再看这个阵列，前锋是三排弩兵，后卫也是三排弩兵，右翼有两列士兵，一列朝前，一列面墙而立，左翼也有一列士兵，面向外。整

pattern, similar to the epaulets worn by today's military officers. Based on these facts, we can infer that the Qin army had a fairly comprehensive system of military rank, with organizational management approaching levels of modern armies.

The equipment of the Qin army is flawlessly refined. Over 40,000 bronze weapons of all varieties have been excavated from the Terracotta Army pits. These weapons were smelted using a combination of copper and tin, making them extremely sturdy; furthermore, the specifications of each weapon are identical. It is thus evident that the State of Qin had already achieved standardized weapons production by this time. The Qin crossbow was an extremely lethal weapon. It had a range of 300 meters and an effective killing range of 150 meters, three times that of a regular bow and arrow. With an exquisite trigger mechanism and aiming device, the Qin crossbow was the most accurate long-range weapon on the ancient battlefields. Inside the pit, the war horses—each of which measures 133 centimeters in height—raise their heads and whinny, coming to life and amazing onlookers.

The Qin army not only boasted advanced weaponry, but the combination of its battle arrays and the coordination of different combat arms were extremely rigorous and precise. One of the Terracotta Army pits contains an army unit comprised solely of 64 chariots, with no infantry following behind. The attack speed of this independent chariot unit was equivalent to that of cavalrymen. Now, take a look at this battle array: the vanguard and rearguard each consists of three rows of archers; the right flank contains two rows of soldiers, one row facing forward and another facing the wall; and the left flank consists of one row of soldiers facing outward. The entire unit, imbued with stern and awe-inspiring vigor, stands

小贴士 世界第八大奇迹 1978年9月，法国总统希拉克在参观秦兵马俑后留下这样的赞词："世界上曾有七大奇迹，秦俑的发现，可以说是'第八大奇迹'了，不看金字塔不算真正到过埃及，不看秦俑不算真正到过中国。"从此，"第八大奇迹"便成为秦始皇兵马俑的代名词。

个军阵严阵以待、气势凛然。这种阵形既可以提防大军的左右两翼遭遇敌人的突然袭击,又可以在前锋、后卫和两翼的护卫下,保护阵中主力部队。阵列攻守平衡,破坏力和震慑力都极为强大,应该是古代战争中最经典的军阵范例。

1980年12月,在秦始皇陵西侧还出土了两组彩绘铜车马。这两辆铜车是根据秦始皇生前的御用车辆仿制的,除了大小是真车真马的一半之外,在形制上跟真车真马一模一样,号称中国考古史上发掘出的最精美的铜车马,被誉为中国古代的"青铜之冠"。

秦始皇陵兵马俑规模宏大、内涵丰富、世所罕见,被誉为"世界第八大奇迹"。1987年秦始皇陵被联合国教科文组织列入《世界文化遗产名录》。

in combat readiness. This kind of formation could prevent the left and right flanks of the Qin army from befalling a sudden attack by the enemy; and could also safeguard the army's main force under the protection of the vanguard, rearguard and flanks. With its mighty destructive power, fear-based deterrence and ingenious balance between offense and defense, this formation can be considered the most classic battle array of ancient combat.

In December 1980, two sets of painted bronze chariots and horses were also unearthed on the west side of the Mausoleum of Qin Shi Huang. These two bronze chariots were modeled after the chariot used by Qin Shi Huang during his lifetime. Aside from the fact that the chariot and horse are half-size miniatures, their shape and structure are indistinguishable from those of real-life chariots and horses. They are regarded as the most exquisite bronze horses and chariots unearthed in China's archaeological history, and are described as "the best of the bronzes" of ancient China.

Reputed as the "Eighth Wonder of the World", the Terracotta Army is grand in scale, rich in meaning, and unique within the world. In 1987, the Mausoleum of the First Qin Emperor was inscribed to the UNESCO World Heritage List.

TIPS | **The Eighth Wonder of the World** In September 1978, after visiting the Terracotta Warriors, the former French President Jacques Chirac commented: "There used to be 7 wonders in the world. Since the discovery of the Terracotta Warriors, there's an eighth one. One cannot be considered to have been to Egypt until he visits the pyramids; without visiting the Terracotta Warriors, one cannot be considered to have been to China." Since then, the Terracotta Warriors has been taken as the "Eighth Wonder of the World".

周口店"北京人"遗址
Peking Man Site at Zhoukoudian

  周口店"北京人"遗址位于北京西南48公里处,遗址的科学考察工作至今仍在进行。到目前为止,科学家已经发现了中国猿人属"北京人"的遗迹,他们大约生活在中更新世时代,同时发现的还有各种各样的生活物品,以及可以追溯到公元前18,000年到公元前11,000年的新人类的遗迹。周口店遗址不仅是有关远古时期亚洲大陆人类社会的一个罕见的历史证据,而且也阐明了人类进化的进程。

世界遗产委员会评价

  周口店"北京人"遗址,位于北京市房山区周口店村的龙骨山,距北京城约50公里。这里处于山区和平原接壤部位,附近山地多为石灰岩,在水力作用下,形成大小不等的天然洞穴,成为埋藏"龙骨"的仓库,故名龙骨山。山上有一个东西长约140米,南北宽2.5~42米不等的天然洞穴。这个洞穴是50

  Scientific work at the site, which lies 48 km southwest of Beijing, is still underway. So far, it has led to the discovery of the remains of Sinanthropus pekinensis, who lived in the Middle Pleistocene, along with various objects, and remains of Homo sapiens dating as far back as 18,000–11,000 B.C. The site is not only an exceptional reminder of the prehistorical human societies of the Asian continent, but also illustrates the process of evolution.

  The Peking Man Site at Zhoukoudian is located at Longgushan (Dragon Bone Hill) in Zhoukoudian Village, Fangshan District, Beijing, about 50 kilometers from Beijing proper. The area lies at the border

小贴士 "北京人"的生存环境 50万年前北京的地质地貌与现在基本相似,在丘陵山地上分布有茂密的森林群落。但也曾出现过面积广阔的草原和沙漠,其中有鸵鸟和骆驼栖息的遗迹。这表明在这段漫长的岁月里,北京曾出现过温暖湿润和寒冷干燥的气候状况,可见当时北京猿人的生存环境非常艰辛。

Date of inscription: 1987
Heritage category: 文化遗产 C
Criteria: C(III)(VI)

万年以前北京猿人栖息的地方,他们先后在洞穴里群居了四十多万年。后来,这个洞被塌方的泥沙和崩落的石块所埋。

between mountainous terrain and plains. The nearby mountains consist predominantly of limestone; under the action of water, many natural caves of various sizes were formed, creating a large warehouse of "dragon bones", hence the name "Dragon Bone Hill." (The dragon is the symbol of the Chinese people.) On the hill, there is a natural cave that is about 140 meters long from east to west and 2.5 to 42 meters long from south to north. This cave was inhabited by Peking Man and his contemporaries 500,000 years ago; they lived gregariously here for more than 400,000 years, leaving behind left-over food, used wares and their own remains. Later, the cave was buried by collapsed sediment and fallen stones.

In 1987, the Peking Man Site at Zhoukoudian was inscribed to the UNESCO World Heritage List.

Among all the sites of ancient human remains discovered to date in the world, the Peking Man Site at Zhoukoudian contains the richest and most vivid human fossils, boasts the most plant fossil varieties, and has produced the most in-depth research. The most well-known is the first site of Zhoukoudian—Peking Man Site. In 1929, Pei Wenzhong, a Chinese paleontologist, discovered the first complete cranium of Peking Man here, which stirred the world. In later excavations, more ancient relics were discovered in the Ape Man Cave on the north slope of Dragon Bone Hill, including approximately 200 human fossils respectively representing 40 ape-men, about 10,000 stoneware articles, and roughly 200 animal fossils.

The appearance of Peking Man and his contemporaries can be inferred from the excavated crania. They had a low and flat forehead, bulky and extruding eyebrow bones covering deep-set eyes, forward extruding lips, strong teeth, and a thick skull—roughly twice as thick as that of modern man.

1987年,联合国教科文组织将周口店"北京人"遗址列入《世界遗产名录》。

周口店遗址是世界上迄今为止人类化石材料最丰富、最生动,植物化石门类最齐全,研究最深入的古人类遗址。1929年,中国古生物学家裴文中在这里发现"北京人"的第一个完整的头盖骨,轰动了世界。在其后的挖掘中,在龙骨山北坡的猿人洞内还发现了更多的远古遗存,其中包括近200件人类化石,分别代表40个猿人个体,还有上万件石器和近200种动物化石。

从挖掘出来的头骨可以推测北京猿人的外

TIPS The living environment of Peking Man The geological environment and geo-morphological structure of Beijing has not changed much during the past 500,000 years. This area is a range of undulating hills overgrown with lush forests. However, traces of ostriches and camels indicate that there used to be vast pastures and desert area. This also proves that in such a long history, the climate of Beijing had climates from warm and humid to cold and dry. It can be seen that the living circumstance of Peking Man were rather tough and difficult.

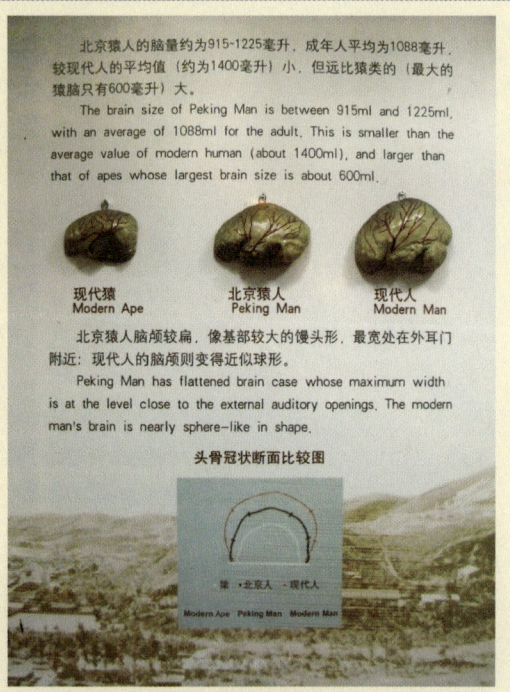

北京猿人的脑量约为915-1225毫升，成年人平均为1088毫升，较现代人的平均值（约为1400毫升）小，但远比猿类的（最大的猿脑只有600毫升）大。

The brain size of Peking Man is between 915ml and 1225ml, with an average of 1088ml for the adult. This is smaller than the average value of modern human (about 1400ml), and larger than that of apes whose largest brain size is about 600ml.

现代猿　　北京猿人　　现代人
Modern Ape　Peking Man　Modern Man

北京猿人脑颅较扁，像基部较大的馒头形，最宽处在外耳门附近；现代人的脑颅则变得近似球形。
Peking Man has flattened brain case whose maximum width is at the level close to the external auditory openings. The modern man's brain is nearly sphere-like in shape.

头骨冠状断面比较图
猿·北京人·现代人
Modern Ape　Peking Man　Modern Man

貌，他们前额低平，眉骨粗大突出，遮盖着深陷的双眼，嘴唇向前伸出，牙齿粗壮，脑壳很厚，大约比现代人要厚一倍。"北京人"的脑容量大约只有现代人的80%，但是和猿类相比则又要大得多。根据脑壳模型来推测，他们应该有了简单的语言。"北京人"的身材并不高大，男性156厘米，女性144厘米，寿命很短，超过40岁的不多，儿童死亡率非常高。

在"北京人"遗址发现的用火遗迹，将人类用火的历史提前了几十万年。遗址中发现有5个灰烬层、3处灰堆遗存以及大量的烧骨，灰烬层最厚处可达6米。这些遗迹表明"北京人"不仅懂得用火，而且会保存火种。

遗址中还出土了数以万计的石制品。石器是"北京人"文化的主要代表。石器和骨器的制作和使用，是人类和猿的根本区别。正是由这些简

The cranial capacity of Peking Man was about 80% of that of modern man but much larger than that of the ape. According to skull models, it can be concluded that they used simple language. The stature of Peking Man and his associates was short—156 centimeters for males and 144 centimeters for females. Furthermore, they had a short lifespan; few of them lived beyond the age of 40 and the death rate of children was extremely high.

Traces of fire use discovered at the Peking Man Site brought forward the recorded history of human fire use by several hundreds of thousands of years. At the site, five ash layers, three ash piles and many burnt stones were discovered; the thickest point of the ash layers measures up to six meters. These relics indicate that Peking Man not only knew how to use fire but also had the ability to maintain fire.

On the site, tens of thousands of stoneware articles have also been excavated. Stoneware is the main representative of the culture of Peking Man. The making and use of stoneware and bone implements

小贴士　"北京人"的进化　"北京人"生存在距今70～20万年前，其间发生过至少一次"间冰期"（地球冰川回旋）。他们属石器时代的人类，穴居，能制造工具。这些本领使"北京人"能够适应周口店地区自然环境的变迁。他们懂得用火，不但能取暖度过严寒，且能烧烤食物，而熟食又使"北京人"大脑得以进化。

陋的工具开始，人类文明的序幕被缓缓拉开。

自达尔文的进化论问世以来，科学和宗教关于人类起源的争执一刻也没有停息。19世纪末，"爪哇猿人"的发现，不但没有平息这一争执，反而在科学界的内部也有了不同声音。北京猿人头盖骨化石的发现，不仅平息了爪哇人的争论，更是进化论观点在自然世界的投影，为人类起源提供了大量富有说服力的证据。大量事实表明，"北京人"生活在距今50万年前到20万年前之间，是属于从古猿进化到智人的中间环节的原始人类。

1930年，在龙骨山顶部发掘出生活于两万年前后的古人类化石，并命名为"山顶洞人"。"山顶洞人"的发现，再次在科学界引起了轰动。在"山顶洞人"遗址发现了三个成年男女完整的头盖骨和残骨，尸骨周围发现撒有红色的赤铁矿粉末。洞内还发现"山顶洞人"用过的骨针、穿孔的骨坠、鱼骨、牙饰、石珠串联而成的"项链"，这些足以证明他们已学会缝制兽皮衣

constitute the fundamental difference between man and ape. It was these simple tools that slowly began the prelude of human civilization.

Since the beginning of Darwinism, dissension between science and religion about the origin of human beings has not ceased for a single moment. At the end of the 19th century, the discovery of Java Man did not quiet down this dissension; rather, it activated different voices in the scientific community instead. The discovery of the cranium of Peking Man not only calmed the dissension regarding Java Man but also reflected Darwinism from nature and provided substantial and persuasive evidence for the origin of humankind. A large body of evidence offers proof that Peking Man lived between 500,000 years and 200,000 years ago and was the transitional primitive human between ancient ape and Homo sapiens.

In 1930, ancient human fossils dated to 20,000 years ago were unearthed in the upper cave on Dragon Bone Hill and were named "Upper Cave Man." The discovery of Upper Cave Man again stirred the scientific circle. On the Upper Cave Man site, the complete crania and skeletons of three adults, around which was spread red hematite powder, were discovered. In addition, bone needles, perforated bone ornaments, fish bones, tooth ornaments and necklaces of stone balls in series used by Upper Cave Man were also found in the cave. These sufficiently prove that they had learned to make hide clothes to maintain warmth and understood how to dress up, reflecting the origins of the primitive art of Upper Cave Man. According to scientific estimates, the body of the Upper Cave Man was not

TIPS **The evolution of Peking Man** Peking Man lived 200,000 to 700,000 years ago, and during that period there was at least one interglacial period between glacial periods. Peking Man lived in the Stone Age and inhabited in caves. They could make tools, which enabled them to adapt to the changing environment around Zhoukoudian area. They knew how to make fire, so they could cook food and get heating in the cold winter. Eating cooked food also helped their brain develop and evolve.

服御寒，懂得装扮自己，反映出"山顶洞人"原始艺术的萌芽。根据科学估测："山顶洞人"的躯体特征和现代人无明显区别，他们是原始的黄种人；他们生活在距今18,000年前，比"北京人"又大大前进了一步。

1973年，科学家又发现了介于北京人和山顶洞人年代之间的"新洞人"。"新洞人"的化石发现较少，最主要的是这三颗牙齿，同样证明了人类进化的延续和发展。

周口店遗址不仅是有关远古时期亚洲大陆人类社会的一个罕见的历史证据，而且也阐明了人类进化的进程。时至今日，对周口店的挖掘和探索仍然没有停止，周口店就像一个取之不尽的原始人类文化宝库，为我们揭示了一个又一个不为人知的秘密。

obviously different from that of modern man. As the primitive yellow race, they lived 18,000 years ago and are much closer to modern man than Peking Man.

In 1973, scientists made another discovery—the so-called New Cave Man, who lived between the periods of Peking Man and Upper Cave Man. Despite the limited number of New Cave Man fossils discovered, these three teeth, in and of themselves, offer evidence of the continuous development and evolution of humankind.

The Peking Man Site at Zhoukoudian not only offers a rare piece of evidence proving the existence of human society on the Asian continent in ancient times, but also serves to clarify the course of human evolution. To the present day, excavation and exploration at the site are still ongoing. Zhoukoudian, an infinite treasure house of primitive human culture, has provided and will continue to provide us with the answers to many of world's deepest mysteries.

收录时间 Date of inscription：1987
遗产类别 Heritage category：双重遗产 CN
收录理由 Criteria：C(I)(II)(III)(IV)(V)(VI);N(III)

泰 山
Mount Taishan

庄严神圣的泰山，两千年来一直是帝王朝拜的对象，山中的人文杰作与自然景观完美和谐地融合在一起。泰山一直是中国艺术家和学者的精神源泉，是古代中国文明和信仰的象征。

世界遗产委员会评价

泰山位于中国山东省中部，东西绵延200多公里，南北宽约50公里。蹲坐在华北平原上，具

The sacred Mount Tai (or Mount Taishan, 'shan' means 'mountain') was the object of an imperial cult for nearly 2,000 years, and the artistic masterpieces found there are in perfect harmony with the natural landscape. It has always been a source of inspiration for Chinese artists and scholars and symbolizes ancient Chinese civilizations and beliefs.

Mount Tai, situated in central Shandong Province, stretches across over 200 kilometers from east to west and about 50 kilometers from north to south. Rising above the North China Plain, Mount Tai is the most respected of the Sacred Mountains of China and is a holy land for the Chinese people.

Mount Tai has a broad base and a structure that is colossal and concentrated, giving people a feeling of stability in spite of any fluctuations occurring in the world or universe. The fracturing of rock strata resulted in Mount Tai's deep valleys and precipitous slopes, with the highest precipice reaching up to 800 meters, creating an illusion that it is extending upward into the heavens.

Mount Tai, which was formed 2.5 billion years ago, possesses the oldest geological stratum on the planet, providing tremendous value for geological investigation. The features of these rocks show traces left by flowing magma in ancient times. These fossils, meanwhile, present a record of life on earth some

 小贴士 封 帝王在山顶堆土筑坛，登坛祭天，答谢上天赐予他执掌天下的权利，这个仪式称作封。禅 在山下的小土丘扫土祭地，回报土地山川的滋养之恩，这个仪式称为禅。

有五岳独尊的地位，是中华民族通天的圣地。

泰山基础宽阔，形体庞大而集中，给人天压不倒、地动不摇的安稳感。岩层的断裂使其谷深壁陡，切割最深处达800米，在视觉上给人一种峻急于天、直冲霄汉的感觉。

形成于25亿年前的泰山拥有地球上最古老的地层，地质科学研究价值具有世界意义。泰山上千变万化的岩石形态就是当年岩浆涌动留下的痕迹。而那些多彩多姿的化石则记录了五亿年前生命的形态。

泰山的自然形态，拓展了中国人的想象空间，使它承载起一个古老民族的精神世界。

公元前219年，中国的第一位皇帝秦始皇登上泰山，昭告天下统一中国的伟业。从此，封禅泰山成为中国封建王朝最高规格的祭祀大典。泰山也因此成为"中华第一山"。在泰山脚下的天地广场上，竖立着12根龙柱，它们代表中国历史上曾经封禅或拜祭过泰山的12位皇帝。据说泰山封禅的隆重程度，超过了历代帝王登基的仪式。

"泰山安，天下安"的信仰让泰山上的石头具有了震妖驱邪的神力。很多中国人都喜欢在居住的地方立一块泰山石，以求驱邪避难，保佑平安。

泰山的美吸引了古往今来的文学家、艺术家，他们登临泰山，描绘泰山。在中国文化典籍中，留下了歌咏泰山的诗文两千多篇。泰山

500 million years ago.

The imaginations of the Chinese people have been widened by the natural features of Mount Tai. The mountain carries with it the spiritual world of this ancient people.

In 219 BC, Qin Shi Huang, the first emperor of China, ascended Mount Tai and proclaimed the great exploit of unifying China. From then on, offering sacrifices to heaven and earth on Mount Tai became the highest-scale sacrificial ceremony for China's feudal dynasties. This is also the reason why Mount Tai became the "No. 1 Mountain in China." There are 12 sculptured dragon pillars standing on the Heaven and Earth Square at the foot of Mount Tai; these pillars represent the 12 emperors who worshiped or held sacrifices on the mountain. It is said that heavenly worship at Mount Tai was even grander and more solemn than emperors' enthronement ceremonies.

The belief that "If Mount Tai is stable, so is the entire country" brought Mount Tai supernatural powers which could drive out evil spirits. Many Chinese people place a stone from Mount Tai in their

小贴士 五岳 中国五大名山的总称。即东岳泰山、南岳衡山、西岳华山、北岳恒山、中岳嵩山。传说为神仙所居，历代帝王多往祭祀。

TIPS | "*Feng*" refers to a ritual that the emperor stepped on the altar built on the top of a mountain to offer sacrifices to Heaven. In this way, the emperor expressed his gratitude for Heaven that he was granted the power to rule the country. "*Shan*" refers to another ritual of offering sacrifices to Earth by sweeping a mound at the foot of a mountain and to repay the favor of the earth, as everything grew on the earth was nourished by the soil and water.

泰山

上下遍布碑刻800余块，崖刻1,000余处，行走在山中，就像徜徉在书法艺术的博物馆。泰山上现存最壮观的一块刻石，是唐代第七位皇帝唐玄宗留下的。这篇《纪泰山铭》被刻在一座山崖的陡壁上，高13米多，宽近6米，有1,000字，虽经风雨磨砺，一千多年前涂的金粉仍金光灿灿。

每年农历四月十八，泰山都会出现万众朝山的宏伟场面。据说这天是泰山老奶奶碧霞元君的生日。传说碧霞元君敢于惩暴除恶，保护弱小，救苦救难，是道教中地位最高的女性神灵。对女性的崇拜，折射着原始的太阳崇拜、东方崇拜和生命崇拜。在普通中国人的心里，泰山是孕育他们生命，安抚他们心灵的母亲。

dwelling places, believing that it will offer protection against evil as well as blessings of peace and safety.

Through the ages, the natural beauty of Mount Tai has attracted artists and writers to scale its slopes and depict it through art and literature. In ancient Chinese texts, there are more than 2,000 poems glorifying Mount Tai. From the foot of the mountain to its summit, there are over 800 inscribed stone tablets and more than 1,000 cliff-side inscriptions. As visitors climb up the mountain, they may feel as though they are wandering through a Chinese calligraphy museum. This cliff-side inscription is the most spectacular inscription surviving on Mount Tai; it was written by Emperor Xuanzong, the seventh emperor of the Tang Dynasty. This inscription, entitled *Ji Tai Shan Ming*, is carved on the wall of a steep cliff. Measuring 13 meters high and six meters wide, it contains over 1,000 Chinese characters. Despite having been exposed to and hardened by nature, the gold powder painted on the cliff over 1,000 years ago is still just as bright and dazzling as ever.

Every year, on the 18th day of the fourth lunar month, thousands of people come to Mount Tai, creating a magnificent spectacle. As the story goes, this date is the birthday of Mount Tai's *Bixia Yuanjun* (the Primordial Lady of Emerald Clouds and Heavenly Immortal Jade Maiden). According to legend, and Jade Maiden is brave and courageous; she punishes cruelty and thwarts evil; helps the needy and relieves the distressed; and protects the weak and the small. She is the highest ranking female deity of Taoism. Adoration of females is a reflection of primordial adoration of the sun, of the eastern direction, and of life. For ordinary Chinese people, Mount Tai is a motherly figure, giving them life and nurturing their soul.

TIPS | The **Five Sacred Mountains** refer to the five famous mountains in China, Mount Tai in the east, Mount Heng in the South, Mount Hua in the west, Mount Heng in the north and Mount Song in the Central Plains. It is said that gods lived in those sacred mountains, so the imperial emperors of all dynasties went to these mountains to offer sacrifices to gods and ancestors.

小贴士 公元110年，汉武帝首次提出，举行泰山封禅必须具备三个条件：一是扫平宇内、天下一统。二是天下太平、长治久安。三是不断有祥瑞出现。

　　人们说登泰山是人生的一种境界，从山脚到山顶，共6,293级台阶，10公里的路程。在这里登山就像登天。利用山体断层设计的三个天门是三个境界。跨过一天门，人就离开了尘世。越过中天门就踏上了天梯。这一步一个台阶的登攀就像努力进取、自强不息的生命历程。登山路两旁有许多充满人生哲理的石刻。

　　"登高必自"意思是往高处攀登一定得从低处开始；往远处行走一定得从近处起步。"从善如登，从恶如崩"意思是美德的提高，就像登山一样，越往上越艰难；但恶习的放纵，就像山崩一样瞬间就溃退到底。

　　泰山上的挑山工都是山脚下的普通村民。自古以来，泰山上所有的生产生活用品，包括建筑材料，都是靠他们挑上去的。为了减少体力的消耗，他们在台阶上走折尺形路线，这在无形中比游人又多走了一倍的路程。

People say that the ascent of Mount Tai offers a new realm of life. From the foot of the mountain to the summit, there are a total of 6,293 steps spanning a distance of 10 kilometers. At Mount Tai, climbing a mountain is like ascending to heaven. The three Gates to Heaven, designed to utilize the mountain's geological fault, offer three different realms. As one crosses the First Gate to Heaven, one effectively steps out of the material world. Crossing the Middle Gate to Heaven is just like climbing a divine staircase to the heavens. Step-by-step ascension of the mountain is akin to one's own life course—working hard and tirelessly while making unremitting efforts to improve. Large numbers of stone inscriptions, imbued with life philosophy, can be found on either side of the mountain trail. The phrase *"deng gao bi zi"* means that, in order to reach great heights, one must begin at a low point; and in order to travel afar, one must begin at a place nearby. The phrase *"cong shan ru deng, cong e ru beng"* means that improving one's morality and virtues

小贴士 岱庙 泰安城的岱庙是登泰山的起点。据说岱庙是仿造宋代皇宫建造的。其正殿天贶殿双层屋檐、四坡屋顶、九开间、五进深，与天子的宫殿同等规格。在现存的中国古代建筑中，只有北京故宫的太和殿与它相似。

TIPS | In 110 A.D., Emperor Wu Di of the Han Dynasty first proposed that there should be 3 prerequisites before offering sacrifices to Heaven and Earth on Mount Tai. The first one was having united the state, the second one was having established a stable and orderly society, and the last was that there appeared constant auspicious signs.

is like scaling a mountain—the higher up you climb, the more difficult the journey becomes. In contrast, self-abandonment and reckless behavior are like an avalanche, wreaking havoc in a mere instant.

These mountain porters are villagers who live near the foot of Mount Tai. Since ancient times, all of the production supplies, household goods and construction materials have been carried up the mountain by these men. In order to conserve energy, they take a route that resembles the shape of a folding ruler, like the letter "Z"; this enables them to conserve energy, but at the same time also makes their route twice as long as that of sightseers.

A precipitous flight of Eighteen Mountain Bends (Shibapan) leads to the third Gate to Heaven—the South Gate to Heaven. Immediately after crossing the South Gate to Heaven, a scene of the Heavenly Palaces, the Heavenly Sky, and the Heavenly Trail will spread out before your eyes. As you dance under the skies without a care in the world, it may be hard to suppress the feeling that you, too, have become an immortal.

TIPS | **Daimiao Temple** Daimiao Temple is the starting point when climbing Mount Tai. It is said that Daimiao Temple imitates the style of the imperial palace in the Song Dynasty. Tiankuang Hall, the main hall in the temple, has double eaves and hipped roof. It has a width that nine times that of a usual room and the distance from the entrance to the rear is five times that of a usual one. The main hall is of equal scale of the imperial palace. In the extant ancient architectures in China, only the Hall of Taihe in the Forbidden City is of similar design.

登上险陡的十八盘就到了泰山的第三个天门——夹在两座雄峰间的南天门——的确很像天庭的大门。南天门一过，满眼看到天宫、天界、天街，不由得飘飘然如同做了神仙。

泰山顶上有中国唯一一座高山文庙，庙里供奉的是儒家学说创立者孔子。儒家学说影响了中国人的思想几千年。在相当长的时间里，儒学即国学，孔庙就是文庙。

两千年来，泰山一直是中国帝王朝拜的对象，是中华民族的精神源泉。直到今天，泰山仍然给人无比庄严和神圣的感觉，让人感到生命的活力和召唤。

1987年，联合国教科文组织世界遗产委员会第11届会议通过泰山为世界文化与自然双重遗产。

This building, which stands on the summit of Mount Tai, is China's only Confucian temple located on a mountaintop. Confucius, the founder of Confucian philosophy, is worshiped at this temple. Confucian philosophy has influenced the Chinese people's thinking for thousands of years. For a very long time, *ruxue* (Confucian studies) and *guoxue* (Sinology) were equivalent for practical purposes. Confucian temples are also known as *wenmiao* (literally "culture temple" or "temple of literature").

For 2,000 years, Mount Tai was worshiped by China's emperors and served as a source of spirituality for the Chinese people. Even today, we can still feel the supreme grandeur and sacredness of Mount Tai, enabling us to feel life's vitality and beckoning call.

In 1987, at the 11th session of the UNESCO World Heritage Committee, Mount Tai was inscribed as a World Cultural and Natural Heritage Site.

收录时间 Date of inscription：1990
遗产类别 Heritage category：双重遗产 CN
收录理由 Criteria：C(II);N(III)(IV)

黄 山
Mount Huangshan

　　黄山，在中国历史上文学艺术的鼎盛时期（公元16世纪中叶的"山水"风格）曾受到广泛的赞誉，以"震旦国中第一奇山"而闻名。今天，黄山以其壮丽的景色——生长在花岗岩石上的奇松和浮现在云海中的怪石而著称。对于从四面八方来到这个风景胜地的游客、诗人、画家和摄影家而言，黄山具有永恒的魅力。

世界遗产委员会评价

　　登黄山，天下无山。

　　明朝旅行家徐霞客，在遍阅名山大川后，唯独给了黄山如此高的赞誉。

　　黄山位于安徽省南部，是长江与钱塘江两大水系的分水岭，面积约1,200平方公里，四季多

Mount Huangshan, known as "the loveliest mountain of China", was acclaimed through art and literature during a good part of Chinese history (e.g. the Shanshui "mountain and water" style of the mid-16th century). Today it holds the same fascination for visitors, poets, painters and photographers who come on pilgrimage to the site, which is renowned for its magnificent scenery made up of many granite peaks and rocks emerging out of a sea of clouds.

"There is no mountain worth visiting after ascending Mount Huangshan."

These were the words of the Ming Dynasty traveler Xu Xiake. Only after having visited all the famous mountains and rivers did he bestow this

小贴士 黄山分温泉、玉屏、北海、松谷、云谷、西海六大景区，有七十二峰（三十六大峰和三十六小峰）、二十四溪、三瀑、二湖以及众多的岩、洞、潭、泉，景色雄奇，风光秀丽。

雨，属亚热带季风气候。人们通常所说的黄山是指黄山中段已经开放的那一部分，是整个黄山山系的精华，面积约154平方公里。

黄山集众多名山胜景于一身，晴雨无常、四季迥异，素以奇松、怪石、云海、温泉"四绝"闻名天下。

黄山素有"无松不奇"的美誉，许多古松姿态优美，性格各异。它们有的破石而出，有的倒悬于绝壁当中，有的耸立于高山之巅……严酷的自然环境，使得黄山松生长速度极其缓慢，一棵高不盈丈的黄山松，树龄往往高达百年，甚至数百年。黄山古松中著名的迎客松，高10米，寿龄800余年，如人伸出手臂欢迎远道而来的客人，是黄山标志性景观。

黄山的石头可谓鬼斧神工，它们似兽、似禽、似人、似物，惟妙惟肖、逼真有趣。松鼠

highest praise on Huangshan.

Located in southern Anhui Province, Huangshan serves as the dividing ridge of the Yangtze River and the Qiantang River. The Huangshan mountain range, which covers an area of about 1,200 square kilometers, is rainy throughout the year and subject to the tropical monsoon climate. When people talk about Huangshan, they are usually referring to the section open to tourists in the middle of the Huangshan mountain range. Covering an area of 154 square kilometers, this section is the quintessence of the entire mountain system.

The Huangshan mountain range integrates scenic wonders of various famous mountains, with changing weather and distinct seasons. It has always been renowned for its "Four Wonders": peculiar pines, bizarre rocks, the sea of clouds (Yunhai), and hot springs.

It has been said that "there would be nothing

小贴士 连心锁 黄山山路两旁的护栏铁链上扣着许多连心锁，是年轻情侣表示互相忠贞的一种方式。系锁人将锁扣好后，将钥匙抛入悬崖之下，以表示永结同心。

TIPS There are six famous scenic spots in Huangshan, which are the Hot Spring, Yuping, the North Sea, the Pine Valley, the Cloudy Valley, and the West Sea. Other scenic spots worth visiting include the 72 peaks (36 large peaks and 36 small ones), 24 brooks, 3 waterfalls, 2 lakes and numerous rocks, caves, ponds and springs. Huangshan is famous for its magnificent and extraordinary scenery.

跳天都、猴子观海、梦笔生花，以及仙人指路、仙人晒靴，人们几乎给每一块黄山的石头，都取了悦耳动听的名字，而每个名字背后都有一个美丽的神话传说或历史故事。

变化莫测的云雾是黄山的神来之笔，为黄山平添了一份悠远神秘的意境。

黄山一年中的云雾天多达两百多天，在亚热带温湿气候条件下，大气中水汽经常凝结成云。每当云雾漫上群峰，远远望去就像大海生起波涛，山岩和古松在云海之上隐约浮现，仿佛有不可知的生命神游其间。这时就连平日气度非凡的天都峰、光明顶也成了小小的孤岛，让人一时天上人间，真幻莫辨。

黄山有很多看云海的理想地点，玉屏楼观南海，清凉台望北海，排云亭看西海，白鹅岭赏东海。由于山谷地形各不相同，同一时刻各处的云

wonderful about Huangshan without its pines." Many of these ancient pines are elegant in posture and distinct in style. Some spear out from the rocks, some hang upside down on the precipice, and some rise on the top of the mountains.... The extreme environment greatly slows down the pines' growth. As a result, a pine no taller than four meters may be over one hundred or even several hundreds of years in age. The well-known Welcoming Pine, which measures 10 meters in height and is over 800 years old, is the symbolic scene of Huangshan. Its posture looks like an arm stretching out to welcome guests coming from afar.

The fascinating and lifelike rocks at Huangshan are an incredible masterpiece of nature, with shapes that closely resemble beasts, birds, human beings and objects. Nearly every rock at Huangshan has been given a beautiful name, such as "the Squirrel Jumping on the Celestial Peak", "the Monkey Gazing at Sea", "Flowers Blossoming in a Dream", "the Immortal Showing the Way" and "the Immortal Drying a Boot." Every name has a beautiful legend or historical story behind it.

The changeable clouds are the most attractive scene of Huangshan, adding a sense of remoteness and mystery to it.

Huangshan may have up to 200 misty or cloudy days every year, as vapor in the air frequently condenses into clouds under the moist subtropical climate. Whenever the clouds are floating among the peaks, as you gaze from afar, you will feel as though you were looking out at a wavy sea. Rocks and pines emerge indistinguishably above the sea of clouds, as if there were unknown creatures wandering joyously in it. At this moment, even the Celestial Peak and the Bright Summit Peak, which are magnificent on normal days, will turn into small isolated islands,

TIPS **The Couple's Lock** There are many locks shaped in two linked hearts locked onto the iron guardrails alongside the mountain paths. Young couples lock up the heart-shaped locks and throw away the keys over the cliff. The lock is used to show the bond of love of a couple.

海往往彼此迥然不同。

当浩浩荡荡的云海与日出或夕阳交相辉映，一卷卷浮云被万道霞光照彻，如同一团团红叶托着一轮红日漂浮群峰之间，那又是一种壮丽绚烂的景象。

黄山四季个性分明，各有特色，最令人叫绝的恐怕要数黄山的冬季。黄山冬雪之妙在于它与黄山四绝巧妙结合，令它们在冬日里呈现出匪夷所思的全新面貌。雪后的黄山银装素裹，格外迷人。莲花峰宛如一朵盛开的雪莲，天都峰瞬时化作一位洁白无暇的神女，九龙峰则如一条蜿蜒的玉龙，飞舞白云之上。冬天的黄山，不仅可以看到冰挂、雾凇、雪莲等奇景，云海、佛光等现象也比平时出现得更加频繁。当气温降到零下时，浓重的雾气凝结在树木、石块、草丛等物体上，立即冻结成了白色固体冰晶，这便是雾凇景观。每当雾凇出现，整个黄山就变成了一个洁白盛大的珊瑚世界。

黄山与宗教文化有着密切关系，仙道故事流传千年，影响深广，许多山峰由此得名，如轩辕峰、浮丘峰、炼丹、仙都等。

making it difficult to distinguish heaven from earth, or reality from illusion.

There are several ideal spots to enjoy the sea of clouds at Huangshan: Yuping Pavilion to view the South Sea (Nanhai), Qingliang Pavilion to look out at the North Sea (Beihai), Paiyun Pavilion to gaze upon the West Sea (Xihai), and Bai'e Ridge to admire the East Sea (Donghai). Owing to the valley's diverse landscapes, these spots provide vastly different views of the sea of clouds even at the same time.

When the grandiose sea of clouds intersects with sunrise or sunset, the floating clouds are lightened by the rosy glow of dawn or dusk, respectively, like clusters of red leaves carrying the red sun as it floats among the peaks. This is another glorious scene of Huangshan.

Huangshan features four distinct seasons, each of which has its own unique characteristics. The season most favored at Huangshan, however, is winter. The merit of the snow here is that it integrates well with the Four Wonders of Huangshan and thus gives them an incredible and brand-new image in winter. After a snowfall, Huangshan, clad in white, is extraordinarily amazing, with the Lotus Peak (Lianhuafeng) like a blossoming white lily, the Celestial Peak a pure fairy, and the Nine Dragon Peak (Jiulongfeng) a winding white dragon soaring above the clouds. In wintertime, Huangshan will present before your eyes not only wonderful views like glaze ice, rime and white lilies, but also more frequent appearances of the sea of clouds and Buddha's Light (Foguang). The rime is formed when dense fog condenses on trees, rocks or grass, and is immediately frozen into ice crystals as the temperature falls below 0°C. When rime appears, the whole Huangshan becomes a giant white world of corals.

Intimately related to religious culture, Huangshan

小贴士　据说，华夏先祖轩辕黄帝曾在此炼丹，历经480年后，终于炼成仙丹，得道升天。信奉黄老学说的唐玄宗对此深信不疑，便在公元747年6月，下诏将此山命名为"黄山"。

据记载，佛教早在南朝就传入黄山，历代先后修建寺庙近百座。僧徒中，能诗善画者甚多，有大量作品传世。

黄山之美令无数诗人画家为之倾倒，从盛唐到晚清的1,200年间，诗人咏叹黄山的诗词达两万首之多，而以黄山为题材的绘画作品更是数不胜数。黄山在中国的山水文化中占有重要地位，特别是对中国传统山水画的发展产生过很大影响，被称为中国山水画的摇篮。

1990年联合国教科文组织世界遗产委员会第14届会议，通过黄山为世界文化和自然双重遗产。

enjoys stories about immortals and Taoism which have been handed down over generations with profound influence, often giving rise to the names of mountain peaks, including Xuanyuanfeng (Xuanyuan Peak), Fuqiufeng (Floating Hillock Peak), Liandan (Elixir Tempering Peak) and Xiandu (Fairy City Peak).

According to records, Buddhism was introduced to Huangshan as early as the Nan Dynasty, and since then, almost one hundred temples were built over subsequent dynasties. Many Buddhist monks excel at poetry and painting and they have left behind numerous works.

The picturesque sight of Huangshan has overwhelmed countless poets and artists. Over the 1,200 years from the peak of the Tang Dynasty to the late Qing Dynasty, the number of poems extolling Huangshan climbed to over 20,000, while the number of paintings depicting Huangshan is beyond count. This mountain range plays an important role in China's landscape painting culture and has greatly influenced traditional landscape painting in China. Huangshan is reputed as the cradle of Chinese landscape paintings.

In 1990, at the 14th session of the UNESCO World Heritage Committee, Huangshan was recognized as a World Cultural and Natural Heritage Site.

TIPS According to legend, Huangdi, the ancestor of the Chinese nation, used to make pills of immortality here. It took him 480 years to successfully make such a pill and he finally become immortal. Emperor Xuanzong of the Tang Dynasty, who had a deep faith in Taoist philosophy of Huangdi and Laozi, named this mountain "Huangshan" in June of 747 A.D..

九寨沟风景名胜区
Jiuzhaigou Valley Scenic and Historic Interest Area

　　九寨沟位于四川省北部，绵延超过72,000公顷，曲折狭长的九寨沟山谷海拔超过4,800米，因而形成了一系列形态不同的森林生态系。它壮丽的景色因一系列狭长的圆锥状喀斯特溶岩地貌和壮观的瀑布而更加充满生趣。沟中现存140多种鸟类，还有许多濒临灭绝的动植物物种，包括大熊猫和四川扭角羚。

世界遗产委员会评价

　　九寨沟风景区位于四川省西北部南坪县。全区面积约720平方公里，大部分为森林所覆盖。这里佳景荟萃，自然纯净，尤以水景最为奇丽，素有"中华水景之王"的美称。

　　九寨沟主沟呈"Y"字形，总长50余公里，散落着114个美丽的高山湖泊，当地人把它们称为"海子"。

Stretching over 72,000 hectares in the northern part of Sichuan Province, the zigzag Jiuzhaigou Valley reaches more than 4,800 meters above sea level, thus comprising a series of diverse forest ecosystems. Its superb landscapes are particularly interesting for their series of narrow conic karst landforms and spectacular waterfalls. More than 140 bird species inhabit the valley, and a number of endangered plant and animal species are found here, including the giant panda and the Sichuan takin.

　　The Jiuzhaigou Valley Scenic Area is part of Jiuzhaigou County (formerly Nanping County), located in northwestern Sichuan province. The area covers 720 square kilometers, the majority of which is forested land. The valley concentrates natural beauty and gorgeous scenery, and is especially known for its strange and beautiful waterscapes; it is thus known as "the King of China's Waterscapes."

　　The main valley of Jiuzhaigou, shaped like the capital letter "Y", stretches over 50 kilometers in length. It contains 114 beautiful alpine lakes, which are known by the local people as *haizi* (literally "little seas").

　　According to legend, a long time ago there lived a deity named Dage, who was in love with the goddess Semo. To show his affection, Dage gave her a mirror made out of wind, but an abhorrent devil caused

小贴士 　九寨沟森林茂密，石灰岩地层含大量碳酸，对湖水有很强的净化作用。有关数据表明，九寨沟湖水的透明度可达30余米。

Date of inscription: 1992
Heritage category: 自然遗产 N
Criteria: N(III)

传说，在很久以前，男神达戈用风云磨成一面宝镜，送给心爱的女神色嫫。可是魔鬼作祟，女神不慎将宝镜打碎，碎片散落到崇山峻岭中，化成了如梦似幻的湖泊。

清晨，一切似乎都还沉浸在睡梦中，镜海的水面没有一丝涟漪，似乎在等待着女神来对镜梳洗。

被吸引来的不仅是女神，还有可爱的熊猫。山上长满了熊猫爱吃的箭竹。熊猫们在饱餐一顿后来到附近的海子喝水，发现水里竟然还有一只熊猫也在喝水，为了和水里的熊猫争抢，它不停地喝、不停地喝，最后竟胀得走不动，只能倒在旁边休息。当地人把这叫做"熊猫醉水"。"熊猫海"也由此得名。

trouble and Semo carelessly broke the mirror. The broken pieces scattered across the steep mountain and were transformed into beautiful, dreamlike lakes.

In the early morning, when the world is still deep in slumber and all is still, Mirror Lake is quiet and ripple-free, as if waiting for Semo to come and comb her hair in front of the mirror.

It is not only the goddess Semo who was attracted to Jiuzhaigou but also the cute and adorable pandas. The mountain is filled with arrow bamboo, which pandas love to feed on. After reaching their satiation point, pandas would come to a nearby lake to drink some water. It is said that when a panda looks into the crystal clear lake, he discovers that there is another panda drinking water, too. The panda then begins to "compete" against his own shadow by drinking non-stop. By the time he has finished, his stomach is so full of water that he is unable to walk, and takes a rest beside the lake. This phenomenon, known by the local people as "the panda inebriated on water", is how Panda Lake got its name.

Long Lake, located in the top-left corner of the valley's "Y" shape and running a length of three kilometers, is the largest "fragment" of the broken mirror. The lake's long and slender shape enables it to accommodate both the blue sky and large glaciers in its body. Long Lake has no outgoing waterways or inlet port; however, the water level always remains the same, even during rainstorms and droughts. People liken Long Lake to a magic gourd that can neither be completely filled up nor emptied dry.

Hidden in the verdant forest not far from Long Lake is a small and exquisite body of water—Five-Color Pond. Despite its modest dimensions, Five-Color Pond possesses a splendor and grace lacked by Long Lake. Often garnering the highest praise from sightseers, even the birds in the forest have a special

TIPS Jiuzhaigou Valley is covered with lush forests. There is a great amount of carbonic acid in the limestone layer in the scenic area, which purify the water in the lakes. According to statistics, the water in the lakes of Jiuzhaigou Valley is so limpid that one can see clearly more than 30 meters deep under water.

位于"Y"字左上方的长海，是宝镜最大的一块碎片，长达3公里。修长的身材使它能将蓝天和大冰川一起纳入胸怀。长海没有出水口，也没有入水口，但无论碰到暴雨还是干旱，这里的水总是保持原样。人们都说长海是一只装不满、也漏不干的宝葫芦。

就在长海不远处的翠林里，藏着一块小巧玲珑的海子——五彩池。虽然在体量上它无法和长海相比，但是它的绚丽秀美也非长海所具。它常常能获得游人最多的赞美，就连林中的小鸟也对这里情有独钟。

在九寨沟，唯一能和五彩池争艳的只有五花海。它就像是大自然的调色盘，在同一块水域可以呈现出鹅黄、墨绿、深蓝、藏青各种颜色，斑驳迷离，色彩缤纷，仿佛一只展翅开屏

fondness for Five-Color Pond.

In Jiuzhaigou Valley, only Five Flower Lake could hope to rival Five-Color Pond in a "beauty contest" of nature. Five Flower Lake is like nature's color palette; inside this one body of water, you will find a plethora of colors, including light yellow, dark green, ultramarine, and navy blue. It's as if the lake is a dazzling peacock, spreading its colorful plumage for all to see.

Although Jiuzhaigou Valley lures visitors with the aesthetic beauty and serenity of its lakes, it also exhibits a more passionate side. The majestic falls you are looking at are called the Nuorilang Falls—Jiuzhaigou's largest waterfall. In the Tibetan language, *Nuorilang* means "powerful and majestic", and is often used to describe men of great physical strength.

Another site filled with passion is Pearl Shoal—even though its style is completely different. As its waters flow along, they are filled with a fresh and invigorating rhythm. According to legend, people witnessed spindrift splashing out of the shoal and thought it was an abundance of pearls. They busily set

的孔雀。

九寨沟的海子给人以宁静秀丽的美感，但是，它也有激情的一面。壮丽的诺日朗瀑布，是九寨沟最大的瀑布。"诺日朗"在藏语中是雄壮的意思，常常用来形容强壮的男性。

充满激情的还有珍珠滩。但这里完全是另外一种风格。水在流动中充满了清新的律动。珍珠滩之所以得名，是因为传说有人看见顺滩而下激起的浪花，以为是一颗颗珍珠，赶忙拿篮子去捞，结果当然是竹篮打水一场空。但是珍珠滩的美名就这样留了下来。

有些海子，要见识它的美需要时间。我们只有在太阳斜照的时候，才能看到闪烁着波光，好像火花的火花海。

同样，我们在冬天去上季节海，夏天去下季节海，等待我们的不是蓝色的湖水，而是一块适合放牧的草地。

在这114个海子中，汇集了九寨沟精华的要属

out to catch these "pearls" with a basket, but their efforts were obviously in vain. Nevertheless, the beautiful name Pearl Shoal has remained.

For some of the lakes, it is essential to go at a certain time to witness their beauty. One such example is Sparkling Lake; only under the rosy glow of the setting sun can we behold its sparkling, shimmering water.

Similarly, we can visit the Seasonal Lakes—the Upper Seasonal Lake in winter and the Lower Seasonal Lake in summer. However, instead of being greeted by a blue lake, one will find a meadow well-suited for pasturing.

Of all the 114 lakes of Jiuzhaigou, the Shuzheng Lakes are the cream of the crop. The water starts from the Shuzheng Waterfall, flows into 19 lakes of all sizes (forming a ladder-like shape) in Shuzheng Gully, and stretches five kilometers, with a vertical drop of over 100 meters. The water flows along the bank, forming a series of water curtains; the azure lake water is rife with willows, cypresses, pines and fir trees. The lake water at the front end crosses the

树正群海。水流从树正瀑布奔流而下，流入树正沟大大小小19个呈阶梯状分布的海子，偎依相衔，长达5公里，高低落差达100余米。水流顺堤跌荡，形成幅幅水帘，湛蓝的水中长满了柳树、柏树、松树和杉树。上部海子的水翻越湖堤，从树丛中溢出，激起白色的水花，在青翠中跳跳蹦蹦，穿梭奔窜。在水中生长的这些树木，不能不说是个奇观。它们之所以能在水流中生长，秘密就在那些红色根须。这些特殊的树根使树木即便是泡在水中也能呼吸和吸收养分。

在树木掩隐中，藏着一个古老的磨房。利用水的落差加工粮食，是旧时人们利用自然造福的一种方式。如今，磨房已经成为过去生活的回忆，但在这个人间仙境中却带给我们一丝生活的气息。

embankment and floods out into the grove, causing white spray to whirl and fly against a backdrop of verdant green. Witnessing these trees living and growing in the water is truly a marvelous spectacle. The reason that they can survive in the water lies in these red-colored tree roots. These special roots enable the trees to respire and absorb nutrients even under water.

Hidden inside the woods is an ancient grinding mill. Utilizing the drop in water level for the purpose of grain processing was one way that the people of yore exploited nature to their benefit. Today, although the grinding mill can only serve as a memory of days gone by, it is the only place in this earthly paradise that offers signs of human life and activity.

Because there were once nine Tibetan ethnic villages distributed in this area, it came to be known as *Jiuzhaigou* (literally "Valley of Nine Villages"). In Jiuzhaigou, colored prayer flags flapping in the wind

小贴士 | 据说，只要转动一圈转经筒就相当于向佛吟诵了一遍经文，转动越多越能体现对佛的虔诚，得到佛的庇佑。

九寨沟之所以得名，是因为这里曾经分布着九个藏族村寨。在这里，我们到处都能看到一种在风中飘曳的彩条，这就是经帆，是藏民们祈求幸福的信物。只要有藏民居住的地方就能看到经帆，当然还有转经筒和白塔。藏传佛教信奉自然神灵。也许，因为有了对佛的虔诚，上天才把梦幻般的美景给了九寨沟；也正是因为对自然的敬畏，淳朴的人们才将它保护得如此完美，让更多的人受惠于这上天的恩赐。

1992年，联合国教科文组织世界遗产委员会第16届会议，通过九寨沟风景名胜区为世界自然遗产。

are everywhere to be seen; these were used by the Tibetan people to pray for happiness. These prayer flags can be seen in any place inhabited by ethnic Tibetans; of course, there are also the prayer wheel and white dagoba. Tibetan Buddhism worships natural deities. Perhaps God was willing to give the dreamlike Jiuzhaigou to the pious Tibetans to reward their devotion to Buddha. It is because of their reverence to nature that the pure and honest local people have protected Jiuzhaigou so well, so that more people can enjoy this gift of God.

In 1992, at the 16th meeting of the World Heritage Committee, Jiuzhaigou Valley was declared a UNESCO World Heritage Site.

TIPS It is said that rotating the prayer wheel one time equals to chanting the whole Buddhist scripture once. The more times one rotates the wheel, the more piety one shows for Buddha. It is believed that Buddha will bless his pious followers.

黄龙风景名胜区
Huanglong Scenic and Historic Interest Area

  黄龙风景名胜区，位于四川省西北部，是由众多雪峰和中国最东部的冰川组成的山谷。在这里人们可以找到高山景观和各种不同的森林生态系，以及壮观的石灰岩构造、瀑布和温泉。这一地区还生存着许多濒临灭绝的动物，包括大熊猫和四川疣鼻金丝猴。

世界遗产委员会评价

  在中国四川省西北部高原，有一个叫做黄龙的地方。这里景观奇特、资源丰富、保存完整，具有重要的科学价值和美学价值。

  1992年，联合国教科文组织世界遗产委员会第16届会议，通过黄龙风景名胜区为世界自然遗产。

Situated in the northwest of Sichuan Province, the Huanglong Valley is made up of snow-capped peaks and the easternmost of all the Chinese glaciers. In addition to its mountain landscape and diverse forest ecosystems, spectacular limestone formations, waterfalls and hot springs can also be found. The area also has a population of endangered animals, including the giant panda and the Sichuan golden snub-nosed monkey.

In the northwest plateau of Sichuan Province, there is a place called Huanglong. With a peculiar landscape, plentiful resources and a high degree of preservation, it possesses important scientific and aesthetic value.

In 1992, at the 16th meeting of the UNESCO World Heritage Committee, the Huanglong Scenic and Historic Interest Area was inscribed as a World Heritage Site.

Huanglong is located on a plateau at an altitude of over 3,000 meters. The area retains extensive and distinct Quaternary glacial remains. Among them, Mount Xuebaoding is China's most easterly protection

小贴士 黄龙风景区位于四川省阿坝州松潘县境内的黄龙沟，与九寨沟风景名胜区一山相隔。但因雪山阻隔，需经公路绕行100公里后方可到达。

收录时间 Date of inscription：1992
遗产类别 Heritage category：自然遗产 N
收录理由 Criteria：N(III)

黄龙地处海拔3,000米以上的高原，这里广泛保留着清晰的第四纪冰川遗迹。其中，雪宝鼎是中国最东部的现代冰川保护区。终年覆盖冰雪的雪宝鼎是藏民心中的圣山。山上的雪水是形成黄龙最奇丽的钙华景观的源泉。数万年来，雪山上流下的雪水大量溶解了石灰岩中的碳酸钙，在水温和压力的作用下，水中结晶出的碳酸钙依附于石块、落叶，甚至是羽毛上，形成钙华，它们围滴成池，下流成滩，塌陷成瀑，形成五光十色的钙华景观。这里有世界上最大的高原边石坝彩池群，世界上最大的钙华滩岭，还有中国落差最大的钙华瀑布，这里就是一座天然的钙华博物馆。

钙华景观分布最集中的是黄龙沟。这条金色的巨龙，长约3.6公里，是世界上规模最大、结构

area of modern glaciers. Mount Xuebaoding, covered year-round ice and snow, is a sacred mountain in the hearts of Tibetans. The mountain's snow water is the source of Huanglong's most spectacular calcified sight. For tens of thousands of years, snow water flowing down the mountain dissolved vast amounts of calcium carbonate contained in the limestone. Under suitable conditions of water temperature and

TIPS The Huanglong Scenic Area is located in the Huanglong Valley in Songpan County, Aba Profecture, Sichuan Province. There is only a mountain between it and the famous scenic area—Jiuzhaigou valley. As the snow mountain is very difficult to climb, visitors have to make a detour of about 100 kilometers to reach the other side.

最完整、造型最奇特的喀斯特地貌景观。传说，古时候黄龙帮助中国的治水英雄大禹治水成功后，便来到这里修炼成仙，后人称为黄龙真人。为了纪念他，人们在这里修建道观黄龙古寺，黄龙也由此得名。黄龙古寺是考察历代道教文化演变的重要遗址。

黄龙真人成仙而去，给人间留下五色山水。黄龙寺后的五彩池也许就是真人留给人间的宝贝。五彩池面积2.1万平方公里，拥有693个彩池，是黄龙最大的一个彩池群。白色、淡黄色的堤坝簇拥着层层叠叠的浅水，反射着淡蓝、墨绿、浅绿、鹅黄，宛如一块块玉盘。

在彩池中有两对石塔和石屋，大部分已经被钙华淹没，只留下塔尖和飞檐屋顶立于碧海之中，显得久远而神秘。据考证，石塔和石屋建于明朝，距今已有六百多年历史。

在离五彩池不远处的绿荫中还隐藏着一个仅4平方米大的水池 ——万花池。由于泉水涌动，落在水面上的花瓣和树叶会向不同的方向旋转。据说年轻男女会在这里占卜爱情，如果两人抛入水中的树叶能旋转到一起，就说明他们会成为美满的一对。

pressure, the calcium carbonate that crystallized in the water adhered to the surfaces of rocks, fallen leaves, and even feathers, forming travertine. The water formed into pools, shoals and waterfalls, creating a brilliant and multicolored travertine sight. With the largest cluster of colorful ponds in plateau-lying rimstone dams in the world, the largest travertine streams in the world and the waterfall with the highest drop in elevation in China, Huanglong is indeed a

小贴士 传说，住在天宫的王母也嫉妒人间有五彩池这样的美景，要把它收归天庭。雪宝鼎山神的女儿达美为了给人间留下这一美景，取下父亲神杖上的五颗珍珠化成彩池让王母带回天庭，五彩池才得以留在人间。

"nature's travertine museum."

The area in which travertine landscapes are most concentrated is Huanglonggou (Yellow Dragon Gully). This giant golden dragon, measuring approximately 3.6 kilometers in length, is the world's largest-scale karst landform, which also has the most complete structure and the most peculiar shape. Legend has it that, in ancient times, the Yellow Dragon helped Yu the Great, China's water-control hero, to successfully prevent flooding. The Yellow Dragon then came to Huanglonggou to cultivate vital energy and became an immortal. Later generations referred to him as Huanglong Zhenren ("the Immortal Yellow Dragon"). To commemorate him, the local people built a Taoist temple, called the Ancient Huanglong Temple. The Ancient Huanglong Temple is an important site for investigating the development of Taoist culture through the ages.

Huanglong became an immortal and, as he departed from this world, he left behind multicolored mountains and rivers. Five-Color Pond (Wucai Chi) behind Huanglong Temple may be one of the treasures that Huanglong gave to the world as a parting gift. Five-Color Pond covers an area of 21,000 square kilometers and contains 693 colorful pools, making it Huanglong's largest cluster of colorful pools. White and light yellow dykes cluster around layer upon layer of shallow water, reflecting baby blue, dark green, light green and light yellow, like a set of jade plates.

Situated among the colorful pools are two stone pagodas and stone houses. They are mostly submerged by travertine deposits; only the spires and rooftops with upturned eaves stand above the azure water, appearing ancient and mysterious. According to research, the stone pagodas and stone houses

从龙首一路往下，沿途金色的钙华中散落着形态各异、色彩斑斓的彩池，水底沉积物、山色、天光和云影赋予了这里最绚丽的颜色。

在黄龙沟的中段，有一条长约1,300多米的钙华滩流，人称"金沙铺地"。这是世界上目前发现的同类历史结构中状态最好、面积最大、距离最长、色彩最丰富的地表钙华滩流。这里就好像

TIPS According to legend, Queen Mother of the Heaven felt jealous that there was such beautiful scenery as the Five-Color Lake on earth. She wanted to take it back to the Heaven. In order to keep this beautiful scenery on earth, Damei, the daughter of God of Xuebaoding Mountain, took off five pearls on the magic wand of her father and turned them into a colorful lake, and let Queen Mother take it back to the Western Heaven. Thus the Five-Color Lake remained on earth.

是龙的脊背，鳞片隆起，水波跳动，似乎这条巨龙随时都可能飞腾而起。

从金沙铺地下陷的钙华流在这里突然塌陷，形成了洗身洞这个目前世界上最长的钙华塌陷地。洗身洞之所以得名，是因为在这个钙华塌陷地上有一个小洞口，传说这是仙人净身的地方。这里也是本波教信徒心中的一大圣地。

过了迎宾池，穿过原始森林，我们几乎就已经到了龙尾。传说如果能绕着黄龙走一圈，心中默念的愿望就能实现。

黄龙不仅拥有自然美景，它所在的松潘土城也是历史上有名的兵家重镇。高大古老的城墙还在展示着它昔日重要的军事地位。

这里也是民族交融的地方。当年，松赞干布就是在这里迎娶唐朝的文成公主进藏，成为民族融合的典范。这种融合一直保留至今。

were built in the Ming Dynasty and date back over 600 years.

In the grove, not far from the Five-Color Pond, is hidden a pool measuring only four square meters in area—Ten-thousand Flower Pool (Wanhua Chi). Because the spring water gushes out, flower petals and tree leaves falling on the water's surface rotate and swirl in different directions. It is said that young boys and girls once practiced divination to foretell the fate of their love. If the leaves that each of them tossed into the water swirled together, it meant that they would be a perfect couple.

Moving down from the "dragon's head", colorful ponds of all shapes and sizes are scattered along the golden travertine; sub-aqueous deposits, celestial light, the mountain's hue, and the cloud's shadows combine to reveal the most splendid colors one can imagine.

In the middle section of Huanglonggou is a rare travertine stream, known as Jinshapudi, which measures 1,300 meters in length. Of all the surface travertine streams of the same historical structure discovered in the world to date, this one is the most colorful, boasts the greatest area and longest distance, and is in the best condition. This seems to be the dragon's back, with bulging "scales." As the water waves pulsate, it seems as though the dragon might soar into the sky at any moment.

小贴士 | 黄龙所处地理位置特殊，使之成为野生动物栖息和繁衍的理想地区，其中国家级保护动物有大熊猫、金丝猴、牛羚、云豹、白唇鹿等近百种。

The travertine stream that falls from Jinshapudi suddenly drops down at this point, forming Xishen Cave—presently the longest collapsed travertine area in the world. The name of Xishen Cave derives from the fact that this travertine area has a small cave, which is where, according to legend, immortals cut off their testes. Xishen Cave is also a holy land for followers of the Benbo religion.

After having passed Yingbin Lake and traversed the primeval forest, we have almost reached the dragon's tail. According to legend, if you are able to walk a loop around Huanglong, your silent prayers will be answered.

In addition to boasting natural beauty, Huanglong is situated in a town of military importance—Songpan County. The large ancient city walls still reveal their important military status of former days.

This is also a place where different ethnicities blended together. It was here that Songtsen Gampo received his bride, Tang Dynasty Princess Wencheng, before going to Tibet—serving as a classic example of ethnic blending. This kind of blending has continued and is still prevalent today.

Songpan is an ancient city inhabited by Tibetan, Hui and Qiang people. We not only can find ancient architecture of the Han people, but also can see Tibetan wooden buildings, Qiang military watchtowers, and Bai mosques.

Even this small city can give us a world-class surprise. The heterophonic Qiang folk songs discovered here have negated the belief that Chinese people lack heterophonic song performances. This is the most ancient kind of singing in the history of Chinese ethnic music; with thousands of years of history, it is the precious wealth of the Chinese people.

松潘是藏、回、羌混居的古城，我们不仅能看到汉族的古典建筑，也能看到藏寨木楼、羌族的碉楼和白族的清真寺。

就是这样一个小城，也能给我们一个世界级的惊喜。在这里发现的羌族多声部民歌，打破了中华民族没有多声部演唱的认识。这是中国民族音乐史上最古老的一种唱腔，至今已有数千年的历史，是中华民族的宝贵财富。

TIPS Huanglong Valley is an ideal place for wild animals, among which animals under state protection are giant panda, golden snub-nosed monkey, cow-horned antelope, clouded leopard, and white-lipped deer.

武陵源风景名胜区
Wulingyuan Scenic and Historic Interest Area

　　武陵源景色奇丽壮观，位于中国中部湖南省境内，连绵26,000多公顷，景区内最独特的景观是3,000余座尖细的砂岩柱和砂岩峰，很多都有200余米高。在峰峦之间，沟壑、峡谷纵横，溪流、池塘和瀑布随处可见，景区内还有40多个石洞和两座天然形成的巨大石桥。除了迷人的自然景观，该地区还因庇护着大量濒临灭绝的动植物物种而引人注目。

世界遗产委员会评价

　　在中国中部的湖南省，有一处奇特的自然景区——武陵源。这里的峰石直立而密集，连绵万顷，给人以层峦叠嶂的磅礴气势。在这360多平方公里的面积中，有山峰3,000多座，垂直400米以上的石峰1,000余个。

　　武陵源风景区由张家界森林公园和索溪峪、天子山两大自然保护区组成。1992年，联合国教科文组织世界遗产委员会第16届会议，通过武陵源风景名胜区为世界自然遗产。

　　在武陵源，几乎每个景区都开通了缆车。坐缆车上山你

A spectacular area stretching over more than 26,000 ha in China's Hunan Province, the site is dominated by more than 3,000 narrow sandstone pillars and peaks, many over 200 meters high. Between the peaks lie ravines and gorges with streams, pools and waterfalls, some 40 caves, and two large natural bridges. In addition to the striking beauty of the landscape, the region is also noted for the fact that it is home to a number of endangered plants and animal species.

In central China's Hunan Province, there is a unique natural scenic area called Wulingyuan. Its stones stand erect and are densely concentrated, spanning thousands of hectares and offering a superb mountain view. In its area of over 360 square kilometers are over 3,000 mountains, more than 1,000 of which have a vertical height in excess of 400 meters.

The Wulingyuan scenic area consists of Zhangjiajie Forest Park as well as the

小贴士　武陵源这片奇特的风景名胜区，直到1979年才被著名画家吴冠中发现，当时，这片山水还没有名字。1984年，另一位著名画家黄永玉建议把这片神奇的区域命名为武陵源。

Date of inscription: 1992
Heritage category: 自然遗产 N
Criteria: N(III)

能看到不一样的风景。郁郁葱葱的森林在你脚下缓缓移动,形态各异的峰柱与你擦肩而过。遇到大雾天气,你的四周白茫茫一片,仿佛置身于虚幻仙境。缆车到达的终点站叫天子山,是武陵源的主要景区之一。从这里举目远眺,武陵源的千山万壑,尽收眼底。因而,它成为了许多摄影师和游客最喜欢的地方。

特殊的峰柱结合曼妙的云雾,使中国的艺术家在这里找到了传统水墨画的真实景象。每当雨过转晴,或阴雨连绵时,幽幽山谷中生出云烟,云雾飘缈在层峦叠嶂间,时浓时淡、时隐时现,景象变幻万千。

Suoxiyu and Tianzi Mountain natural protection areas. In 1992, at the 16th session of the UNESCO World Heritage Committee, the Wulingyuan Scenic and Historic Interest Area was inscribed as a World Heritage Site.

At Wulingyuan, almost every scenic area is equipped with a cable car. Sitting in the cable car, you will be able to witness scenery of a different sort. The lush forest moves slowly under your feet while stone pillars of variously shapes pass right by your shoulders. If it happens to be a day of heavy fog, you will find yourself surrounded by a vast expanse of whiteness, as if you had set foot in a fairyland. The terminal of the cable-car ride is called Tianzi

TIPS Wulingyuan Scenic Area remained unknown until a famous Chinese artist Wu Guanzhong discovered this spectacular scenery in 1979. At that time, the place did not have a name yet. In 1984, another famous artist Huang Yongyu suggested that this beautiful and miraculous lanscape be named "Wulingyuan".

小贴士　武陵源景区与美国黄石国家公园、科罗拉多大峡谷等著名世界遗产并称为"地球最后的奇迹"。

雾使晴日下坚硬的山峰变得妖娆、飘逸和神秘。

武陵源这些奇异的自然地貌是怎样形成的呢？科学家在金鞭溪附近发现了一块岩石，表面有被海流冲刷过的痕迹。后来，又陆续发现了古生物化石。经过对金鞭溪岩石成分的分析检验，专家们做出推断，在距今大约三亿五千万年前的古生代中期，这里是濒临大海的沙滩。这里的石英砂是由远古时期的河流从内陆带来的泥沙形成的，这些泥沙中含有大量的石英，经过数千万年的沉积固结，慢慢形成了平整的石英砂岩地层。

在这里我们随处都可以发现褶皱岩层。它是造山运动留下的证据。这说明距今2亿年前，这里发生过造山运动。造山运动使石英砂岩地层被拖出地表，形成山脉并发生断裂，最终形成方向一致的峡谷。

Mountain, one of the main scenic areas of Wulingyuan. As you enjoy a bird's-eye view from high up in the sky, Wulingyuan's innumerable mountains and valleys come fully into view. Not surprisingly, Wulingyuan has become a favorite location for photographers and tourists.

Distinctive stone pillars gracefully shrouded in mist have provided Chinese artists with real-life scenes to create traditional Chinese ink paintings. When the sun comes out after a rainfall—or even if it has been cloudy and drizzly for days on end—a cloudy mist rises from the valleys and flows along the mountaintops. The mist is in a constant state of flux; sometimes dense and sometimes thin, it appears for a time before disappearing again, creating a variegated and ever-changing spectacle.

Misty fogs under the bright sunshine give the rigid mountain peaks an air of enchantment, elegance and mystery.

How did these amazing natural features possessed by Wulingyuan come into being? Scientists found a rock near Jinbian Stream, the surface of which had erosion marks left by sea water. Later, a series of fossils of ancient organisms were discovered. After performing analytical tests on the Jinbian Stream rocks, experts deduced that approximately 350 million years ago, during the mid-Paleozoic

小贴士　**金鞭溪**　因标志性景点金鞭岩而得名，是一条十余公里长的溪流，从张家界沿溪可以一直走到索溪峪，两岸峡谷对峙，红岩绿树倒映溪间，别具风味，是整个景区的精华游路。金鞭岩，金鞭溪边的一块岩石，拔地而起，有棱有角，酷似一条高300余米直插于地的金鞭。

TIPS Wulingyuan Scenic Area, ranking with many world famous relic spots such as the Yellowstone National Park and Colorado Grand Canyon of the USA, is regarded as one of "the world's last wonders".

武陵源风景名胜区

接下来，水对武陵源地貌的形成起了很大的促进作用。站在金鞭溪或索溪域，你仿佛能感受到远古时期，水流冲刷岩壁时的壮观景象。

黄龙洞是地壳运动和水流冲刷形成的巨大岩洞。进入幽深的岩洞，即使在酷暑时节也感到十分清凉。黄龙洞有13个大厅，96条走廊，3处瀑布和1条阴河，顺着地下河游览，四周的岩石千奇百怪。

数亿年沧海桑田所形成的峰云奇观，在未来的地球史上，还会经历怎样的发展和变化呢？地质学家们根据地壳演化的规律推测，这些山峰将随着时间的延续而逐渐变形缩小，最终变成沙石，随溪流注入江海。

今天，武陵源漫山遍野处处入眼的还是茂密的森林，这里生长了几千年的森林，一直无人砍伐，森林覆盖率高达97.9%。被称为活化石的水杉、银杏等古稀植物比比皆是。走在密林中不经意触到的也许恰恰是某种珍稀植物的叶子。

era, this site was once a beach facing out to sea. The quartz sand was formed by sediment brought by the water tide from the inner land during ancient times. This sediment contained a large quantity of quartz; over the course of thousands of years of deposition and fixation, a flat stratum of quartz sandstone was gradually formed.

The many "wrinkled" rock strata that we can see here offer evidence of mountain making. This indicates that, 200 million years ago, mountain-making activity occurred at this site. As the quartz sandstone stratum was dragged out from the surface, a mountain range was formed; and as fissures occurred, this unidirectional gorge that you are looking at was formed.

Thereafter, water factored heavily in promoting the formation of Wulingyuan's physical contours. Standing beside Jinbian Stream or the Suoxiyu area, you can easily imagine the magnificent sight of water currents washing out the cliff.

This massive grotto, called Yellow Dragon Cave, was formed by tectonic movement and water erosion. Even during sweltering summer heat, you will feel cool and refreshed as you enter the depths of the grotto. Yellow Dragon Cave contains 13 halls, 96 corridors, three waterfalls and one underground river. As you tour along the underground river, you will encounter all kinds of strange and bizarre rocks.

Hundreds of millions of years of transformations have led to the marvelous spectacle of Wulingyuan. In the future, what kinds of changes and developments will it encounter? Based on regular patterns of tectonic evolution, geologists have inferred that, over the course of time, today's mountain peaks will gradually contract and become deformed, ultimately

TIPS Jinbian Stream is named after the symbolic spot Jinbian Rock in this area. It winds along more than 10 kilometers. A best tourist route is set out from Zhangjiajie, walking along the Jinbian Stream and finally reaching Suoxiyu. There are forests on both sides of the valley alongside the stream, and red rocks and green trees are reflected in the stream. All this forms a scenery of unique charm and beauty. Jinbian Rock is a huge rock pillar by the Jinbian Stream soaring into the air more than 300 meters high, which looks like an erecting gold whip.

　　森林为野生动物提供了良好的繁衍栖息之地。武陵源拥有极为丰富的野生动物资源。这里居住着28种国家级保护动物。有一种长得并不很可爱的动物叫大鲵，是世界上现存最大的两栖类动物。大鲵的肤色随环境而变，一般为棕褐色，背部有花斑。因为叫声像婴儿的啼哭，所以人们一般叫它娃娃鱼。

　　武陵源世代居住着土家族、苗族等少数民族。"毛古斯"舞是土家族最原始的戏剧。毛古斯带有浓厚的祭祀色彩，表达土家族对自然与祖先的崇拜。

　　土家族的年轻人用对歌来表达爱情。对于人类，爱情是永恒的。但对于地球，武陵源却只有一次。

being carried by the rivers out into the sea.

　　Today, visitors will be met with the eye-catching sight of lush forests covering Wulingyuan. They have grown for thousands of years without lumbering and the area's forest coverage is as high as 97.9%. Rare ancient plants, such as metasequoia and gingko, which have been extolled as living fossils, are everywhere to be found. As you walk through the dense forest, you might find yourself accidentally brushing past the leaves of a rare and exotic plant.

　　The forest provides excellent reproductive and living conditions for wild animals. Boasting rich wildlife resources, Wulingyuan is home to 28 state-protected animals. This awkward-looking animal, called the giant salamander, is the largest existing amphibian in the world. The giant salamander's skin color changes in response to changes in the environment; it is usually brown, with stain patterns on the back. Since the sound it makes is similar to babies' wailing, people also refer to it as the "baby fish" (*wawayu*).

　　Several ethnic minorities, including the Tujia people and the Miao people, have lived on Wulingyuan for generations. This is the *Maogusi* dance, the earliest form of theater of the Tujia people. Maogusi incorporates rich sacrificial elements, expressing the Tujia people's adoration of nature and veneration of their ancestors.

　　Young people of the Tujia ethnic group sing in antiphonal style to express feelings of love. For the human race, love lasts an eternity. But on planet Earth, there is only one Wulingyuan.

| 收录时间 Date of inscription：1994
| 遗产类别 Heritage category：文化遗产 C
| 收录理由 Criteria：C(II)(IV)

承德避暑山庄及周围寺庙
Mountain Resort and its Outlying Temples, Chengde

承德避暑山庄，是清王朝的夏季行宫，位于河北省境内，修建于公元1703年到1792年。它是由众多的宫殿以及其他处理政务、举行仪式的建筑构成的一个庞大的建筑群。建筑风格各异的庙宇和皇家园林同周围的湖泊、牧场和森林巧妙地融为一体。避暑山庄不仅具有极高的美学研究价值，而且还保留着中国封建社会发展末期的罕见的历史遗迹。

世界遗产委员会评价

避暑山庄及周围寺庙坐落在中国北部河北省的承德市，始建于公元1703年，历经中国清朝康熙、雍正、乾隆三代帝王，历时89年建成，是中国现存最大的皇家园林和寺庙群。

The Mountain Resort (the Qing Dynasty's summer palace), in Hebei Province, was built between 1703 and 1792. It is a vast complex of palaces and administrative and ceremonial buildings. Temples of various architectural styles and imperial gardens blend harmoniously into a landscape of lakes, pastureland and forests. In addition to its aesthetic interest, the Mountain Resort is a rare historic vestige of the final development of feudal society in China.

The Chengde Mountain Resort and its outlying temples are situated in Chengde City, in northern China's Hebei Province. Its construction began in 1703 AD and lasted for 89 years through the reigns of emperors Kangxi, Yongzheng and Qianlong of the Qing Dynasty. It is China's largest existing imperial garden and cluster of temples.

Chengde Mountain Resort is also known as Rehe Xinggong (*xinggong* means "temporary imperial dwelling palace"). Every year in midsummer, the emperors of the Qing Dynasty came

小贴士　避暑山庄的"避"字多写了一横。在清代,两个"避"字同时使用,无论用哪一种写法都是正确的,这是一种异体字现象。康熙皇帝多写一横是为了追求书法上的美观、漂亮。

避暑山庄原称"热河行宫"。每逢盛夏,清朝的皇帝一般都会从北京故宫来此避暑,因此改称为避暑山庄。与其他皇家园林不同,这里既有大气恢弘的皇家建筑,也有精致典雅的园林景观;既有满、蒙、回、藏等少数民族特色的庙宇,也有传统的汉式楼阁,汇集了中国古代建筑、园林、宗教艺术精品,享有"中国地理形貌之缩影"的美誉。一位英国特使觐见乾隆皇帝时称赞避暑山庄犹如"精美的人工盆景"。1994年,避暑山庄及周围寺庙被联合国教科文组织列入《世界文化遗产名录》。

避暑山庄占地5.64平方公里,宫墙高7米、宽仅3米,绵延20里,共有建筑120余处,主要分为宫殿区和园林区两部分。

宫殿区是整个避暑山庄的核心,集中在山庄的南部,包括正宫、松鹤斋、万壑松风和东宫四组建筑。与故宫的富丽堂皇不同,避暑山庄的宫殿大都用普通的青砖和灰瓦修筑,简单而内敛。阅射门是皇帝观看皇子皇孙射箭比赛的地方。门上匾额有四个鎏金大字——"避暑山庄",是由康熙皇帝御笔亲题的,在蓝色的映衬下显得格

外遒劲。门前威风凛凛的铜狮显示着皇家的威严。穿过阅射门有一个苍松遍布的方形庭院,庭院北边屹立着山庄正宫的主殿——澹泊敬诚殿。这里是皇帝处理朝政、接见使节和举行大典的地

here from the Imperial Palaces in Beijing to escape the summer heat; it was thus renamed as Chengde Mountain Resort. In contrast to other imperial gardens, it has both grandiose imperial buildings as well as exquisite gardens; and it features temples of various ethnic minorities—such as Manchu, Mongolian, Hui and Tibetan—as well as traditional Han-style pavilions. Combining the best of ancient Chinese architecture, gardens and religion, the resort is reputed as the "epitome of China's geographical landscapes". One British envoy, when having an audience with Emperor Qianlong, compared Chengde Mountain Resort to an "exquisite man-made bonsai". In 1994, the Chengde Mountain Resort and its outlying temples was inscribed to the World Heritage List by the UNESCO World Heritage Committee.

Chengde Mountain Resort covers an area of 5.64 square kilometers. The enclosing walls are seven meters in height, three meter wide, and stretch for 10 kilometers. There are more than 120 buildings, which are divided into two main parts: the palace area and the garden.

The palace area, the core of the whole mountain resort, is concentrated in the south part of the resort. The main buildings include Zhenggong (the Front Palace), Songhezhai (the Pine-Crane Hall), Wanhesongfeng (the Whispering Pine Valley) and Donggong (the Eastern Palace). In contrast with the grandeur and magnificence of the Forbidden City, most palaces in the mountain resort are built simply and modestly using ordinary green bricks and grey tiles. Yueshe Gate is the place where the emperor watched his sons and grandsons participate in archery competitions. The tablet hung on the gate is inscribed with four gilt characters reading "Bi Shu Shan Zhuang" (meaning "mountain resort"), which were written by Emperor Kangxi and appear even more forceful

小贴士　中国地理形貌之缩影　从地形上看,避暑山庄是中国山河的一个缩影:西部是山区,地势高敞、沟壑纵横,仿佛是中国的西部高原;东北部地势平坦、林木茂盛,就像内蒙草原、东北森林;东南部是湖区,如同中国的江南水乡。

TIPS There is an extra stroke in the Chinese character "避" in "避暑山庄", which is the variant form of the character. There were two different forms of the character used in the Qing Dynasty, and either one was correct. Emperor Kangxi wrote this extra stroke for the sake of calligraphic beauty.

承德避暑山庄及周围寺庙

under the reflection of the blue sky. The majestic-looking bronze lions in front of the gate demonstrate the power and influence of the imperial family. Crossing the Yueshe Gate, there is a square yard sheltered by pines; and, at the north of it, there stands the main building of the Front Palace, Danbojingcheng Hall, where the emperor dealt with administrative affairs, received foreign envoys, and held ceremonies. The whole hall is constructed with *nanmu*, waxed, and carved with delicate designs of bats and the Chinese character "万" (pronounced *wan*, literally "ten thousand"), symbolizing auspiciousness and longevity. The rear part of the Front Palace is the dwelling place of the emperor, empress and concubines. The biggest palace building there is Yanbozhishuang Palace, the imperial sleeping palace. The furnishings in the palace are exquisite and gorgeous, with various pieces of gold, silver and jade as well as porcelain, clocks and antiques. The last building of the palace area is Yunshanshengdi Palace, where the emperor and empress could admire the scenic sights of lakes and mountains. The two-storey building has no stairs; visitors must go upstairs via the stone steps of the rockery in front of it.

方。整座大殿用楠木建造而成，素身烫蜡，雕刻着"万"字、蝙蝠等象征吉祥和长寿的图案，非常精美。正宫区的后半部分是皇帝、皇后以及嫔妃们生活居住的地方，其中最大的宫殿是烟波致爽殿，这里是皇帝的寝宫。殿内陈设考究、富丽堂皇，各代金、银、玉、瓷、钟表、古玩等琳琅满目。云山胜地楼是宫殿区的最后一座建筑，是皇帝、皇后欣赏湖光山色的地方，两层楼，楼内没有楼梯，需要沿楼前假山上的磴道上楼。

园林区多散落在湖泊附近，山环水抱，是皇帝休闲娱乐的地方。园林一般根据森林、草原、溪流、湖泊、山石、地形等自然形态和走势进行建造，使之与周围的景色融为一体。如意洲里面有很多别有情致的上古建筑。每逢酷暑，清风直通殿内，夏日的炎热则悄然散

Scattered by lakes and featuring both mountains and water, the garden served as the emperor's place of recreation. Most of the gardens were

TIPS **A miniature of China's topography** The Summer Mountain Resort can be regarded as a miniature of China's topography. West of it is the mountain area, with highland and crossing canyons, just like the western plateau in China; its northeast part is expanding with flat land and forest, just like the Mongolia pasture and the northeast forest; the southeast part is the lake area, which is comparable to the south of the Yangtze River.

小贴士 京剧 京剧是一种综合性表演艺术，将唱（歌唱）、念（念白）、做（表演）、打（武打）、舞（舞蹈）融为一体，通过程式化的表演叙演故事、刻画人物，表达人"喜、怒、哀、乐、惊、恐、悲"的思想感情。京剧是中国最大的戏曲剧种。

去。在如意洲北侧青莲岛上的烟雨楼颇具江南烟雨楼的神韵，装饰朴素，结构不拘定势。楼外堆砌大型假山，旁边设有一片荷塘。西侧墙上的小门就像一个画框，移步换景，远处的荷花、山石、碧水变换着不同的画面吸引着你。沧浪屿是仿照闻名天下的苏州园林修建的，小巧别致，清幽秀雅。清音阁大戏楼是山庄内最大的戏楼，是乾隆皇帝下令修建的。凉风习习，清音入耳，好不惬意！山庄里有一个三面临湖的小岛——金山岛。它完全是靠人工堆砌而成的。湖区最好的观光点就是小岛上的上帝阁，登高望远，山庄的湖光山色尽收眼底。

在避暑山庄的周围有12座寺庙，其中有8座是由清政府直接管理的，因而称这八处京师之外的庙宇为"外八庙"。这些庙宇风格各异、

constructed in accordance with the natural landforms and trends of forests, grasslands, streams, lakes, mountains and landscapes, in order to integrate the gardens with nearby scenery. On Ruyi Islet, ancient buildings with distinctive features were built. In the hot summer, the cool wind blows straight into the palace, dispersing the heat of summer. On Qinglian Island, north of Ruyi Islet, lies the Yanyu Tower (" the Tower of Mist and Rain"), with the charm of pavilions south of the Yangtze River, simply decorated and variegated in structure. Outside the tower, there is a large rockery, beside which is a lotus pond. The small gate on the west wall is just like a picture frame; as you change your position, you will be attracted by different views of the lotuses, rocks and waters which transform before your eyes. The tranquil and elegant Canglang, ("Surging Wave") Islet was built in imitation of the famous Suzhou Gardens. The biggest opera tower in the resort is Qingyin ("Crystal Sound") Pavilion Opera Tower, which was built under the mandate of Emperor Qianlong. How enjoyable it is when the cool wind blows the melodious sound into your ears! In the resort, there is an islet which faces the lake on three sides, namely, Jinshan ("Gold Mountain") Islet, which was entirely piled up artificially. The best sightseeing spot for the lake area is the islet's Shangdi ("Heavenly Emperor") Pavilion, where the whole beautiful scene unfolds before your eyes as you gaze far into the distance from above.

There are 12 temples near the Chengde Mountain Resort, eight of which were directly administrated By the Qing government. Therefore, the eight temples outside of Beijing were called the "Eight Outer Temples." These temples vary in flavor but all are splendid and magnificent, and embody imperial style. Puning Temple is the first temple that Emperor Qianlong built in the mountain resort. The statue

小贴士 避暑山庄72景 避暑山庄于康熙年间开始建造，到乾隆时期最后完成，大小建筑有120多组，康熙和乾隆分别在园中题了36景。二者合称"避暑山庄72景"。这72景是避暑山庄的精华所在。

TIPS: **Peking Opera** Peking Opera is a kind of art performance that combines singing, chanting, acting, martial arts and dancing. By stylized performance, it depicts stories and portrays figures and expresses emotions such as joy, anger, sadness, surprise and fear. Peking Opera is regarded as the most important traditional opera in China.

承德避暑山庄及周围寺庙

金碧辉煌、气势宏伟,极具皇家风范。普宁寺是乾隆皇帝在避暑山庄修建的第一座寺庙,里面供奉着一位千手千眼观音菩萨,这是世界上最大的金漆木雕大佛。佛像高22.28米,腰围15米,用松、柏、榆、杉、椴五种木材120立方米雕成,重达110吨。更有意思的是,菩萨头顶上还端坐着一位小佛。据说这是观世音的老师——无量寿佛,放在头顶以示对先师的尊敬。普陀宗乘之庙建于公元1770年,是为庆贺乾隆六十寿辰接待各少数民族王公贵族建造的。建筑形式与布局仿照西藏拉萨布达拉宫,有"小布达拉宫"之称。须弥福寿之庙是乾隆皇帝为欢迎西藏宗教领袖六世班禅前来祝贺七十寿诞时修建的,供班禅日常拜佛、居住使用。

今天的避暑山庄秀美依然,不再是皇家禁地,已经成为中外游客消夏避暑的好去处。

enshrined here is the thousand-handed Guanyin Bodhisattva, the world's largest wood-carved Buddha statue in golden lacquer. It has a height of 22.28 meters, a waistline of 15 meters, weighs 110 tons, and is carved with 120 cubic meters of pine, cedar, elm, fir and linden. What is more interesting is that on the head of this statue, there sits a little Buddha. It is said to represent Buddha Amitayus, the teacher of Guanyin, and that it was placed on the head as a sign of respect. This Temple of the Potaraka Doctrine was constructed in 1770 AD by Emperor Qianlong for receiving nobles of various national minorities at his 60th birthday. The formation and arrangement of the temple follow the example of the Potala Palace and it is reputed as the "Little Potala Palace." The Temple of Sumeru Happiness and Longevity was built by Emperor Qianlong to welcome the Sixth Panchen Lama, the religious leader of Tibet, who came to celebrate Qianlong's 70th birthday. The Panchen Lama used this temple for daily Buddha worship and as his living quarters.

Still elegant and beautiful, the mountain resort is no longer an imperial "forbidden area", but a summer resort favored by tourists from both home and abroad.

TIPS **The 72 scenes in the Summer Mountain Resort** The construction of the Summer Mountain Resort began during the reign of Emperor Kangxi, and was finally completed during the reign of Emperor Qianlong. There are more than 120 groups of buildings in this royal garden. Emperor Kangxi wrote inscriptions for 36 scenes and Emperor Qianlong for another 36, thus came the 72 scenes in the Mountain Resort. All these 72 scenes embody the essence of the architectural style of the Summer Mountain Resort.

孔庙、孔府、孔林
Temple and Cemetery of Confucius and the Kong Family Mansion

孔子是公元前6世纪到公元前5世纪中国春秋时期伟大的哲学家、政治家和教育家。孔子的庙宇、墓地和府邸位于山东省的曲阜。孔庙是公元前478年为纪念孔夫子而兴建的，千百年来屡毁屡建，到今天已经发展成超过100座殿堂的建筑群。孔林里不仅容纳了孔子的坟墓，而且他的后裔中，有超过10万人也葬在这里。当初小小的孔宅如今已经扩建成一个庞大显赫的府邸，整个宅院包括了152座殿堂。曲阜的古建筑群之所以具有独特的艺术和历史特色，应归功于2,000多年来中国历代帝王对孔夫子的大力推崇。

世界遗产委员会评价

The temple, cemetery and family mansion of Confucius, the great philosopher, politician and educator of the 6th–5th centuries BC, are located at Qufu, Shandong Province. The Qufu complex of monuments has retained its outstanding artistic and historic character due to the devotion of successive Chinese emperors over more than 2,000 years.

In the city of Qufu, China's Shandong Province, there is a large architectural complex that has preserved the ancestral temple, family mansion and cemetery of Confucius and his descendents. In 1994, the Temple and Cemetery of Confucius and the Kong Family Mansion (the Mansion of Confucius' Family)—jointly referred to as the "*San Kong*" (three Confucius')—were entered in the UNESCO World Heritage List.

Confucius, born in 551 BC, is the greatest philosopher, politician and educator of ancient China, as well as the founder of Confucian doctrine.

The Temple of Confucius was originally built in 478 BC to worship Confucius during the ancient Chinese feudal dynasties. Successive feudal emperors continued to increase Confucius' rank and paid homage to him, while expanding construction of the Temple to yield the grand architectural complex of today. Currently consisting of more than 100 ancient buildings and over 460 rooms and occupying 6,000 square meters of land, it can be considered a paragon

小贴士 《论语》是一部记载孔子及其若干弟子言行的书，是中国古代儒学经典。这部书是孔子死后，由他的弟子和再传弟子辑录而成的，大约编定于战国初期。《论语》的"仁政"思想是儒学的思想核心。

收录时间 Date of inscription：1994
遗产类别 Heritage category：文化遗产 C
收录理由 Criteria：C(I)(IV)(VI)

在中国山东省的曲阜市，有一个庞大的建筑群。这里保留着孔子及其后裔的宗庙、宅邸和墓地，即孔庙、孔府与孔林，合称"三孔"。1994年，三孔被联合国教科文组织列入《世界文化遗产名录》。

孔子，生于公元前551年，是中国古代最伟大的哲学家、政治家和教育家，也是儒家学派创始人。

孔庙是中国古代封建王朝祭祀孔子的庙宇，始建于公元前478年，后世封建帝王不断对孔子加封膜拜，扩建孔庙，使之成为一个规模宏大的建筑群。现存古建筑100余座460余间，占地6,000平方米，堪称中国古代大型祠庙建筑的典范。

孔庙的主体建筑贯穿在一条南北中轴线上，左右对称，布局严谨。大成殿是孔庙的核心建筑，黄瓦飞檐，气势非凡。殿内神龛里供奉着近两人高的孔子彩绘塑像。殿前的十根盘龙石柱非常引人注目：每根石柱均用高6米、直径近1米的整石雕刻而成；每根石柱雕有两条巨龙，飞腾于云彩和波涛之间。十根龙柱气势雄壮，无一雷

of architectural excellence among large-scale ancient Chinese temples.

The Temple of Confucius' main building is carefully laid out on a central axis that runs north-south in strict symmetry. Dacheng Hall is the core architecture of the Temple; with its yellow tiles and imposing eaves, the energy it radiates can be described as extraordinary. In a shrine inside the Hall sits a consecrated full-color statue of Confucius with a height of almost two people. In front of the Hall, visitors are mesmerized by the ten *panlong* (coiling dragon) stone pillars. At a height of six meters and a diameter of nearly one meter, each pillar is made from a whole piece of stone carved with two giant dragons soaring between the colorful clouds and billowing waves. The ten dragon pillars exude a majestic force. They each have their own distinguishing qualities, and are the best pieces of ancient Chinese stone carvings. A tall outdoor platform was the altar used for sacrificial offerings to Confucius during ancient times. On September 28th of each year, advocate representatives of Confucianism from all over the world would gather to participate in a sacrificial ceremony to Confucius.

TIPS *The Analects* is a classic work of Confucianism, which records the words and acts of Confucius and his followers. This classic work was compiled by Confucius' disciples after his death and finally finished in the early Warring States Period. The core idea of *The Analects* is the "policy of benevolence".

小贴士 杏坛 "杏坛"当时是孔子聚众讲学的地方,现在延伸为"教育"的代称。在汉语中有不少类似的用法,如"梨园"代指戏曲,"杏林"代指中医。

同,各具特色,是中国古代石雕艺术中的极品。当年祭祀孔子的祭坛是一处露天高台。每年9月28日,世界各地崇尚儒学的代表云集于此,一起参加祭孔大典。很难想象,这样盛大的祭祀仪式已经延续了2,500多年!大成殿东西两侧的房间里面供奉着156位中国历代儒学名家的牌位。殿前有一条神道长约166米,寓意着儒家思想的源远流长。神道正中央的这座亭子叫"杏坛",相传是孔子讲学的地方。孔庙神道两侧古树参天,苍翠挺拔,穿行其间,庄严肃穆之感油然而生。孔庙存有历代碑刻两千多块,上面有历代皇帝、大臣和文人雅士题写的诗词,堪称中国古代书法、绘画和雕刻艺术的宝库。

孔府又称"衍圣公府",是孔子嫡系长孙世代办公居住的府邸,占地240亩,有厅、堂、楼、房463间,前后有九进院落。"衍圣公"是朝廷授予孔子嫡系长孙的封号。孔府布局

It is hard to imagine that such grand ceremonies have continued for more than 2,500 years! In the rooms east and west of the Dacheng Hall, memorial tablets of 156 Confucian scholars from China's past dynasties are consecrated. The *shendao* (passageway) in front of the Hall is about 166 meters long, implying that Confucian thinking is long-lasting as well as far-reaching. At the center of the *shendao* is the Xingtan Pavilion, which is the place where Confucius is said to have taught. On both sides of the Temple's *shendao* are towering trees and upright greenery, encouraging stately reverent feelings to flourish. The Temple of Confucius has over 2,000 stone tablets from successive dynasties, with inscriptions of poetry from past emperors, ministers, scholars and other gentlemen, making it a veritable treasure chest of ancient Chinese calligraphy, paintings and sculpture arts.

The Kong Family Mansion is also known as *Yanshenggong Fu*, and is the official office and residence of Confucius' direct eldest male descendant, which is passed down from generation to generation. It occupies 240 *mu* of land, with about 463 buildings that are mainly halls, mansions, tower and chambers, and nine *jin yuanluo* (courtyards) at the front and the back. *Yanshenggong* is the official title granted by the courts to

小贴士 衍圣公 孔子后代赐爵始于公元前195年(汉高祖十二年)刘邦封孔子九世孙孔腾为奉祀君,代表国家祭祀孔子。宋仁宗至和二年(1055年)改封"衍圣公"。

TIPS **The Apricot Altar** "The Apricot Altar" is the place where Confucius gave lectures and instructions to his disciples and followers, and now it is used as a metonymy to refer to "education". Many words in Chinese are used similarly, such as "the pear garden" (referring to Chinese traditional operas), "the apricot forest" (referring to traditional Chinese medicine).

孔庙、孔府、孔林

很有特点，前面是官衙，后面是私宅。衙署大堂是衍圣公迎接皇帝圣旨、接见官员、审理案件以及举行庆典仪式的地方。大堂两旁摆放着斧头、刀枪等仪仗用具，象征着孔府主人的地位。在私宅和官衙之间，有一道禁门，任何人不准擅自出入。禁门西侧有一个特制石槽，挑水夫把私宅所需的生活用水从墙外倒入石槽，穿墙流入私宅。如此严密的守卫就是为了保证衍圣公后代有纯正的血统。私宅的第一个房间是衍圣公接待亲朋好友的地方。院内有一幅特殊的壁画，上面画着一

个怪兽，名叫贪，以此告诫子孙不要贪赃枉法。私宅的第二个院落是家族成员居住的地方，房间布置得富丽堂皇，有各种珍奇的书画墨宝和生活用品。现在室内的陈设布置还保持着当年的原貌。孔府后院有一座花园，布局独具匠心，清幽雅致。花园里保存着一幅清代壁画。无论从哪一个角度看，观赏者都会觉得画中的小路正对着自己，很有情趣。

the direct eldest male descendant of Confucius. The layout of the Kong Family Mansion features the office at the front and residence at the back. Yashu Hall is the place where Yanshenggong would receive the Emperor's *shengzhi* (decree), meet with government officials, hear cases and hold celebratory ceremonies. Placed on both sides of the Hall are axes, knives, spears and other ceremonial weaponry, symbolic of the status of the Mansion's master. Between the Hall and the residence is a "banned door" that prohibits any unauthorized entry and exit. On the west side of the banned door is a specially built stone trough where the water carrier would throw all the daily requirements for the residence into the stone trough from the outside wall, then the water would flow through the wall to the residence inside. This security feature is to safeguard the descendents of Yanshenggong and their genuine lineage. The first room of the residence is used by Yanshenggong to greet family relatives and good friends. Inside the courtyard is a special mural, where a monster is painted called the "greedy cat", which is used to warn the family's future generations not to be greedy or break the law. The second courtyard in the residential area is the living quarters for family members; their rooms are decorated beautifully, with a variety of rare calligraphy, paintings and other necessities. The indoor furnishings of the rooms still maintain their original appearance. There is a garden in the Kong Family Mansion's backyard with a distinctive layout and a peaceful and elegant atmosphere. A Qing Dynasty mural is preserved in the gardens. It is interesting to note that no matter from which angle visitors choose to see it, they will feel that the little path in the painting is directly facing them.

The Cemetery of Confucius has a stone memorial arch named *Wanguchangchun* where the

TIPS **Yanshenggong** "Yanshenggong" is the noble title inherited by Confucius' offsprings. In 195 B.C., Emperor Liu Bang of the Han Dynasty first conferred the title of "Fengsi Jun" to Kong Teng, Confucius' ninth-generation descendant and authorized him to offer sacrifices to Confucius on behalf of the country. In the year of 1055 A.D., Emperor Renzong of the Song Dynasty changed the title to "Yansheng-gong".

小贴士 贪 本义指爱财，这里指一种传说中的怪兽，它见物即吞，贪得无厌，最终因贪而死。孔府的这幅壁画旨在告诫后人要清廉，不要贪赃枉法。

这是孔林中的"万古长春"石牌坊，六柱五间，古朴大气。方柱上的蟠龙浮雕，生动鲜活，呼之欲出。孔林又称"至圣林"。帝王们为了彰

ancient atmosphere transcends among the pillars and spaces. The coiling dragon sculptures on the square pillars are fresh and vivid, and come alive in your eyes. The Cemetery is also called *Zhishenglin* ("Extremely Holy Forest"). For the manifestation of Confucius' thinking, emperors not only renovated the Temple of Confucius and expanded the construction of the Kong Family Mansion, on numerous occasions, they also bestowed burial lands to the descendents of Confucius. With burial grounds in excess of 3,000 *mu*, more than 100,000 graves and mausoleums of varying sizes and over 3,600 tombstones, this cemetery boasts the longest lasting, best-preserved, and largest scale ancestral clan tombs in the world. The Cemetery of Confucius holds the grave burials of successive dynasties in China, and has become a museum of ancient Chinese tombs.

The grave of Confucius is surrounded by low red walls and a tombstone erected at the front engraved with "Tomb of the Great Holy *Wenxuan Wang*". On the east side lays his son, the *Sishui Hou* (bestowed title)

小贴士 逝者如斯夫 出自《论语》"子在川上曰：逝者如斯夫，不舍昼夜"。现在人们多用来指时间像流水一样不停地流逝，感叹人生世事变幻之快，也有珍惜时间的意味。

TIPS | *Tan* "Tan" is a legendary animal that would swallow anything it sees. Because it is so greedy that it finally dies of greed. The mural painting of "Tan" in the family mansion of Confucius is to tell the descendents that one should be honest and upright, and should not take bribes and bend the law.

孔庙、孔府、孔林

显儒家思想，除了新修孔庙、扩建孔府，还多次赐给孔子后裔墓田。墓地达3,000余亩，大小墓冢累计有十万余座，墓碑3,600多块，成为世界上延续时间最长、保存最完整、规模最宏大的家族墓地。中国历代墓葬在这里都能看到，孔林已成为中国古代墓葬的博物馆。

孔子墓地周围环绕红色垣墙，墓前立一座石碑，上刻"大成至圣文宣王墓"。东侧为其子"泗水侯"孔鲤的墓地，前边为其孙"沂国述圣公"孔伋的墓地。据说，这种墓葬布局是按照古代当地风俗设计的，取"携子抱孙"之意。

逝者如斯夫！虽然圣人已逝，但孔子创立的儒家思想和儒家文化已经穿越历史时空影响着世人。孔庙、孔府、孔林不仅尽显中国历代建筑艺术之美，也将儒家思想的精髓固化下来。

Kongli's grave, and in front lays his grandson, the *Yiguoshusheng Gong* (bestowed title) Kongji's grave. It is said that this type of tomb design is laid out in accordance with the ancient local customs, with the implied meaning of "carry the son and embrace the grandson."

A Confucius disciple recorded, *Shi zhe ru si fu* ("It passes on just like this!"). Even though the holy one has died, the philosophy and culture founded by Confucius have been preserved through history and time to influence the people of the world. The Temple and Cemetery of Confucius and the Kong Family Mansion are not only beautiful masterpieces of the architectural art of successive Chinese dynasties, but also serve to solidify the essence of Confucian thinking.

TIPS | *Shi zhe ru si fu* This line is a quotation from *The Analects*. The original verse goes like this, "Confucius said on the bank of the river: 'The passage of time is just like the flow of water which goes on day and night'". Nowadays people quote this line to mean that time passes just like the ever-changing life, therefore we should value time.

拉萨布达拉宫和大昭寺
Historic Ensemble of the Potala Palace, Lhasa

布达拉宫，坐落在拉萨河谷中心海拔3,700米的红色山峰之上，是集行政、宗教、政治事务于一体的综合性建筑。它由白宫和红宫及其附属建筑组成。布达拉宫自公元7世纪起就成为达赖喇嘛的冬宫，象征着西藏佛教和历代行政统治的中心。优美而又独具匠心的建筑、华美绚丽的装饰、与天然美景间的和谐融洽，使布达拉宫在历史和宗教特色之外平添几分风采。大昭寺是一组极具特色的佛教建筑群。建造于公元18世纪的罗布林卡，是达赖喇嘛的夏宫，也是西藏艺术的杰作。这三处地点风景优美，建筑创意新颖。加之它们在历史和宗教上的重要性，构成一幅和谐的融入了装饰艺术之美的惊人胜景。

世界遗产委员会评价

The Potala Palace, Winter Palace of the Dalai Lama since the 7th century, symbolizes Tibetan Buddhism and its central role in the traditional administration of Tibet. The complex, comprising the White and Red Palaces with their ancillary buildings, is built on Red Mountain in the center of Lhasa Valley, at an altitude of 3,700 meter. Also founded in the 7th century, the Jokhang Temple Monastery is an exceptional Buddhist religious complex. Norbulingka, the Dalai Lama's former summer palace, constructed in the 18th century, is a masterpiece of Tibetan art. The beauty and originality of the architecture of these three sites, their rich ornamentation and harmonious integration in a striking landscape, add to their historic and religious interest.

在海拔3,700多米的雪域高原上，矗立着世界上海拔最高的宫殿——布达拉宫。它是拉萨乃至整个青藏高原的标志。它的独特魅力让无数人为之神往。

1994年，联合国教科文组织世界遗产委员会第18届会议，通过拉萨布达拉宫为世界文化遗产。

布达拉宫坐落在拉萨市区西北的红山上。整座宫殿依自然地势而建，从平地直达山顶，是一座集宫殿、城堡、寺院于一体的建筑群。

The Potala Palace stands on a snowy plateau 3,700 meters above sea level, making it the highest-altitude

小贴士　在藏语中，"布达拉"是观音菩萨的居住地，当时的藏传佛教徒认为，他们的首领松赞干布是观音菩萨在人间的化身，因此把他居住的宫殿叫布达拉宫。

收录时间 Date of inscription：1994；2000；2001
遗产类别 Heritage category：文化遗产 C
收录理由 Criteria：C(I)(IV)(VI)

公元7世纪，松赞干布为迎娶唐朝文成公主而修建了布达拉宫。布达拉宫中的一幅壁画描绘了当时的热闹场面。可惜，松赞干布所建的布达拉宫后来毁于战火，现在仅存一座法王洞。法王洞是当年松赞干布修行的房间。现在，里边供奉着松赞干布和文成公主的塑像。这些塑像表情生动、衣褶流畅，是难得的艺术珍品。

布达拉宫的重建是在17世纪。1652年，西藏的宗教领袖五世达赖来到北京觐见，顺治皇帝封他为"达赖喇嘛"，并赋予他管理西藏的行政权力。顺治皇帝赐予五世达赖喇嘛金册和金印。金印重达8公斤，上面刻有汉、藏、满、蒙4种文字，至今收藏在布达拉宫内。

从北京回到西藏后，五世达赖喇嘛下令重建布达拉宫作为自己的居所。从那时起，布达拉宫成为历代达赖喇嘛的冬宫居所，象征着西藏佛教和历代行政统治的中心。重建后的布达拉宫显现出藏族在建筑方面的才华和审美观。

这座建筑群主要由白宫和红宫两大部分组成。白宫，因外墙为白色而得名。它是达赖喇嘛生活起居和政治活动的场所。共有七层。最顶层是达赖的寝宫——日光殿。日光殿的陈设十分豪华，墙壁和柱子全部用红色的毛呢包裹着，配以各种金银饰品，看上去金碧辉煌。殿内纯金的佛像、玉雕的观音、古代瓷器、西方钟表和锦缎被褥等都是当年的原物，依然按原样摆放着。

palace in the world. It is the symbol not only of Lhasa but also of the entire Qinghai-Tibetan Plateau. The palace's distinctive charm has captivated the spirits of countless people.

In 1994, at the 18th session of the UNESCO World Heritage Committee, the Potala Palace was inscribed to the UNESCO World Heritage List.

The Potala Palace lies on the Red Hill (Marpo Ri) in the northwestern suburbs of Lhasa. The whole palace was built based on the area's physical features, from ground level up to the summit. The Potala Palace is an architectural complex, consisting of a palace, fort and temple.

In the 7th century AD, Songtsen Gampo had the Potala Palace built for Tang Dynasty Princess Wencheng before he wedded her. The palace's fresco depicted the lively scenes of the time. Unfortunately, the palace was later destroyed in the flames of war and, today, the Fawang Cave is all that remains. Fawang Cave is the room where Songtsen Gampo engaged in self-cultivation. The room now contains

TIPS　In Tibetan language, "Potala" is the place where Guanyin lives. The Tibetan Buddhists in the old days believed that their head Songtsen Gampo was the incarnation of Guanyin on earth, so the palace where he lived was named "Potala Palace".

红宫的外墙为红色，它是供奉神佛和举行宗教仪式的地方。宫中的灵塔殿内供奉着八座灵塔，是藏传佛教信徒们心中的圣地。

今天徜徉在布达拉宫里，人们似乎是在参观一座艺术的殿堂。墙壁上绘满了壁画，或讲述佛教故事，或记述历史传说，笔法细腻，线条流畅，历经千年而亮丽如新。

大昭寺是拉萨市中心的一座藏传佛教寺院，传说是拉萨城内最早的建筑，在西藏有"先有大昭寺，后有拉萨城"之说。在大昭寺的广场上，我们能看到无数从各地前来朝拜的藏传佛教徒，他们默念着佛经，虔诚地低下自己的头，祈求佛祖的保佑。

大昭寺的金顶是它作为宗教圣地的典型标志。金顶是靠信徒们捐献黄金在不同时期建筑而成的。远远望去，金色的屋顶在高原的阳光

statues consecrating Songtsen Gampo and Princess Wencheng. With lively facial expressions and lifelike clothing, they are truly a pair of rare artistic treasures.

The Potala Palace was rebuilt in the 17th century. In 1652, Tibet's religious leader, the Fifth Dalai, came to Beijing to visit Emperor Shunzhi. The emperor bestowed the Fifth Dalai with the title of "Dalai Lama" and conferred him administrative powers over Tibet. These are the golden certificate of appointment and the golden seal bestowed by the emperor to the Fifth Dalai Lama. On the eight-kilogram golden seal are printed four different scripts: Chinese, Tibetan, Manchu and Mongolian. Even today, it is still kept in the Potala Palace.

After the Fifth Dalai Lama left Beijing and returned to Tibet, he ordered the rebuilding of the Potala Palace to serve as his personal residence. From then on, the Potala Palace has been used as the residence of each successive Dalai Lama, representing the center of Buddhism and of the historical administration of Tibet. The reconstructed Potala Place reveals the Tibetan people's talent and aesthetic standards in architectural design.

This architectural complex consists mainly of the White Palace (Potrang Karpo) and the Red Palace (Potrang Marpo). The White Palace, which contains seven storeys, derives its name from its white-colored exterior walls. It served as the living quarters of the Dalai Lama and a place where he conducted political activities. The top storey of the White Palace is the Sunlight Palace, the Dalai's sleeping palace. The Sunlight Palace is luxuriantly adorned, with walls and pillars covered in red woolen cloth and decorated with gold and silver accessories. Today, the pure gold Buddha statue, jade-carved Guanyin, ancient porcelain work, Western clocks and brocaded beddings can all be found in their original positions.

小贴士 **唐卡** 一种特殊的卷轴画，色泽艳丽，画面繁复而精致，是藏族文化中一种独具特色的绘画艺术形式。布达拉宫内珍藏着不同工艺、不同材质的唐卡近万部。

The Red Palace has red-colored outer walls, and is the place where sacrifices to Buddha were made and religious ceremonies were held. Eight stupas are found in the palace's Lingta Hall, which is a holy land for Buddhists.

Today, roaming the Potala Palace is akin to visiting a palace of art. The palace's fully painted walls relate Buddhist stories and historical legends. With exquisite brushwork and smooth lines, the images still look brand new even after more than one thousand years.

Jokhang Temple, a Tibetan Buddhist temple located in central Lhasa, is said to be the city's oldest building. In Tibet, there is a saying that "First there was Jokhang Temple, and then there was Lhasa." On the plaza at Jokhang Temple, we can see countless Buddhists coming from near and far to worship. They chant scriptures in a low voice, as they piously lower their heads and pray for the blessing of Lord Buddha.

下灿灿生辉，无比夺目。大殿的寺顶，采用了典型的汉族屋顶的建筑风格，以镏金的金瓦、法轮等装饰，不仅将中原古典建筑艺术与藏式建筑融为一体，而且带有尼泊尔、印度等地的风格，显示出多元文化的交融。

今天，拉萨人休闲时，喜欢到西郊的罗布林卡去。这里是达赖喇嘛的夏宫。从七世达赖喇嘛开始，历代达赖喇嘛夏天时都要移居此处，在这

The golden roof of Jokhang Temple is a typical symbol of religious holy lands. The golden roof was constructed multiple times using gold donated by Buddhists. As one looks at the temple from afar, the golden roof glistens and dazzles the eyes over the sunlit plateau. The temple's peak utilizes typical Han-style roof architecture and is decorated with gold-plated tiles, prayer wheels and other adornments. The temple not only amalgamates the classical architectural style of the central plains with that of Tibet, but also combines elements of Nepali and Indian styles, exhibiting a fusion of many cultures.

Today, the people of Lhasa enjoy

TIPS   **Tangka** It is a special kind of scroll painting which features in rich color, and exquisite and delicate pictures. It's a unique artistic form of Tibetan culture. There are about 10,000 scrolls of Tangka kept in Potala Palace. They were made in different technologies and of various textures of material.

里处理政务和举行宗教活动。罗布林卡的布局具有藏汉结合的浓郁风格，既有西藏高原建筑的特点，又吸取了内地造园的传统手法。运用建筑、山石、水面、陵墓构成一组组别致的景色，创造出不同的意境。其中，宫殿建筑和园林建筑错落有致，或宫墙庭院、绿树成荫，或亭台掩映、湖光水色，两种风格迥异的建筑和谐地融为一体，相得益彰。

visiting Norbulingka, in the city's west suburbs, in their leisure time. Norbulingka is the Dalai Lama's summer palace. Beginning with the Seventh Dalai Lama, each successive Dalai Lama spent their summers at this palace, where they handled government affairs and held religious activities. The layout of Norbulingka mixes the rich styles of both the Han and Tibetan; it possesses characteristics of Tibetan architecture while absorbing traditional gardening methods from inland China. The buildings, rockwork, lakes and mausoleums form an array of novel scenery, creating a unique artistic mood. Whether through the palace walls and courtyards offsetting the lush greenery, or the interlaced pavilions juxtaposing against glistening lake waters, Norbulingka demonstrates the harmonious integration of two vastly different architectural styles.

武当山古建筑群
Ancient Building Complex in the Wudang Mountains

收录时间 Date of inscription：1994
遗产类别 Heritage category：文化遗产 C
收录理由 Criteria：C(I)(II)(VI)

　　武当山古建筑中的宫阙庙宇集中体现了中国元、明、清三代世俗和宗教建筑的建筑学和艺术成就。古建筑群坐落在沟壑纵横、风景如画的湖北省武当山麓，在明代逐渐形成规模，其中道教建筑可以追溯到公元7世纪，这些建筑代表了近千年的中国艺术和建筑的最高水平。

世界遗产委员会评价

　　武当山，在中国中部省份湖北的西北、长江最大的支流——汉水之滨。方圆321平方公里，主峰天柱峰海拔1,612米。环绕在天柱峰周围的群山，从四面八方向主峰倾斜，形成"七十二峰朝大顶，二十四涧水长流"的天然奇观。

　　1994年，联合国教科文组织世界遗产委员会通过武当山古建筑群为世界文化遗产。

The palaces and temples which form the nucleus of this group of secular and religious buildings exemplify the architectural and artistic achievements of China's Yuan, Ming and Qing dynasties. Situated in the scenic valleys and on the slopes of the Wudang Mountain in Hubei Province, the site, which was built as an organized complex during the Ming Dynasty (14th–17th centuries), contains Taoist buildings from as early as the 7th century. It represents the highest standards of Chinese art and architecture over a period of nearly 1,000 years.

Mount Wudang is located in the northwest of Hubei Province in central China on the banks of the Han River—the biggest tributary of the Yangtze River. The mountain has a total area of 321 square kilometers. Its main peak, Heavenly Pillar, is 1,612 meters above sea level. Every surrounding peak

小贴士 **真武大帝** 在道教传说中，武当山主神本是古代净乐国的太子，在武当山修炼42年得道成仙，号玄武君，因后世有一位皇帝的名字中有"玄"字，为了避讳又将玄武改为真武。

武当山上曾有33个建筑群，现存的36处道教宫观，大多建于14到16世纪的明代，是中国现存最完整、规模最大、等级最高的道教古建筑群。这些建筑或建于高山险峰之巅，或隐于悬崖绝壁之内，或依托于山水之俏丽，或映衬于丛林之苍翠，体现了人文建筑与自然景观的高度和谐。

地处偏远的武当山为什么会受到古代中国人的青睐，要在这里大兴土木呢？这得从传说中的仙说起。在中国传统文化中，"仙"是指那些长生不老、具有神奇本领的高人。他们原来都是普通人，通过苦心修道，最终成仙。而他们修炼时，必须远离尘世，身处仙境。武当山地处亚热带，气候温暖湿润，山峰常年笼罩在云雾之中，若隐若现，加上这里环境清幽，自古以来，中国人就把这里看成是神仙的居所。

据记载，从公元200多年的东汉开始，就有教徒在这里搭建房子，潜心修道。

公元14世纪，明朝皇帝朱棣在北京修建紫禁城的同时，又在武当山上为道教的玄武神修建了另一座紫禁城。这座紫禁城，以山下的净乐宫为起点，至天柱峰金顶，规模超过北京紫禁城一倍以上。

bows to it, yielding an extraordinary sight of "72 peaks paying homage to the big crown and 24 ravines of flowing water."

In 1994, the Ancient Building Complex in the Wudang Mountains was inscribed as a World Heritage Site by the UNESCO World Heritage Committee.

Mount Wudang was once home to 33 complexes of buildings. The 36 Taoist temples that remain were built mostly between the 14th to 16th centuries in the Ming Dynasty. It is the most complete, largest-scale and highest-tier ancient Taoist building complex in China. These buildings—whether standing on the top of steep peaks, hidden by cliffs, backed with beautiful landscapes, or set off by dark green jungles—are the superb integration of human architecture and natural landscape.

Why was the remote Mount Wudang favored by the ancient Chinese people? Why did the ancient people build so many magnificent temples here? To answer these questions, we must first examine the immortal beings of Chinese legends. In traditional Chinese culture, "immortals" refer to people with miraculous powers who never grow old. According to legend, they began as ordinary people and, through moral cultivation, rose to heaven and became immortal beings. During their cultivation, it was imperative for them to be far removed from the material world and dwell in a remote "fairyland". Mount Wudang, located in a subtropical region with a warm humid climate, boasts a pristine and tranquil environment, and the mountain's peaks are shrouded in clouds and mist throughout the year. Since ancient times, the Chinese people have regarded this mountain as the abode of immortals.

According to records, Taoists began building houses and cultivating themselves at Mount Wudang around 200 AD during the Eastern Han Dynasty.

小贴士 朱棣靠在北方发动兵变登上皇帝宝座，声称武当山的主神——真武大帝曾显圣帮助自己。他一登上帝位，就动用军夫30万在武当山建造了一个庞大的建筑群，基本确立了武当山的建筑体系。

TIPS **Zhenwu Dadi** It refers to the Taoist god of Wudang Mountain. According to Taoist legend, the chief god of Wudang Mountain was the crown prince of ancient Jingle Kingdom. The prince had practiced Taoism on Wudang Mountain for 42 years, and was called Xuanwu Jun. Later "Xuanwu" was changed to "Zhenwu" to avoid the taboo word "Xuan", which was a given name of an emperor.

道教讲究顺其自然。保护圣山风水，是武当山上施建的一条法则。所谓风水，就是建筑与环境的和谐。据说，朱棣就曾再三下旨，要求工程人员对山体不要有分毫的修动。

传说紫霄宫是净乐太子修炼成仙、化为玄武神的地方。这里也是武当山规模最大、保存最完整的宫观建筑群。它在纵向陡峭、横向宽敞的地形上成轴线构筑，由下而上依次建有龙虎殿、碑亭、石坊堂、紫霄大殿、父母殿。这些殿堂鳞次栉比，又主次分明，是利用特殊地貌营造建筑的典范。

南岩是武当山三十六岩中风景最美的一岩。南岩宫全部用石头建造，虽为石造但却是惟妙惟肖的仿木结构，梁柱斗拱门窗等都是用青石雕造，最重的构件重达万余斤，他们是怎样被举到

In the 14th century, when the well-known Forbidden City was under construction in Beijing, Ming Dynasty Emperor Zhu Di ordered the construction of another Forbidden City at Mount Wudang for Xuanwu, a Taoist deity. This Forbidden City started with the Jingle Palace at the foot of the mountain and ended at the Golden Summit of Heavenly Pillar Peak, with a scale over twice that of the Forbidden City in Beijing.

Taoism stresses the principle of "letting nature take its course." Protecting the mountain's *feng-shui* has served as a rule for building and construction on Mount Wudang. Feng-shui refers to harmony between architectural structures and the surrounding environment. It is said that Zhu Di issued several decrees and forbade workers to change any part of the mountain's body.

According to legend, Zixiao Palace was the site

TIPS Zhu Di initiated a mutiny in the north and became enthroned, claiming that he was helped by Zhenwu Deity, the Taoist deity of Wudang Mountain. When he became the emperor, he ordered 300,000 soldiers to build a large architectural complex on Wudang Mountain, which set the base of the architectural system in Wudang.

绝壁上，又是如何组接起来的，古人没有留下答案，今人也未能破译。

南岩宫中最显耀的是龙头香。一只香炉被安放在伸出悬崖3米远的一块岩石上。这块悬崖的顶端是龙头，中间是龙颈。据说，要想得偿所愿，就得踏着30多厘米宽的龙颈，将手中的香火插入龙头的香炉，然后，在万丈深渊之上后退三步，回到宫内。由于险情不断，如今，这里已用护栏封闭了起来。

从青石神道攀援而上，翻过一天门、二天门、三天门，就到达武当山的最高处——天柱峰绝顶，武当山最负盛名的金顶便坐落在这里。

金顶也称金殿，建于公元1416年，高5.54米，宽4.4米，进深3.15米，总重量达40余吨，全部用铜铸镏金构建而成，卯榫焊接，浑然一体，密不透风。檐脊立有68个玲珑可爱的铜兽。

金顶是中国现存最大的铜铸镏金建筑，代表了当时世界铸造技术的极致，也是整个武当山的精华和象征。

除了秀丽的自然风光、规模浩大的古建筑

where Prince Jingle cultivated himself and ascended to heaven to become the deity Xuanwu. Situated on a wide, steep side of the mountain, Zixiao Palace is the largest and best-preserved palace complex still standing on Mount Wudang. In terms of its layout, Longhu Palace, Stele Pavilion, Shifang Hall, Zixiao Palace and Fumu Palace were built in turn from bottom to top. These palaces are arranged in perfect order, with a clear demarcation between main and auxiliary buildings. Zixiao Palace is a prime example of a cluster of buildings constructed to take advantage of topographical features.

South Cliff is the most beautiful of the 36 cliffs on Mount Wudang. South Cliff Palace is a vivid imitation of a wooden structure; it was actually built completely with stones, with all of the beams, pillars, arches and windows in the palace made of bluestone. The heaviest component of the building weighs over 5,000 kilograms. How these stones were lifted onto the precipice and connected together remains a secret.

The most famous scenic spot in South Cliff Palace is Longtouxiang ("Dragon's Head Incense Burner"). An incense burner was set on a stone projecting three meters from the edge of the cliff. The peak of this cliff resembles the head of a dragon, while the middle part looks like a dragon's neck. It is said that if one wants to realize one's wishes, one must step onto the "dragon's neck", which is only 30 centimeters in width, insert the incense into the incense burner on the "dragon's head", and then take three steps back over a deep abyss and return to South Cliff Palace. Due to frequent accidents, this scenic spot is now railed off and closed.

After climbing along Bluestone Heaven Road and passing through the First, Second and Third Heavenly Gates, visitors will arrive at Mount Wudang's highest point—Heavenly Pillar Peak (Tianzhufeng). The Golden Summit (Jinding), the most famous scenic

小贴士 内家拳派的创始人是明代初期张三丰。传说他修炼时曾看到喜鹊和蛇的一场争斗，从"喜鹊上下飞击，而蛇轻身闪击"中悟出武功以柔克刚的至理，潜心创制出武当派功夫。

群，武当山最为游客所熟知的还有武当功夫。道士修道往往伴以习武。武当倡导内功修炼，运气养性，以静制动，以柔克刚，后发制人，被称为内家拳派。尤其是太极拳法，看似绵绵无力，却能四两拨千斤，动静之中透露出浓郁的道教气息，为武当功夫平添了一道神秘色彩。

在中国人眼里，武当山是一个充满仙气的地方。这里的一砖一石一草一木，都给人以高深莫测之感，似乎都能带给人好运。千百年来，人们在这里祈福，也把最美好的心愿寄托于这座仙山。

spot of Mount Wudang, is situated here.

The Golden Summit, also called Golden Palace, was built in 1416 AD. With a height of 5.54 meters, a width of 4.4 meters, a depth of 3.15 meters and a total weight of over 40 tons, the whole palace was built using copper casting and gold-plating. Through tenoning and welding, these components were perfectly integrated together. On the ridges of the roof stand 68 adorable and exquisite copper beasts.

As the largest building made of copper and plated gold in China, the Golden Palace represented the finest casting technology in the world at the time of its construction. It is also the essence and the symbol of Mount Wudang.

Besides its beautiful natural landscapes and grand ancient architecture, Mount Wudang is also highly reputed for "Wudang kung fu." Practicing martial arts has often been a part of the cultivation process for Taoists. The Wudang school advocates exercising inner strength to improve the flow of *qi* and cultivate character, following the principles of "stillness breaks movement", "softness conquers rigidity", and "striking only after the enemy has struck." Wudang kung fu is regarded as an "internal style" of kung fu. Although tai chi chuan (shadowboxing) may seem weak and powerless, it takes only a few masters of this skill to defeat countless others. A profound Taoist atmosphere adds a mysterious quality to Wudang kung fu.

In the hearts of the Chinese people, Mount Wudang is a place filled with a supernatural aura. Everything here—every brick, stone, tree, and blade of grass—is mysterious and profound, and seemingly able to bring about good luck. For thousands of years and over countless generations, people seeking happiness have chosen this holy mountain as a destination and place of prayer.

TIPS | The founder of Neijiaquan faction is Zhang Sanfeng who lived in the early Ming Dynasty. It is said that Zhang Sanfeng saw a fight between a magpie and a snake when he self-cultivated. By watching the magpie flinging up and down in fighting, and the snake shunning and attacking nimbly, he realized that the soft could conquer rigidity,which was considered a famous axiom. He studied hard and created a faction of martial art, *Wudang kung fu*.

庐山
Lushan National Park

江西庐山是中华文明的发祥地之一。这里的佛教和道教庙观、代表理学观念的白鹿洞书院，以其独特的方式融汇在具有突出价值的自然美之中，形成了具有极高美学价值的、与中华民族精神和文化生活紧密联系的文化景观。

世界遗产委员会评价

庐山位于江西省九江市，北依扬子江，南临鄱阳湖，90余座山峰绵延25公里，犹如一道优美的中国屏风。庐山诞生于喜马拉雅造山运动，是一座崛起于平地的孤立山系，漫长复杂的地质运动和冰川巨大的剥蚀切割作用，造就了庐山险峻而又秀丽的面貌。

庐山地处亚热带，江湖环绕，雨量充沛，气候温湿，森林覆盖率近80%，动植物类型极其丰富。

Mount Lushan, in Jiangxi, is one of the spiritual centres of Chinese civilization. Buddhist and Taoist temples, along with landmarks of Confucianism, where the most eminent masters taught, blend effortlessly into a strikingly beautiful landscape which has inspired countless artists who developed the aesthetic approach to nature found in Chinese culture.

Mount Lu (also known as Mount Lushan) is situated in the city of Jiujiang in China's Jiangxi Province. Overlooking the Yangtze River to the north and Poyang Lake to the south, the mountain features over 90 peaks and stretches out for 25 kilometers like an exquisite Chinese folding screen. Mount Lu, an independent mountain system that rises abruptly from flatland terrain, came into being during the orogenesis of the Himalayas. Complex and protracted geological activity as well as massive glacial erosion and denudation were responsible for creating the precipitous yet beautiful features of Mount Lu.

Located in a semitropical zone and surrounded by lakes and rivers, Mount Lu features a warm, humid climate and abundant rainfall. With forest coverage of almost 80%, the mountain boasts an incredible diversity of flora and fauna.

Visitors are enchanted by Mount Lu's countless scenic spots, which include Sandiequan, Hanpokou, Jinxiugu, Tianqiao, Shimenjian, Xingyunchi,

小贴士 | 锦绣谷 是一段长约1.5公里的山谷，整个山谷花团锦簇、四季不绝，锦绣谷一名由此而来。

收录时间 Date of inscription：1996
遗产类别 Heritage category：文化景观 C
收录理由 Criteria：C(II)(III)(IV)(VI)

庐山迷人的景点数不胜数，三叠泉、含鄱口、锦绣谷、天桥、石门涧、行运池、黄龙潭……整个庐山可谓十步一景，让游人目不暇接，美不胜收。

五老峰是庐山最著名的山峰，位于庐山的东南侧，海拔1,436米。神奇的地质运动在这里构造出五个彼此独立又相互连接的峰林，五个主峰俨如五位老人并坐，十分安静祥和。

庐山半数以上的山峰都有瀑布，看上去就像一条条洁白的丝绸披挂山间。在这些为数

Huanglongtan. Yielding "one scenic spot for every ten paces," the unimaginable beauty of Mount Lu provides tourists with a veritable feast for the eyes.

Located at the southeastern end of Mount Lu at an altitude of 1,436 meters, Wulaofeng ("Five Old Men Peak") is Mount Lu's most famous peak. Mysterious geological activity at this location created five forested summits, which are independent but also interconnected. The five summits resemble five old men sitting together, producing a tranquil and auspicious scene.

Over half of Mount Lu's summits feature waterfalls, like sheets of pure white silk draped over the mountain. Of the numerous falls, the most peculiar is Sandiequan Waterfall, located below Wulaofeng. This torrential waterfall, divided into three sections, has a vertical drop of 155 meters. It is magnificent beyond compare.

In 381 AD, the Buddhist monk Huiyuan passed by Mount Lu and witnessed its picturesque scenery. He decided to settle down here and deliver sermons. In no time, Buddhists from all over China were coming in flocks. As Buddhism flourished at Mount

TIPS **Jinxiugu** It is about 1.5 kilometers long and is overgrown with all kinds of flowers all year round, which makes the valley a splendid and beautiful place, hence comes the name "Jinxiugu" (in Chinese, jinxiu means beautiful and splendid).

小贴士 | 整个庐山遍布茂林修竹，奇花异草，相传中国杰出诗人陶渊明笔下家喻户晓的乌托邦世界——桃花源，就是以庐山康王谷为原形。

众多的瀑布中，最为奇特的要数五老峰下的三叠泉瀑布，飞瀑分为三级，落差达155米，看上去煞是壮观。

公元381年，高僧慧远路过庐山，见这里山清水秀，便决定在此定居，筑台讲经。一时间中国各地的佛教徒蜂拥而至，庐山佛教大胜，寺庙遍地开花，成为当时中国南方的佛教中心。慧远修建了东林寺，此后三十余年他一直在此研修佛学，创立了净土宗。

藏传佛教也同样在庐山修庙建寺。位于小天池山的诺那塔院，是我国南方唯一对外开放的密宗道场。塔院内供奉的藏密本尊、祖师、护法，在内地的寺院中极为罕见。

除了佛教，庐山也为道教人士所青睐。在距离锦绣谷不远的绝壁上，有一个由山崖构成的天然石洞，传说是著名的道士吕洞宾修仙之处。道教的这一福地洞天，历来都是最为游人喜爱的胜景。

Lu and temples sprung up in large numbers, the mountain became the center for Buddhism in southern China. Huiyuan built East Forest Temple, where he lived and practiced Buddhism for over 30 years. During this period, he founded a branch of Buddhism known as Pure Land Buddhism.

Tibetan Buddhist temples were also built at Mount Lu. Nuona Pagoda, located on Xiaotianchi Mountain, is the only place in southern China open to outsiders where Tibetan Buddhist rites are performed. Inside the pagoda, sacrifices are offered to the founders of Tibetan Buddhism as well as to Buddhist doctrine (and the maintenance thereof), practices rarely seen in inland Chinese temples.

In addition to having strong Buddhist roots, Mount Lu is also a location highly favored by Taoists. On a precipice not far from Jinxiugu, there is a natural stone cavern adjoined to one of the cliffs. According to legend, this was where the famous Taoist priest Lü Dongbin meditated and practiced self-cultivation. This paradisiacal holy land has consistently been the scenic spot most adored by visitors.

小贴士 | 净土宗 强调轮回和因果报应，符合当时中国人的心理需求，因而广受欢迎。后来净土宗教义传入日本。至今，日本东林教仍以庐山东林寺为祖庭。

TIPS | Lush forests and tall bamboos grow all over Lushan Mountain, and there are also exotic flowers and rare herbs everywhere. It is said that the prototype of the well-known Arcadia in a poem written by Tao Yuanming, a famous ancient poet in China, is Kangwang Valley in Mount Lu.

庐山还是一个适合安心做学问的地方。唐朝一个叫李渤的书生曾隐居在此,他在附近开了个书院,因为还养了一只白鹿,后人便称它为白鹿洞书院。公元12世纪,北宋最伟大的哲学家朱熹,辞去官职来到庐山,亲自在白鹿洞书院主持讲学。在此期间,他购买了大量书籍,还邀请全国名师到此讲学,使得白鹿洞书院成为当时思想学术的中心。

Mount Lu is still highly conducive to the leisurely pursuit of scholarly activities. A Tang Dynasty intellectual named Li Bo once lived in seclusion on this mountain. He opened an academy nearby and, because he kept a white deer, later generations called it the White-Deer Cave Academy. In the 12th century AD, Zhu Xi, the greatest philosopher of the Northern Song Dynasty, resigned his official post to come to Mount Lu, and personally lectured at the White-Deer Cave Academy. During this time, he purchased a large volume of books and invited famous teachers from around China to give lectures at White-Deer Cave Academy, turning it into the center of philosophical thought.

After the Ming and Qing Dynasties, places of worship for the Islam, Christian and Catholic faiths

明清以后,伊斯兰教、基督教、天主教也在庐山建堂传教。先后共有20多个国家30多个教会在山上购地建房。教会组织在山上开办培训班,传输宗教信义,同时还创立学校、医院和慈善机构。

庐山是中外闻名的避暑胜地。19世纪末,西方人士开始在庐山牯岭一带修建别墅,到1927年,庐山上已经出现了560多座风格迥异的别

were also built at Mount Lu. In total, more than 30 churches representing over 20 countries bought land on the mountain and erected buildings. Religious organizations have set up training courses on Mount Lu to spread their respective religious faiths. They have also established a variety of schools, hospitals and charitable organizations.

Mount Lu is a summer resort renowned both

TIPS | **Pure Land Buddhism** It believed in the transmigration of life and death, and retribution for sin, which met the psychological needs of Chinese at that time. Therefore, it was popular among people. Later the doctrines of Pure Land Buddhism was introduced to Japan. Nowadays, followers of Donglin School in Japan still respectfully refer to East Forest Temple on Lushan Mountain as their ancestral temple.

墅。今天人们将出现在这里的各国建筑群称为万国建筑博览会。

庐山的独特魅力不仅在于它怡人的气候和仙境一般的水光山色，还在于它绵绵不绝的文化传承和一山兼五教的包容气度。不同时代、不同地域、信仰各异的人们带着他们各自的宗教和文化，在这里创造出一幅人与自然和谐相处的动人画面。

1996年联合国教科文组织世界遗产委员会第20届会议，通过庐山风景名胜区为世界文化景观。

in China and abroad. Near the end of the 19th century, Westerners began to build villas in Mount Lu's Guling region. By 1927, over 560 villas of wide-ranging styles had been constructed. Today, people refer to the multinational diversity of structures appearing here as an "architectural museum of ten thousand nations."

Mount Lu's distinctive charm lies not only in its pleasing climate and heavenly natural scenery, but also in its long and uninterrupted cultural heritage and its embracing attitude, captured by the fact that five different faiths are practiced on this one mountain. People of different eras, homelands and convictions have brought their respective religions and cultures here, creating a moving image of the harmonious coexistence of people and nature.

In 1996, at the 20th session of the UNESCO World Heritage Committee, Lushan National Park was inscribed as a World Heritage Site.

峨眉山—乐山大佛
Mount Emei and Leshan Giant Buddha

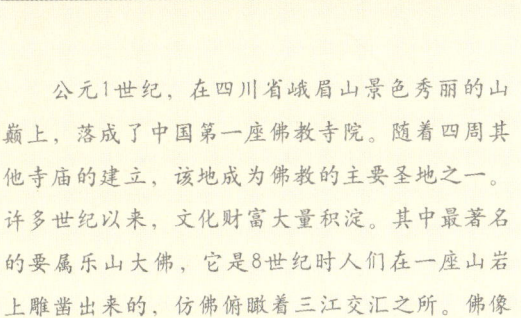

　　公元1世纪，在四川省峨眉山景色秀丽的山巅上，落成了中国第一座佛教寺院。随着四周其他寺庙的建立，该地成为佛教的主要圣地之一。许多世纪以来，文化财富大量积淀。其中最著名的要属乐山大佛，它是8世纪时人们在一座山岩上雕凿出来的，仿佛俯瞰着三江交汇之所。佛像身高71米，堪称世界之最。峨眉山还以其物种繁多、种类丰富的植物而闻名天下，从亚热带植物到亚高山针叶林可谓应有尽有，有些树木树龄已逾千年。

世界遗产委员会评价

The first Buddhist temple in China was built in Sichuan Province in the 1st century AD in the beautiful surroundings of the summit Mount Emei. The addition of other temples turned the site into one of Buddhism's holiest sites. Over the centuries, the cultural treasures grew in number. The most remarkable is the Giant Buddha of Leshan, carved out of a hillside in the 8th century and looking down on the confluence of three rivers. At 71 meters high, it is the largest Buddha in the world. Mount Emei is also notable for its exceptionally diverse vegetation, ranging from subtropical to subalpine pine forests. Some of the trees there are more than 1,000 years old.

　　峨眉山，位于四川省中南部，主峰金顶的最高峰——万佛顶，海拔3,099米。乐山大佛位于峨眉山东麓。峨眉山—乐山大佛，完整体现了佛教传入中国后，在长江流域的影响与演变过程。

　　1996年，联合国教科文组织世界遗产委员会第20届会议，通过峨眉山和乐山大佛为世界文化与自然双重遗产。

　　公元19年，中国的第

一座佛教寺院在峨眉山顶建成。从此,峨眉山一直香火缭绕,与九华山、普陀山、五台山并称为中国的四大佛教圣地。

峨眉山在鼎盛时期,全山共有260多座寺院,数千僧弥供奉着近300尊普贤菩萨的塑像。今天的峨眉山还有30多个寺庙,风格各异,点缀着自然景致。

位于峨眉山脚下的报国寺,宽敞巍峨。位于中山区的清音阁,幽静雅致。而最值得一看的要数万年寺了。

万年寺始建于公元4世纪。公元17世纪,明朝万历皇帝为了庆贺母亲七十大寿,修建了无梁砖殿,并题写了"圣寿万年寺"的金匾。无梁殿为全砖结构,没有梁柱。整个大殿上方是半圆型中空穹隆顶,下方是方型底座,象征天圆地方。穹隆殿顶上绘着四位飞天的仙女。殿内四面的墙壁上万佛围绕,内壁下方有24个佛龛,每个佛龛内放有铁铸的佛像,而他们共同围绕的就是殿内的普贤菩萨。头戴五

Mount Emei is located in south-central Sichuan Province. Its highest summit is Wanfo Peak, with an altitude of 3,099 meters. The Leshan Giant Buddha lies at the eastern foot of Mount Emei. Together, Mount Emei and the Leshan Giant Buddha fully embody the influence of Buddhism and its evolution in the Yangtze River valley after it was introduced to China.

In 1996, at the 20th session of the UNESCO World Heritage Committee, the Mount Emei Scenic Area (including the Leshan Giant Buddha Scenic Area) was listed as a World Heritage Site.

The first Chinese Buddhist temple was constructed on the top of Mount Emei in 19 AD. From then on, Mount Emei has always been wreathed in smoke from burning incense. Mount Emei is one of China's Four Sacred Buddhist Mountains; the others are Mount Jiuhua, Mount Putuo and Mount Wutai.

At the height of Mount Emei's prosperity, the entire mountain had over 260 temples, with thousands of monks offering sacrifices to nearly 300 statues of the Puxian Bodhisattva. Today's Mount Emei has over 30 temples, which vary in style and embellish the surrounding scenery.

Baoguo Temple, located at the foot of Mount Emei, is both spacious and majestic. Qingyin Pavilion, located in the middle part of the mountain, is quiet, peaceful and elegant. The temple most worth visiting, however, is Wannian Temple.

Wannian Temple was constructed in the 4th century. In the 17th century AD, the Ming Dynasty Emperor Wanli built Wuliang Temple to celebrate his mother's 70th

小贴士 | 古时候,将女子细长而弯的眉毛称为"蛾眉",以显示其秀丽,所以,峨眉山素有"峨眉天下秀"的美称。

佛金冠的普贤菩萨比一般菩萨更加华贵美丽，双腿盘曲，坐在莲花宝座上，庄重自然。莲花宝座下一头白色大象俯首帖耳，这座一千多年前铸造的铜象重62吨，它是如何铸造而成的，又是怎样运到山上安放的，至今还是不解之谜。

位于中亚季风气候区域的峨眉山有着丰富的动植物资源，一些珍稀物种，例如枯叶蝶、凤蝶、弹琴蛙、树蛙等都为峨眉山所特有。

在诸多的动植物当中，最有名的莫过于猴群了。峨眉山的猴子身材高大，尾巴短小，毛色棕青，因此又称为大青猴、短尾猴。因为长期生活在佛教名山，这些猴子还得了一个雅号，叫猴居士。野生的猴群往往风餐露宿，以采集植物的叶

birthday, and inscribed the words "*Shengshou Wannian Temple*" on a golden plaque. The structure of Wuliang Temple is constructed solely using bricks, with no beams or columns. The entire upper part of the main hall is a hollow, semicircular dome-shaped roof, while the lower part is a square foundation; together, they symbolize the "round heaven and square earth." Four flying fairies are painted on the roof. Inside the hall, the walls are decorated with countless images of Buddha. In the middle of the temple there are 24 niches, in each of which is placed an iron Buddha statue; these statues collectively encircle the Puxian Bodhisattva. Wearing a golden crown with five Buddhas, featuring a grave and natural bearing, and with both legs coiled on the lotus seat, the Puxian Bodhisattva looks more luxurious and beautiful than ordinary Bodhisattvas. A white elephant beneath the lotus seat appears docile and obedient. This elephant statue, which was cast more than 1,000 years ago, has an impressive weight of 62 tons. To this day, the questions of how the elephant was cast and how it was transported up the mountain remain a mystery.

Located in central Asia's monsoon climate region, Mount Emei is rich in flora and fauna. It is the sole home of some rare and precious species, including the dried-leaf butterfly, the swallowtail, the *tanqin* frog, and the tree frog.

Of the numerous plants and animals on the mountain, the monkeys are certainly the most renowned. Mount Emei's monkeys are tall and big, have short tails and greenish brown fur; they have thus been nicknamed "big green monkeys" and "short-tail monkeys." Having resided on this famous Buddhist mountain for a long time, these monkeys have also received the honor of being nicknamed the "lay Buddhist monkeys." In general, wild monkeys tend to stay and eat in the woods, with leaves, flowers

TIPS | In ancient times, "Emei" was used to address the delicate and fine eyebrows of a woman. And Mount Emei is so called because of its beautiful and delicate scenery.

花果为食，然而，峨眉山的猴子却享受着游客带来的各种现代美食。壮硕的猴王，利用自己的权威，占据了猴区各条道路的中心，轻车熟路地从兴高采烈的大人和孩子手里获得美味。

对于朝山进香的佛教徒来说，峨眉山的金顶是必然前往的地方。金顶在佛语中又称为"光明之鼎""幸福之鼎"，是峨眉山佛教文化的集中体现，也是信众心中的圣地。金顶以高达48米的四面十方普贤圣像为中心，由金殿、银殿、铜殿和朝圣大道组成，整个建筑群面向普贤圣像，雄伟庄严，层次分明。普贤圣像高48米，总重量达660吨，是世界上最高的金

and fruit as their main foods. The monkeys on Mount Emei, in contrast, enjoy all sorts of modern delicacies brought by visitors. The strong and powerful monkey king uses his authority to occupy the central hub of the tourist paths and gorge himself with delicious food supplied by children and adults alike.

As far as Buddhist pilgrims are concerned, Mount Emei's Golden Summit (*Jinding*) is an essential destination. In the Buddhist language, the Golden Summit is also called "peak of brightness" or "peak of happiness"; this peak embodies the convergence of Buddhist culture and is also a holy place for Buddhist followers. At the center of the Golden Summit is a statue of Puxian measuring 48 meters in height. Grand, dignified and with clearly demarcated levels, the Golden Summit is comprised of the Golden Hall, the Silver Hall, the Copper Hall and the Pilgrimage Path; the whole architectural complex faces the Puxian statue. The 660-ton Puxian statue has a height of 48 meters, making it the tallest golden Buddha in the world. The height of 48 meters symbolizes the 48 wishes of the Amitabha Buddha. Divided into three levels, the ten heads of the Puxian statue feature varying expressions and represent the ten different mentalities of human beings.

The Golden Summit is the most concentrated place for marvelous views and wondrous sights on Mount Emei. The rapidly changing weather on the peak gives rise to its sunrise, the sea of clouds, the buddhist light, and the sacred lamp—the four natural wonders of the Golden Summit.

The Leshan Giant Buddha sits at the eastern foot of Mount Emei. Chiseling began in the early Kaiyuan Era during the Tang Dynasty, with the construction lasting 90 years. It is the world's biggest cliff-side statue in existence. The Buddha measures 71 meters in height and faces to the west. Imbued with a dignified

小贴士　20世纪80年代，一名游客偶然发现，乐山大佛四周的山峰恰巧组成了一个仰面而卧的巨型睡佛。睡佛的身躯顺延约1,240米，乐山大佛正处于巨型睡佛的心脏部位。

峨眉山—乐山大佛

appearance, exquisite carving, smooth lines, a well-proportioned body, and far-reaching prestige, it embodies the magnificent splendor of the prosperous Tang Dynasty culture.

Facing the confluence of the Minjiang, Qingyi and Dadu rivers, and with its back to Mount Lingyun, the Leshan Giant Buddha has blessed the local people for hundreds of years. Before the Leshan Giant Buddha was chiseled, this was once a perilous area for boating, with terrifying waves and frequent capsizing accidents. It is said that after the Leshan Giant Buddha appeared, these tragic boating accidents came to an end. Believers think that this is a manifestation of Buddha's mercy. Scientists, however, believe that the Leshan Giant Buddha assumed the role of a bearing indicator for sailors, pointing them in the right direction, and that alteration of the local river environment served to slow down the stream's turbulent waters.

TIPS | In 1980s, a tourist discovered accidentally that the mountain peaks around Leshan Giant Buddha form a shape of sleeping Buddha lying on its back. The body part of this lying Buddha extends about 1,240 meters, and the Leshan Giant Buddha is just sitting in the position of its heart.

佛。通高48米，代表阿弥陀佛的48个愿望，普贤的10个头像分为三层，神态各异，代表了世人10种不同心态。

金顶是峨眉山奇景与神迹最为集中的地方，这里瞬息万变的天气，造就了日出、云海、佛光、圣灯，这最负盛名的金顶四奇。

位于峨眉山东麓的乐山大佛，始凿于唐代开元初年，历时90年才得以完成，是世界现存最大的一尊摩崖石像。大佛通高71米，坐东向西，面相端庄，雕刻细致，线条流畅，身躯比例匀称，气势恢弘，体现了盛唐文化的宏大气派。

大佛背负凌云山，面对岷江、青衣江、大渡河三江交汇之处，千百年来从容祥和地庇佑着这里的人们。在大佛开凿前，这里曾是惊涛骇浪、行船倾覆的险恶之处。据说大佛出现后，船毁人亡的悲剧再也没有发生。信徒们认为这是佛祖慈悲的显现。而科学家们认为，大佛既为船只航行提供了方位指示，也改变了当地的河道环境，舒缓了湍急的水流。

其他地方的弥勒像都是盘腿的坐姿，而乐山大佛却是分腿而坐，这是印度佛教传入中国后本土化的一个表现。大佛的这种坐姿膝部以下呈凹字型，这使得江水冲入后受挫回流，缓和了水流。即便以今天的技术角度而言，乐山大佛的修建也是一项伟大的工程学奇迹。

Buddha statues elsewhere always sit in a cross-legged position. The Leshan Giant Buddha, however, sits with its legs apart. This change in posture is an indication of religious localization after Indian Buddhism was introduced to China. The shape of the statue from the Buddha's knees downward resembles the Chinese character "凹" (pronounced *āo*, meaning "concave"). Water that crushed into the hollow would thus flow back under the counterforce, slowing down turbulent river waters. Even by today's technological standards, the Leshan Giant Buddha is a great wonder of engineering science.

收录时间 Date of inscription：1997
遗产类别 Heritage category：文化遗产 C
收录理由 Criteria：C(II)(IV)(V)

丽江古城
Old Town of Lijiang

古城丽江把经济和战略重地与崎岖的地势巧妙地融合在一起，真实、完美地保存和再现了古朴的风貌。古城的建筑历经无数朝代的洗礼，饱经沧桑，它融汇了各个民族的文化特色而声名远扬。丽江还拥有古老的供水系统，这一系统纵横交错、精巧独特，至今仍在有效地发挥着作用。

世界遗产委员会评价

清晨，高原的阳光还没有铺满这座城市，古城丽江却已经开始了热闹的一天。许多新婚夫

The Old Town of Lijiang, which is perfectly adapted to the uneven topography of this key commercial and strategic site, has retained a historic townscape of high quality and authenticity. Its architecture is noteworthy for the blending of elements from several cultures that have come together over many centuries. Lijiang also possesses an ancient water-supply system of great complexity and ingenuity that still functions effectively today.

In the early morning, before the highland

妇，不远千里，来到丽江拍摄婚纱照。延续了八百多年的古城，就在这样的浪漫气氛中开始了她崭新的一天。

丽江是中国历史文化名城中唯一一座没有城墙的古城。她四面被青山环绕，形状如同一块碧玉大砚，所以又叫做"大研（砚）镇"。据说，古代丽江的统治者姓木，如果筑了城墙，就如同木字加框而成"困"字，这样显得不吉利。丽江最初建于宋末元初，在明清时候开始昌盛。探寻她的过去，人们发现，这片曾被遗忘的"古纳西王国"，远古以来就已有人类生息繁衍。今日的主人纳西民族，是古代南迁羌人的后裔。在千百年的悠长岁月里，他们辛勤劳作，筑起自己美好的家园。

1997年，丽江古城作为文化遗产被联合国教科文组织批准列入《世界遗产名录》。

sunlight has spread over the city, another busy day in the old town of Lijiang has already begun. Scores of newlyweds have traveled vast distances to take wedding photos here. At the old town of Lijiang, with 800 years of history behind it, a brand-new day unfolds in an atmosphere filled with romance.

Among all of China's famous historic and cultural ancient cities, Lijiang is the only one not enclosed by city walls. Instead, it is surrounded by green hills, resembling the appearance of a jade ink-stone; for this reason, it is also called "Great Ink-stone Town." It is said that the ancient governor of Lijiang was surnamed *Mu* ("木", meaning "timber"); if city walls were constructed, the governor's family name would look like the inauspicious Chinese character *kun* ("困", meaning "trapped"). Lijiang, which was first built toward the end of the Song Dynasty and beginning of the Yuan Dynasty, flourished during the Ming and Qing dynasties. Only when we explore the city's history do we notice that in this long forgotten "Ancient Nakhi Kingdom", people have in fact been living and propagating since ancient times. Over the course of thousands of years, they have toiled hard to build up their own beautiful home.

In 1997, the Old Town of Lijiang was registered on the UNESCO World Heritage List.

Like a mesmerizing painting, Lijiang is simple and unadorned, natural and harmonious. Most of the streets and lanes of the old town are situated adjacent to hills and rivers and paved with red breccia, preventing them from becoming muddy during the rainy season or dusty in the dry season. The natural and elegant design of the stones flawlessly coheres with the entire atmosphere of the town. The centrally located Sifang Street (literally "Square Street") is the epitome of Lijiang's ancient streets.

小贴士 ┃ 土司 官名。元朝时开始设置。用于封授给西北、西南地区的少数民族部族首领，土司的职位可以世袭。

As you roam around Lijiang, you will soon discover that this is a flowing city, with rolling rivers everywhere to be seen. The crystal spring water is divided into three main streams, which transform into countless tributaries that interweave with the streets and lanes and wind around courtyards and houses. These interlinking waterways are responsible for the virtual labyrinth of streets in the old town. Lijiang is also called the "Highland Jiangnan," because Lijiang's scenic water vistas closely resemble the Jiangnan area located in the middle and lower reaches of the Yangtze River.

As you look out northward from the old town, you will see the towering Jade Dragon Snow Mountain, which rises to an altitude of 5,596 meters. It is the closest glacial snow mountain to the equator in the northern hemisphere. The mountain's covering of snow and ice, which does not melt even in summer, is a spectacular and magical sight of nature. A local folk rhyme speaks of "one mountain with four seasons and a different view every 10 *li* (equivalent to five kilometers)." Lijiang has long been reputed as a "treasury of flora and fauna" and also boasts a huge natural water reservoir, the source of the old town's flowing waters. Melted snow and underground spring

古朴如画的丽江处处透出自然和谐。古城街道大都依山傍水修建，以红色角砾岩铺就，雨季不会泥泞、旱季也不会飞灰，石上花纹图案自然雅致，与整个城市环境相得益彰。位于古城中心的四方街是丽江古街的代表。

漫步丽江，你会发现这是一座流动的城市，随处可以看到静静流淌的河水。清澈的泉水分三股主流穿城而过，在城区又变幻成无数支流，穿街走巷，入院过墙，流遍万户千家。古城迷宫一样的街道，便是来自于这些交错的水道。有了水的丽江景致很像长江中下游的江南，所以人们把丽江又称为"高原上的江南"。

从古城向北眺望，是高耸云天的玉龙雪山，海拔5,596米，是北半球距离赤道最近的冰川雪峰。山上积雪和冰川终年不化，成就了丽江神奇的自然景观。民谣说它"一山有四季，十里不同天"。这里素有"动植物宝库"的美誉，又是巨大的天然水库。它也正是古城的活水源头，融化的雪水与地下泉水汇聚成黑龙潭，沿着玉河流进古城的每一个街区。

TIPS Tusi It was an official title first set in the Yuan Dynasty and was used to appoint national minority heads in northwest and southwest of in China. The title was hereditary.

小贴士 木府 木府坐西朝东，迎旭日而得暮气，是纳西族传统文化的精神所在。中国很多建筑都呈坐西朝东的姿态，寓意是每天都能迎接从东方升起的红太阳。

丽江人自古以来对水就有一种独特的情感。他们把泉水源头看做是自然之神的居所，并且严格遵守祖先定下来的用水规定，采用"一潭一井三塘水"的用水方法，即头塘饮水、二塘洗菜、三塘洗衣，清水顺序而下，既科学又卫生。居民还以河水洗街，保持街市清洁。

在丽江古城区内的玉河水系上，修建有桥梁354座，密度为平均每平方公里93座。其中以位于四方街东边的大石桥最具特色。这些桥多数是明朝所建。几百年来，古桥默默守护着古城的河流和街巷，随着时光的流逝，显得古老沧桑。

这座气宇轩昂的木府，曾经是古城权力最高的木氏土司的府第。它占地46亩，府内有大小房间共162间。其内还悬挂有历代皇帝钦赐的匾额11块，反映了木氏家族的盛衰历史。

受木府建筑的影响，纳西民居融入了汉、白、藏等民族建筑的精华，凝炼成纳西民族自成一格的建筑经典。当地常见的是"三坊一照壁"和"四合五天井"式民宅。"三坊一照壁"，即主房、左右厢房与照壁围成的三合

water converge to form the Black Dragon Pond. The water flows along the Jade River, reaching each and every corner of the old town.

From ancient times to the present, the people of Lijiang have had a special affection for water. Fountainheads were revered as the abode of the deity of nature and water usage regulations set down by their ancestors were strictly observed. The Lijiang people's method of water usage revolves around "one pool, one well and three ponds". The water in the first pond is used for drinking, the second pond is for washing fruit and vegetables, and the third pond is for washing clothes. This sequential allocation of water is both scientific and sanitary. Local residents even use river water to wash the streets, keeping the town fresh and clean.

Above the old town's Jade River system are 354 bridges, with an average density of 93 bridges per kilometer. The most unique one of all is the Great Stone Bridge, constructed on the east side of Sifang Street. These ancient bridges, which were built during the Ming Dynasty, have watched silently over the old town's rivers and streets for hundreds of years, revealing the bold and rapid changes rendered by the passage of time.

Mu's Residence, with its imposing appearance, once served as the home of this old town's most powerful politician. The residence occupies over three hectares of land and contains 162 rooms of assorted sizes. 11 steles conferred by successive generations of emperors hang inside, reflecting the rise and fall of the Mu family.

Nakhi folk houses, influenced by the architectural features of the Mu Residence, integrate and distill elements of Han, Bai and Tibetan architecture to create the Nakhi people's unique and classic architectural style. Two of the most common building types are

小贴士 东巴 "东巴"在纳西语中意为智者，是纳西人对技师的称呼。东巴文纳西语称"思究鲁究"，可直译为"木迹石迹"。它包含有两层含义：一是指"留记在木头石头上的迹印"；二是"木石之痕迹"，也可引申为"见木画木，见石画石"，即以画物像作为记载交流的工具。

TIPS | **Mu's residence** Mu's residence is located in the west and facing the east, which aims at welcoming the rising sun and gathering the dusk. It is the essence of the traditional culture of Naxi Nakhi. Many buildings in China are set in this manner with the purpose of welcoming the rising sun in the east every day.

丽江古城

院。"四合五天井"是由正房、厢房、左右厢房组成的封闭式四合宅院。石板铺地，青瓦覆顶，红门紫廊的街道，宛如穿越时空隧道，让人回到了美好的人类童年。

"东巴"在纳西语中意为智者，是纳西人对技师的称呼。丽江一带现在还流传着"东巴文"。这种独特文字，是世界上唯一活着的图画象形文，记录着纳西族千百年辉煌的历史文化。

the "triangle courtyard house" and the "quadrangle courtyard house." The "triangle courtyard house" incorporates one main hall, left and right wing rooms and a screen wall. The "quadrangle courtyard house", an enclosed courtyard includes the main hall, south wing room, and left and right wing rooms, all paved with stones, covered by green tiles, and featuring red doors and purple corridors. Wandering through these houses is like walking through a time tunnel, rekindling beautiful childhood memories.

"Dongba", which means "sage" in the Nakhi language, is a title used by the Nakhi people to refer to technicians. Use of the "Dongba" language is still prevalent in Lijiang. This unique language, which features the only hieroglyphic script still in use in the modern world, has recorded the spectacular history and culture of the Nakhi people over the course of thousands of years.

If you are planning to stay overnight in the old town of Lijiang, there is no better activity than to listen to ancient Nakhi music. Every night at eight o'clock, live performances of ancient Nakhi music—usually lasting about two hours—are held at the Dongba Palace. Nakhi music, one of the oldest forms

TIPS | **Dongba** "Dongba" in Nakhi language means "wise man". It is an address for technician by Nakhi people. "Sijiulujiu" in Nakhi language can be translated literally as "wood and stone marks". It contains two meanings. one is "the mark left on the wood or stone", the other is "the mark of the wood or stone". It can also be interpreted as "recording events by making marks on wood or stone", as drawing pictures was a means of recording events and communication in the old days.

住在丽江古城，夜晚最美的安排莫过于听纳西古乐。夜幕降临，每晚8点钟在古城东巴宫内，都会有一场两个小时左右的纳西古乐演出。纳西古乐是是世界上流传至今最古老的音乐之一，是人类文明的音乐活化石。古乐队的成员大多是民间老人。他们来自各行各业，都是喜爱音乐的普通人。这些老人将自己的人生感悟融化在演奏中，使纳西古乐有了一种独特的魅力。

每个去过丽江的人都会有自己心目中的丽江，没有去过丽江的人也会在心中想象着丽江，丽江所包容的多变的地理、丰富的人文和绚丽的民族文化值得我们用一生去追忆。

of music in the world today, is a "living fossil" of human music culture. Most of the band members are senior citizens. They are just ordinary folks who come from all different trades and professions, but share in common a passion for music. These old folks integrate their life experiences into their musical performances, giving ancient Nakhi music a truly distinctive charm.

Every visitor to Lijiang has his or her own understanding of this historic town. Those who have not yet had a chance to visit can tap into the imagination to create their own vivid images. It is certainly worth our time and energy to ponder the diverse geography, rich human culture, and beautiful ethnic traditions of the old town of Lijiang.

平遥古城
Ancient City of Pingyao

收录时间 Date of inscription：1997
遗产类别 Heritage category：文化遗产 C
收录理由 Criteria：C(Ⅱ)(Ⅲ)(Ⅳ)

　　平遥古城是中国境内保存最为完整的一座古代县城，是中国汉民族城市在明清时期的杰出范例，在中国历史的发展中，为人们展示了一幅非同寻常的文化、社会、经济及宗教发展的完整画卷。

世界遗产委员会评价

　　当你登上这个城楼，望着这座古城墙，你可能无法相信，它竟然能够保存至今，而且早在600多年前，它几乎就是你眼前看到的样子。

　　这就是平遥古城，一座具有2,700多年历史的古城。她位于中国北方山西省的中部，是中国境内保留最完整的明清时期的县城。

　　人们说平遥有三宝，古城墙便是其一。城墙建于1370年，是山西现存历史较早、规模最大的一座城墙。明清两代都有补修，但基本还保留着明初的样子。现存的平遥古城墙，周长6.4公里，墙高10米左右。

Pingyao is an exceptionally well-preserved example of a traditional Chinese city, founded in the 14th century. Its urban fabric shows the evolution of architectural styles and town planning in imperial China over five centuries. Of special interest are the imposing buildings associated with banking, for which Pingyao was the major center for the whole of China in the 19th and early 20th centuries.

When you ascend this gate tower and gaze upon this city wall, you may find it hard to believe that not only has it

小贴士 晋商 晋为山西简称。晋商，即山西商人。晋商，尤其是首创中国历史上票号的山西票号商人，曾在中国历史上显赫一时。在宋代，山西商人与徽州商人（又称"徽商"）并称，成为当时中国商业的中坚力量。

鸟瞰平遥古城，令人称奇道绝。这个呈平面方形的城墙，形如龟状，城门六座，南北各一，东西各二。城池南门为龟头，门外两眼水井象征龟的双目。北城门为龟尾，是全城的最低处，城内所有积水都要经此流出。城池东西四座瓮城，双双相对，上西门、下西门、上东门、下东门四个瓮城城门像是乌龟的四条腿。平遥的街巷由四大街、八小街、七十二道小巷构成，呈现着龟甲上的图案，城内最高建筑——高达18.5米的市楼屹立在城市的中心点上，被看做是乌龟的心脏。乌龟乃长生之物，是吉祥、长寿的象征，在中国古人心目中如同神灵一样圣洁。"龟城"寓意金汤永固，长治久安。城墙历经了600余年的风雨沧桑，至今仍雄风犹存。

关公是中国1,800多年前的一位著名将军，在民间被看做勇武和忠义的化身，尊称为"武圣"。他又被商人们视为保护神，因此还有一个称号——"武财神"。古城的几个瓮城内原来都建有关公庙，这个被神化了的历史人物，似乎真的起到了保佑的作用，近代的平遥县城既没有遭受战火，还曾经富甲天下。

出古城北门有镇国寺，它是古城的第二宝。该寺的万佛殿是中国现存排名第三位的古

been preserved until now, but also, that it has looked more or less as you see it now for more than 600 years.

This is the ancient city of Pingyao, a city with a history of over 2,700 years. She lies in the middle of Shanxi Province in northern China, and is the best-preserved county town dating from the Ming and Qing dynasties in the whole country.

It is said that Pingyao has three treasures, one of which is the ancient city wall. Built in 1370, it is comparatively one of the earlier-built, and certainly the largest city wall in Shanxi today. While it had been repaired during the Ming and Qing dynasties, it has essentially retained its early Ming appearance. The Pingyao city wall has a circumference of 6.4 kilometers, and a height of approximately 10 meters.

A bird's-eye view of Pingyao elicits a feeling of admiration. The wall is rectangular and resembles a turtle, with six city gates: one on the north and south sides, and two on the east and west sides, respectively. The south gate is the turtle's head, and the two wells outside the gate symbolize the turtle's eyes. The north gate is the turtle's tail as well as the lowest point of the entire city; all the water from within the city must flow out through there. There are four defense enclosures on the east and west walls, each pair facing the other. The upper west gate, lower west gate, upper east gate, and lower west gate are four defense enclosure gates that form the limbs of the turtle. Pingyao's roads consist of four main streets, eight smaller streets, and 72 alleys, forming a pattern on the turtle's shell. The highest construction inside the city—an 18.5-meter tall building—stands at the center of the city, and is thought of as the turtle's heart. The turtle is life-giving, a symbol for luck and longevity, and in the minds of the ancient people, just as holy as a god. Thus, the "turtle city" is said to be impenetrable, with lasting stability and a history of peace. The city wall has endured more than 600 years of wind and rain, and yet

小贴士 | **龟城** 据说古城四座瓮城城门只有下东门径直向东开，其他城门均向南开。据说是造城时恐怕乌龟爬走，将其左腿拉直，拴在距城二十里的麓台上。这个看似虚妄的传说，闪射出古人对乌龟的极其崇拜之情。

TIPS *Jinshang* Jin is the short form of Shanxi Province. Merchants of Jin refer to the businessmen from Shanxi. Merchants of Jin, especially those who first established firms for exchange and transfer of money in Shanxi, used to be a prominent and influential group of merchants in Chinese history. In the Song Dynasty, Merchants of Jin ranked with merchants of Hui as the nucleus of Chinese commerce at that time.

平遥古城

老木结构建筑，距今已有1,000余年的历史。

　　古城的第三宝是位于城西南的双林寺。该寺修建于公元571年，距今已有1,400多年的历史。双林寺以彩塑雕像闻名天下，保存有元代至明代的彩塑造像2,000余尊，被人们誉为"彩塑艺术的宝库"。

　　平遥，是中国古代商业中著名的"晋商"的发源地之一。

　　古城石板路面上的许多凹痕，并不是人工故意凿出来的，而是清代晚期一百多年的时间里，马车车轮留下的车辙印。当时的平遥是中国著名的金融中心，商贾云集，每天进出城门运送财物的马车无数，平遥城里的金银财宝号称"填不满、拉不完"。在当年一些富商豪宅的院子中

fortunately still exists today.

　　Duke Guan was a famous army general over 1800 years ago in China. He was considered by the people to be bravery and loyalty incarnate, and was dubbed the "military saint." Businesspeople consider him a protector god, hence his other nickname—the "military god of wealth." The defense enclosures of the ancient city all originally had temples dedicated to Duke Guan. This deified historical figure seems to really have the power of protection; the modern Pingyao city not only has never suffered the flames of war, but had been one of the richest cities in the world.

　　Outside the north gate sits the Zhenguo Temple, which is the second treasure of the ancient city. The Wanfo Hall (literally, Hall of the Ten Thousand Buddhas) in this temple is ranked the third among all ancient wooden structures in China that are still standing, and has had a history of over 1,000 years.

　　The third treasure of this ancient city is the Shuanglin Temple located in the southwest part of the city. Built in 571 AD, this temple has a history spanning over 1,400 years. Shuanglin Temple is world-renowned for its painted sculptures. With over 2,000 painted statues from the Yuan and Ming dynasties, it has been called the "treasure-house of painted sculptures."

　　Pingyao is one of the birthplaces of the *Jinshang* (a term of tribute for merchants from Shanxi Province for their achievements in building China's commercial culture), who were famous throughout ancient China.

　　These depressions in the flagstone streets weren't chiseled by man on purpose, but are left by over one hundred years' worth of carriage wheels from the late Qing Dynasty. The Pingyao of those days was one of China's financial centers and a hub of commerce. Countless carriages bearing loads of wealth entered and exited the city walls each day, and the valuables

TIPS *Turtle City* Among the four defense enclosures outside the ancient city of Pingyao, only the gate of the lower east one opens eastward, while the other three are all southward. It is said that at the time when the city was being built, people pulled the left hind leg of the tortoise straight and tied it to to a platform 20 ‖ away from the city in fear that it would run away. This legend reflects the ancients' respect and worship for the tortoise.

央，我们还能看到石刻的元宝，古时商人们以此祈求日日招财进宝，岁岁富贵荣华。

雷吕泰原是一家染料店的掌柜。1823年，雷吕泰筹集白银30万两，在平遥城内开创了日升昌票号。"日升昌"是平遥第一家票号，也是全中国第一家具有现代意义的银行。在"日升昌"票号的带动下，平遥的票号业发展迅猛，鼎盛时期这里的票号竟多达22家，控制了中国一半的流通货币。今天的平遥古城就是研究中国近代金融发展史的最大的博物馆。

如果说在明清时期平遥是山西的经济中心，那么文庙就是平遥古城的文化中心。文庙原称孔庙，是春秋时期儒教创始人孔子的家

were in endless supply. In those days, many wealthy merchants had central courtyards in their mansions, where today, we can still see some of the carved gold and silver ingots (used as money in ancient China). The people of that time used these to ask that each day usher in wealth and prosperity, and each year bring honor, glory, and splendor.

One of these mansions belonged to Lei Lütai, who was originally the keeper of a dye shop. In 1823, Lei collected 300,000 *liang* of silver and started the Rishengchang Exchange Shop in Pingyao. Rishengchang was Pingyao's first exchange shop, and is also the first bank established in China with modern significance. Following in Rishengchang's lead, the exchange industry in Pingyao exploded. At its peak, there were over 22 shops, which controlled half of all circulating currency in China. The Pingyao of today is the largest museum for research into the financial development of China in modern times.

If the Pingyao of the Ming and Qing dynasties was the economic center of Shanxi, then Wenmiao Temple (literally "Temple of Confucian Learning") was the cultural center of Pingyao. Wenmiao, the original name of which was Kongmiao (the Temple of Confucius), is the ancestral temple of Confucius (known as Kong Zi in Chinese), who founded Confucianism during the Spring and Autumn Period. The main hall of the temple was rebuilt 800 years ago and has kept its original appearance until now. It is the oldest Confucian temple in all of China, as well as the tallest ancient building in Pingyao. A large Chinese character, "kui", is imprinted on the back wall of the main hall, allegedly written by Wen Tianxiang's hand in the Song Dynasty. "Kui" means "number

TIPS | 古城大街 古城南大街上鳞次栉比的店铺，是明清时期商业街的真实写照。如今依然热闹非凡，只不过自行车取代了昔日的马车。

庙。其主建筑大成殿于800年前重建，至今保持着原貌，是中国现存最古老的文庙建筑，也是平遥古城内最早的古建筑。大成殿的后壁上有一个硕大的"魁"字，传说是宋代文天祥手书的。"魁"的意思是第一，文天祥本人曾经高中状元，也就是全国科举考试的第一名。传说在这个"魁"字前，曾挂着一面大鼓，只有状元才有资格敲响它。但是，当年的平遥商业气氛浓厚，大批人材弃文从商，在明清两朝五百多年科举考试中，山西竟没有一个人得中状元，当然那面大鼓也就长期保持沉默了。

平遥古城黑砖灰瓦，经过千百年岁月的磨炼，虽然没有鲜艳明亮的色彩，但是，当你徜徉其中，会有一种时光倒流、超然现实的感觉，你会慢慢感受到，中国传统文化那永不褪色的光芒。

1997年12月，平遥古城被列入《世界遗产名录》。

one"; Wen Tianxiang once scored the highest in an imperial examination. As legend has it, there used to be a drum hanging in front of the character "kui" that only the highest ranked scholar had a right to beat. But the Pingyao of those days was dense with an air of commerce; large numbers of people abandoned literature for business, and Shanxi did not produce a single top-ranking scholar in 500 years of imperial examinations during the Ming and Qing dynasties. Thus, the drum remained silent for a long time.

Pingyao's black bricks and gray tiles have been weathered by thousands of years. They lack bright colors, but when you wander among them, you will feel a surreal sense of time flowing backwards. Gradually, you will feel the never-fading rays of China's traditional culture shine on you.

In December 1997, the Ancient City of Pingyao was added to the UNESCO World Heritage List.

TIPS Ancient city street Rows upon rows of stores and shops on the South Street of the ancient city gives a true picture of the commercial street in the Ming and Qing dynasties. It is now still as busy and bustling as in the old days, However, today the bicycles have taken the place of the horse-drawn carts in the ancient times.

苏州古典园林
Classical Gardens of Suzhou

　　没有哪些园林比历史名城苏州的九大园林更能体现出中国古典园林设计的理想品质。咫尺之内再造乾坤，苏州园林被公认是实现这一设计思想的典范。这些建造于11至19世纪的园林，以其精雕细琢的设计，折射出中国文化中取法自然而又超越自然的深邃意境。

世界遗产委员会评价

　　上有天堂，下有苏杭。苏州是一个充满国际化和时尚化的现代都市，但在一些小巷中也隐藏着一处处清幽之地，碧水潺潺、亭榭相映，这就是闻名天下的苏州园林。

　　苏州园林一般都不大，大的四五亩，小的不足一亩，但造园艺术却极为讲究，深受中国文学和绘画艺术的影响。一抹青山、一池碧

Classical Chinese garden design, which seeks to recreate natural landscapes in miniature, is nowhere better illustrated than in the nine gardens in the historic city of Suzhou. They are generally acknowledged to be masterpieces of the genre. Dating from the 11th-19th century, the gardens reflect the profound metaphysical importance of natural beauty in Chinese culture in their meticulous design.

"There is Heaven above, Suzhou and Hangzhou below." Suzhou is an internationalized modern and fashionable metropolis. Hidden between its laneways are locations of peace and tranquility, with jade green waters that flow by and reflect nearby pavilions. These are the world-famous Suzhou Gardens.

In general, Suzhou gardens are not very big. The

小贴士　**写意山水画**　中国画的一种，是用毛笔、墨水把自然界的山水美景传神地描绘出来，而不是一笔一画如实地去临摹、渲染。中国画是用中国所独有的毛笔、水墨和颜料在特制的宣纸或绢上作画，常常留有空白。

收录时间 Date of inscription：1997；2000
遗产类别 Heritage category：文化遗产 C
收录理由 Criteria：C(I)(II)(III)(IV)(V)

水，花木扶疏、楼台掩映，就像一幅幅写意山水画。苏州园林取法自然而又超越自然，人们都说它是"立体的画、有形的诗、凝固的音乐"。

据记载，苏州园林始建于公元前6世纪，最多时达到五百多座，因而称苏州为"园林之城"并不为过。苏州园林是私家园林的代表，精致小巧，清新秀雅。拙政园、留园和狮子林等九处作为苏州园林的典型例证先后于1997年和2000年被联合国教科文组织列入《世界文化遗产名录》。

拙政园是苏州园林中面积最大的一座，布局以水为中心，疏落相宜，清新雅致。拙政园分为三个园，最有名的要数中园了。占中园面积1/5的水池宛如烟波浩淼的湖泊，环水而建的房屋把江南水乡拢进一园，十六座不同式样的桥，或直或曲、或飞或跨，让游人在十几分钟内就能遍赏小桥流水人家的神韵。园中的荷花亭亭玉立，清香四溢。中国古人常常借用荷花"出淤泥而不染，濯清涟而不妖"的特点来比喻人的洁身自好、不与世

larger ones occupy four to five *mu* (1 *mu* equaling to 0.0667 hectare or 1/6 acre) of land, while the smaller ones are less than one *mu*. Particular attention is paid to the gardens' artistic design, which is deeply influenced by Chinese art, literature and paintings. Imagine a green hill in the distance, and flowers and shrubs surrounding a pool of emerald water that reflects nearby buildings and platforms. It's comparable to traditional freehand landscape paintings. Suzhou gardens use natural landscapes but also transcend nature. People say that it is similar to a "three-dimensional painting, poetry in a physical form, or music that you can touch."

According to historical records, development of Suzhou gardens began in the 6th century BC. The number of gardens reached a peak of over 500 and thus it is no surprise that Suzhou came to be called the "City of Gardens." Suzhou gardens are representative of private gardens—delicately compact, refreshing and elegant. The Humble Administrator's Garden, Lingering Garden and Lion Grove Garden are some of the nine classical examples of Suzhou gardens registered in the UNESCO World Heritage List in 1997 and 2000.

The Humble Administrator's Garden has the largest area amongst the Suzhou gardens with its layout mainly focusing on the water features. It is fresh and elegant with buildings scattered in a perfect arrangement. This garden is divided into three parts, and the most famous is the Central Garden. Occupying one-fifth of the Central Garden area is the pool which looks like a lake with a vast expanse of mists and ripples. Houses built along the water bring the characteristics of the water villages of south of the Yangtze River into the garden: 16 different styles of bridges—straight or bent, overhead or

TIPS **The Landscape Painting of Freehand Brushwork** It is a kind of traditional Chinese painting, which aims at catching the spirit of the nature and landscape by using brush and ink, instead of imitating the original scenery exactly. Chinese painting employs the paintbrush, ink and pigment to draw on cloth, paper or wood board. You may find blank space in a Chinese traditional painting.

俗同流合污的高贵品格。

留园更具特色。小小的前庭、暗暗的走廊、窄窄的天井，半漏半遮，让人产生很多猜想。令人称奇的是，门和窗构成了一幅幅风景

画。苏州园林中有很多这样的设计，这叫框窗，用门框或窗框把风景框起来，从这个角度看是一幅画，从另一个角度看又是另一幅画。这叫移步换景，人动画变。

网师园虽然占地面积最小，但建筑却非常精美。园林的设计处处显示着中国古人的文化理念。大门门槛的高低是用来表示主人身份的。古时有身份的人要乘坐轿子，而且一直到轿厅才下轿。大堂是主人见客和家庭举行重要活动的地方，布置非常讲究。如果是家庭活动，辈分最高

ground level, etc.—allowing visitors to appreciate the charm of the local people's lifestyle in less than twenty minutes. The lotuses in the garden stand erect and elegant with their fragrance reaching everywhere. The ancient Chinese would often describe the lotus flower and compare it to people: "(The lotus) grows out of the mud but is never contaminated; (it) rises out of the water without seeming too fragile." The message is to encourage people to stay pure and clean, and maintain an elegant character that will not be tarnished by worldly impurities.

The Lingering Garden has a small vestibule, darkened corridors, and a half-sheltered narrow courtyard. It is fascinating to see through the doors and windows as though one is looking at a landscape painting. Suzhou gardens have many such designs, called *kuangchuang*; doors or windows are used to frame the scenery. Viewed from a certain angle, it looks like one painting, and from another angle it looks like

小贴士 私家园林 中国园林主要有皇家园林和私家园林两种。私家园林是由王公、贵族、地主、富商、士大夫等私人修建的园林，现存者以江南地区成就更高。私家园林精致小巧，清新秀雅，苏州园林是其代表。

another painting. When the location is changed, the scenery adjusts; the painting is thus "altered" by people's movements.

Although the Master-of-Nets Garden occupies the smallest area, the buildings are exceptionally beautiful. The garden's design fully demonstrates the ideas of ancient Chinese culture. The height of the front door's threshold is used to show the owner's rank. In ancient times, people of status would ride sedan chairs, and they would only disembark at the Sedan Chair Hall. The grand reception hall is where the owner would greet visitors or hold important family activities, with very particular decorations. For family activities, the highest ranking male and female hosts would sit on the chairs facing south; for meeting distinguished guests, the hosts would sit on the left side of the honored guest, and the others would sit on the chairs facing east or west. The *taishiyi*, a chair with handrails on both sides, is the seat for the highest ranking individual.

The Master-of-Nets Garden is called "Number One Building in South of Yangtze River", where on the bricks are engraved with historical stories as well as designs of birds, animals, flowers and shrubs. These are not only used for decorative purposes, but also to express people's wishes for blessing.

The Mountain Villa with Embracing Beauty has man-made mountains that look like imposing high peaks, exhibiting spontaneous energy from treacherous cliffs, dells and deep lakes, making it difficult to distinguish from natural mountains. Ancient skilled craftsmen could, based on the size, shape, crevice, and texture of the rocks of Taihu-lake,

的男女主人坐在靠北向南的椅子上；如果是见尊贵的客人，主人在左贵客在右，其他人坐在东西两侧的椅子上，两边有扶手的太师椅是规格最高的座椅。

网师园的门楼人称"江南第一门楼"，砖上刻着历史故事和鸟兽花卉图案，既起装饰作用，又表达祈福的心愿。

环秀山庄的假山看上去峰峦起伏、气势雄健、危崖绝壁、幽谷深潭，与自然的山难辨真假。古代的能工巧匠按照太湖石的大小、形状、缝隙、纹理巧妙地进行拼对、勾连、镶嵌，把一块块大小不等的石头堆砌成宛若天成的假山极品。

沧浪亭是苏州园林中最古老的一座，始建于公元9世纪，是宋朝一位叫苏舜钦的高官修建的。

TIPS **The private gardens** Chinese gardens can be divided into two categories: royal gardens and private gardens. Private gardens are those built by nobles, officials and rich people, and most of the masterpieces exist in the south of Yangtze River today. The private gardens are exquisite, refined, elegant and tasteful in design, among which the gardens in the historic city of Suzhou are typical.

小贴士 花窗 苏州园林有很多精美的花窗，纹饰各异，有丁裂纹、柳条纹、海棠花纹、梅花纹、万字纹，还有各种组合的花纹。

沧浪亭的命名源于诗句"沧浪之水清兮，可以濯我缨；沧浪之水浊兮，可以濯我足"，寓意顺乎自然的归隐人生。沧浪亭松柏森森、青草离离、水色濛濛，108个花窗没有一个重样，千姿百态的门洞好像信手拈来，极小的空间如诗如画，曲折的长廊随意蜿蜒。

skillfully match, connect, and embed stones of varying sizes and build them into excellent pieces to construct these man-made mountains which appear to have been made in heaven.

The Canglang Pavilion is the oldest amongst the existing Suzhou gardens, built in the 9th century AD by a high-ranking Song Dynasty official named Su Shunqin. The Pavilion's name came from a poem about the natural life of a recluse. The Pavilion is surrounded by pine trees, green grass and ethereal water scenery. It consists of 108 lattice windows, without a duplicating design, which are as beautiful and picturesque as paintings and poetry. There are also long corridors that twist and turn, meandering effortlessly.

The Lion Grove Garden has a series of awesome peaks, many resembling the shape of lions. The man-made mountains occupy one-fifth of the Lion Grove Garden. It is the largest man-made rock mountain in China, and is divided into upper, middle and lower levels. Complete with nine winding mountain trails spiraling, assembling, dispersing and entangling in the body of the mountains, with complicated lines weaving through, it may be easy to enter but not easy to come out. There are also 11 caves hidden in peculiar summits and secluded ravines, making it resemble a labyrinth

小贴士 太湖石 太湖石多为灰色，玲珑剔透、重峦叠嶂，适合做园林石材，因产于太湖而得名，与灵璧石、昆石、大理石一起被称为中国古代四大玩石。

TIPS | **Engraved windows** There are many delicate and exquisite engraved windows in the gardens of Suzhou. They were made in various patterns and designs, for examples, the pattern like the shape of the Chinese characters "丁"or "万", the pattern of the willow branches, the Chinese flowering crabapple, and the Chinese plum flower etc. Some were made of a combination of different patterns.

苏州古典园林

狮子林园内石峰林立，多状似狮子。狮子林中有一片假山，占全园面积的1/5，是中国现存最大的石假山，假山分上、中、下三层，九条山径曲折盘旋，聚散纠缠在山体间，线路错综复杂，进去容易出来却没那么简单，十一个洞穴掩藏在怪峰幽壑间，更使得假山像迷宫一样。

藕园中有一座假山，为苏州园林当中最大的黄石假山，像这样单独叠成一座山，在苏州园林中并不多见。艺圃中的延光阁是苏州园林中最大的水榭，无论是古代还是今天，坐在这里品茶观鱼，任凭温润的风抚在脸上，真是诗意的享受。"退思园"中的贴水建筑更是匠心独运，人置身其上如碧波踏浪。

在过去的几百年中，园林的主人在此起居宴饮、会见宾客、读书写作。清风明月、柳浪荷香，多么富有诗情画意！这种人与自然和谐、生活与艺术统一的人居环境即使在今天也是人们所向往和追求的。

rather than a man-made mountain.

The Couple Garden Retreat has the largest yellowstone man-made mountain of Suzhou gardens. It is rare to find another one which has been piled up individually like that. The artistic *Yanguangge* is the largest water pavilion amongst Suzhou gardens. Whether during ancient times or in the present day, to be able to sit and enjoy a cup of tea or observe the fish while letting the warm and moist breeze caress your face is a delight usually found only in poetry. *Tuisiyuan*, built on the water banks, captures the essence of the craftsmen; one almost has the feeling of treading on emerald waves.

Over the past several hundred years, the masters of the gardens have enjoyed their daily lives there: feasting, drinking, meeting guests, reading and writing. One can enjoy a refreshing breeze, a clear moonlit night, swaying willows, and fragrant lotuses—how poetic and picturesque! Harmony between man and nature, a living environment that unifies life and the arts... these are precisely the ideals, of which modern people are in pursuit.

TIPS | **Taihu-lake stone** Taihu-lake stone, a kind of porous stone from Taihu-lake is famous for use in rockeries. Theses stones are grey and in various shapes, which are used as the main materials in gardening architecture. Taihu-lake stone was considered one of the four ornamental stones in ancient China, the other three were Lingbi Stone, Kun Stone and Dali Stone.

颐和园
Summer Palace

北京颐和园，始建于公元1750年，1860年在战火中严重损毁，1886年在原址上重新进行了修缮。其亭台、长廊、殿堂、庙宇和小桥等人工景观与自然山峦和开阔的湖面相互和谐、艺术地融为一体，堪称中国风景园林设计中的杰作。

世界遗产委员会评价

颐和园旧称"清漪园"，位于北京城区西北郊，始建于1750年，是中国清朝皇家花园和行宫。

历经两次战争洗劫，颐和园损毁严重，几经重修扩建。今天，充满历史厚重感与沧桑感的颐和园显得更加雄伟壮观、富丽恢弘。

颐和园占地2.97平方公里，有各式宫殿、寺

The Summer Palace in Beijing – first built in 1750, largely destroyed in the war of 1860 and restored on its original foundations in 1886 – is a masterpiece of Chinese landscape garden design. The natural landscape of hills and open water is combined with artificial features such as pavilions, halls, palaces, temples and bridges to form a harmonious ensemble of outstanding aesthetic value.

Originally known as Qingyiyuan (the Garden of Clear Ripples), the Summer Palace is situated in the northwestern outskirts of Beijing. Constructed in 1750, it was an imperial garden and temporary dwelling palace for the Qing royal family.

The Summer Palace, twice ransacked and severely damaged during periods of war, underwent several reconstructions. Today, laden with history and imbued with the vicissitudes of time, the Summer Palace has become even more magnificent, grand and expansive.

Covering an area of 2.97 square kilometers, the Summer Palace contains more than 3,000 palaces, temples and gardens of various styles. It is the largest and best-preserved imperial garden in China and has earned the reputation of being an

小贴士 皇家园林 是中国古代皇室家族娱乐休憩的场所，现存者以北京一带最为集中。皇家园林气势雄伟，雍容华贵，最出名的有颐和园、圆明园、承德避暑山庄等。

收录时间 Date of inscription：1998
遗产类别 Heritage category：文化遗产 C
收录理由 Criteria：C(I)(II)(III)

庙和园林3,000多座，是中国现存最为完整、规模最大的皇家园林，素有"皇家园林博物馆"的美誉。1998年，颐和园被联合国教科文组织列入《世界文化遗产名录》。

颐和园主要由万寿山和昆明湖组成，大体分为三个区域：以仁寿殿为中心的勤政区，以乐寿堂、玉澜堂和宜芸馆为主体的生活区，由万寿山和昆明湖等组成的游览区。

仁寿殿是宫廷区的主要建筑，是当年慈禧太后和光绪皇帝坐朝听政、会见外宾的地方。乾隆皇帝在位时叫勤政殿，意为不忘勤理政务。光绪十二年重修，改称仁寿殿，意为施仁者长寿。仁寿殿西侧的乐寿堂是慈禧太后休息的地方，是颐和园生活区的主要建筑。院内有

"imperial garden museum." In 1998, the Summer Palace was inscribed to the UNESCO World Heritage List.

Consisting mainly of Longevity Hill and Kunming Lake, the Summer Palace is roughly divided into three areas: the political area, at the center of which lies Renshoudian (the Hall of Benevolence and Longevity); the living area, comprised mainly of Leshoutang (the Hall of Joyful Longevity), Yulantang (the Hall of Jade Ripples) and Yiyunguan (originally used to collect books for Emperor Qianlong and later used as the sleeping chamber of Empress Longyu); and the sightseeing area, comprised mainly of the Longevity Hill and Kunming Lake.

The Hall of Benevolence and Longevity is the main building of the palace complex and used to be the place where Empress Dowager Cixi and Emperor Guangxu administered state affairs and met foreign guests. During the reign of Emperor Qianlong, the Hall of Benevolence and Longevity was named *Qinzheng* (meaning "assiduous with government affairs") Hall, as a reminder to the emperor to administer the state's political affairs with diligence. Reconstructed in the 12th year of Emperor Guangxu, the hall was given its current name of Renshou, implying that those who were industrious in administering state affairs could

TIPS | **The royal gardens** Royal gardens are places where the royal families of ancient China entertained themselves and took vacations, and these gardens are designed in magnificent and splendid style. Extant royal gardens are mainly in Beijing and the neighboring areas, among which the most prominent are the Summer Palace, the Winter Palace, and the Mountain Resort of Chengde etc.

小贴士 ▎乐寿堂 "乐寿"是出自《论语》中的"智者乐，仁者寿"，意思是说这里就是仁者智者居住的地方。

几株玉兰花，是乾隆皇帝从南方移植过来敬献给母亲的。初春时节，玉兰花悄然绽放，晶莹洁白。玉澜堂是一组别致优雅的四合院建筑，是光绪皇帝的寝宫。戊戌变法失败后，他就一直被囚禁在这里。不远处的德和园戏楼是慈禧太后为方便自己欣赏京剧专门修建的。

万寿山原名翁山。中国古代杰出的工匠在高不足六十米的小山上修建了巨大的主体建筑群。从山脚的"云辉玉宇"牌楼，经排云殿、德辉殿、佛香阁，至顶部的智慧海，重廊复殿、层叠上升、气势磅礴。巍峨高耸的佛香阁八面三层，踞山面湖，位于万寿山的最高点上。凭栏远眺，园内的湖光山色一览无遗。佛香阁里面供奉的是接引佛，就是把诚心礼佛的人接引到西方极乐世界的佛。与佛香阁的庄严肃穆相比，智慧海显得非常地华丽。外墙全部用黄绿两色的琉璃瓦装饰，上面排满了千余尊琉璃佛，在阳光的照耀下色彩绚丽、光彩夺目。

昆明湖原名西湖，占全园面积的3/4。与万寿山上佛教建筑的恢弘不同，昆明湖拥有江南水乡的细致和婉约。十七孔桥像一条彩虹横卧在湖面上，连接着东堤和南湖岛。十七孔桥是园中最大的石桥，由十七个桥洞组成，从中间

achieve longevity. The Hall of Joyful Longevity, located on the west side of the Hall of Benevolence and Longevity, is the place where Cixi rested. It is the main building of the Summer Palace's living area. The Yulan magnolias in the yard were brought from South China by Emperor Qianlong for his mother. In the springtime, these Yulan magnolias silently blossom—sparklingly brilliant and as white as snow. The Hall of Jade Ripples is a *siheyuan* (a residence consisting of a courtyard surrounded by buildings at the four sides) which served as Emperor Guangxu's imperial sleeping chamber. After the Hundred Days' Reform movement failed, Emperor Guangxu was confined here. The nearby Deheyuan (Garden of Virtue and Harmony) opera house was specially constructed for Cixi to enjoy Peking Opera.

The Longevity Hill was originally called Wengshan Hill. On this hill less than 60 meters high, ancient China's outstanding craftsmen built the huge main cluster of buildings. Yunhuiyuyu Archway lies at the foot of the hill, and is followed by Paiyundian (the Hall of Dispelling Clouds), Dehuidian (the Hall of Moral Glory) and Foxiangge (the Pavilion of Buddhist Fragrance) in the middle, and finally Zhihuihai (the Hall of the Sea of Wisdom) on the hilltop; the buildings lie in close proximity to one another and carry great momentum. The towering Pavilion of Buddhist Fragrance, which contains eight sides and three

小贴士 ▎戊戌变法 1898年，维新派代表人物康有为、梁启超、谭嗣同等人通过光绪皇帝实行变法，主要内容是：学习西方，提倡科学文化，改革政治、教育制度，发展农、工、商业等。

| TIPS | **The Hall of Joyful Longevity** "Le shou (joyful longevity)" comes from a verse in *The Analects*. The original verse says, "The wise man lives happily and the benevolent man lives longer." So the name "Leshoutang" implies that it is the place where the wise and benevolent people inhabit. |

的桥洞向两边数都是中国古人最崇尚的阳数九。石桥栏杆上雕刻着有五百多只石狮子，静静地凝望着过往的游客。十七孔桥东侧的铜牛是乾隆时期铸造的，背上刻着大禹治水的故事。作为制伏水患的神仙，两百年来一直守护着昆明湖。石舫是昆明湖上特有的风景，是颐和园中唯一带有

storeys, is located at the top of Longevity Hill, facing Kunming Lake. When looking out over the rails, visitors can admire the beautiful lake and mountain scenery. Inside the Pavilion of Buddhist Fragrance, sacrifices are made to Amitabha Buddha, who guides pious Buddhist believers to the Pure Land of the West. In contrast to the solemnity and stateliness of the Pavilion of Buddhist Fragrance, the Hall of the Sea of Wisdom has a look of incredible magnificence. All of its external walls are decorated with yellow and green glazed tiles. Under the sun's golden rays, over 1,000 colored-glaze Buddhas shine with spectacular colors and dazzling radiance.

Kunming Lake, originally known as the West Lake, covers three-quarters of the area of the Summer Palace. In contrast to the grandeur of the Buddhist architecture on the Longevity Hill, Kunming Lake embodies the exquisite and mellow quality of rivers and lakes south of the Yangtze River. The 17-Arch Bridge, like a rainbow stretching across the lake, connects the east bank with Nanhu Island. The 17-Arch Bridge, as the name implies, consists of 17 arches and is the largest bridge in the Summer Palace. Counting from the central arch to the last arch on either end yields the number "9", the number most favored by the ancient Chinese people. On the stone rails of the bridge are perched over 500 stone lions, silently gazing upon the passing visitors. The copper bull on the east side of the bridge was cast during the reign of Emperor Qianlong, and on its back is engraved the story Da Yu Zhi Shui ("Yu the Great Subdues the Flood"). An immortal creature capable of controlling floods, the bull has kept watching over Kunming Lake for the past 200 years. The Marble Boat (also known as the Boat of Purity and Ease) is a special scene on Kunming Lake and its only Western-style structure. The whole boat was carved out of and

| TIPS | **The Hundred Days' Reform** The reform movement of 1898 was launched by Kang Youwei, Liang Qichao, Tan Sitong and other reformers under the auspices of Emperor Guangxu. The main content of this reform included learning from the West, advocating science and culture, reforming political and educational systems, and developing agriculture, industry and commerce. |

小贴士 清代三大戏楼 中国清代有三大戏楼驰名中外。它们是北京颐和园里的德和园、北京故宫里的畅音阁和河北承德避暑山庄里的清音阁。

西洋风格的建筑。整个石舫都是用大理石雕刻堆砌而成。船身上建有两层船楼，船底花砖铺地，窗户为彩色玻璃。下雨时，落在船顶的雨水通过四角的空心柱子，由船身的四个龙头口静静地流入湖中。

如果说佛香阁和智慧海占了万寿山的灵气，十七孔桥和石舫拥有昆明湖的秀气，那么将万寿山与昆明湖分隔开来的728米长的长廊则完全是人力的巅峰。它体现了中国古代工匠完美的艺术感觉和创作技巧，至今仍然是世界上最长的一条画廊。人在廊中走，两边的风光千变万化，可以让人领略到中国园林特有的移步换景的乐趣。长廊自身也是雕梁画栋。廊上的每根枋梁上都有彩绘，绘有人物典故、西湖美景、花鸟鱼虫一万四千余幅。

谐趣园和苏州街也非常有名。谐趣园是典型的南方园林建筑。南方园林特有的亭、台、堂、榭在这里都可以看见。苏州街和中国南方

built with marble. The two-storey boat has windows inlaid with colored glass, while the bottom of the boat is paved with ornamental tiles. When it rains, four dragon-head-shaped outlets connected to four hollow columns silently drain the rainfall on the roof of the boat into the lake.

If we say that the Pavilion of Buddhist Fragrance and the Hall of the Sea of Wisdom capture the spiritual aura of the Longevity Hill and that the 17-Arch Bridge and Marble Boat carry the elegance of Kunming Lake, then we have to say that the 728-meter Long Corridor separating the Longevity Hill from Kunming Lake represents the zenith of workmanship. It reflects a perfect artistic perception and creative techniques of the ancient Chinese craftsmen. To this day, the Long Corridor remains the longest painted corridor in the world. By walking through the corridor and witnessing the ever-changing scenes on both sides, visitors can experience the first-hand pleasure of "a different view with every step" peculiar to Chinese gardens. The corridor itself is richly ornamented, with every beam and pillar painted in rich color. The paintings, numbering over 14,000 in total, depict figures from stories and tales, beautiful scenes of the West Lake, and of flowers, birds, fish and insects.

The Garden of Harmonious Interest and Suzhou Street are also very famous. The former is a garden typical of southern Chinese garden architecture.

小贴士 "六合太平"和"玉堂富贵" 在乐寿堂的庭院中陈设了很多的东西——铜鹿、铜鹤、铜花瓶，分别借鹿、鹤、瓶的谐音，取意"六合太平"，意思是天下太平。园内还种植有玉兰、海棠、牡丹，取意"玉堂富贵"。

TIPS | **Three Famous Theaters in the Qing Dynasty** There were three famous theaters in the Qing Dynasty, which were De He Yuan in the Summer Palace, Changyin Ge in the Forbidden City, and Qingyin Ge in the Summer Mountain Resort in Chengde, Hebei Province.

颐和园

The pavilions, terraces, halls and *xie* (pavilions or houses built on terraces), characteristic of gardens in southern China, can all be found in the Garden of Harmonious Interest. Suzhou Street is extremely similar to actual commercial streets in southern China. Both banks of the river are lined with stationery stores, shoe boutiques, antique shops and restaurants. Suzhou Street was built specially for the imperial family to allow them to experience the pleasures of civilian life.

真正的商业街——苏州街非常相像，河的两边建有文具店、鞋铺、古玩店、酒楼等门面，当年是给皇家成员体验民间乐趣特意修建的。

漫步昆明湖畔，清风徐来，您可以细细地品味皇家宫殿的富丽堂皇，江南水乡的清丽婉约，宗教寺庙的庄重肃穆，民间住宅的精巧别致……

As you walk along the bank of Kunming Lake, with a fresh breeze blowing towards you, you can experience the grand splendor of the imperial palace, the graceful tenderness of regions of rivers and lakes in south of the Yangtze River, the solemn stateliness of sacred temples, the exquisite novelty of civilian residences—and much more.

109

TIPS | *"Liuhetaiping"* and *"Yutangfugui"* In the yard of Leshoutang (the Hall of Joyful Longevity), bronze deers, bronze cranes, and bronze vases are displayed. People make use of the homophones of them in Chinese to mean "smooth, peaceful and tranquil". Flowers like magnolia, Chinese flowing crabapple and peony are planted in the garden for the same purpose, as their homophones in Chinese mean "Jade and Wealth".

天坛
Temple of Heaven

天坛，建于15世纪上半叶，坐落在皇家园林当中，四周古松环抱，是保存完好的坛庙建筑群，无论在整体布局还是单一建筑上，都反映出天地之间的关系，而这一关系在中国古代宇宙观中占据着核心位置。同时，这些建筑还体现出帝王将相在这一关系中所起的独特作用。

世界遗产委员会评价

天坛始建于公元1420年，是明清两代皇帝祭祀天地之神的地方。

天坛位于北京天安门的东南，占地273万平方米，东西相距1,700米，南北相距1,600米，北部呈圆形，南部呈方形，寓意"天圆地方"。

The Temple of Heaven, founded in the first half of the 15th century, is a dignified complex of fine cult buildings set in gardens and surrounded by historic pine woods. In its overall layout and that of its individual buildings, it symbolizes the relationship between earth and heaven – the human world and God's world – which stands at the heart of Chinese cosmogony, and also the special role played by the emperors within that relationship.

The Temple of Heaven, built in 1420 AD, was where emperors of the Ming and Qing dynasties offered sacrifices to the Gods of Heaven and Earth.

The Temple of Heaven is situated southeast of Beijing's Tian'anmen

---

小贴士 | **天子** 天的儿子，专指皇帝。中国古人认为，"天"是世间万物的主宰，皇帝作为"天"的儿子，受天命统治人间。

收录时间 Date of inscription:	1998
遗产类别 Heritage category:	文化遗产 C
收录理由 Criteria:	C(I)(II)(III)

天坛规模宏伟、富丽堂皇。从规划、建筑以及环境的营造等方面来看，天坛无不体现着中国古代阴阳、五行的思想，营造出一种"天人感应"的理想氛围，承载着古人对"天"的崇敬之情和殷切期盼。天坛不仅是中国古代建筑的珍品，也是世界上最大的皇家祭祀建筑群。1998年，天坛被联合国教科文组织列入《世界文化遗产名录》。

天坛原称"天地坛"，公元1530年，明朝嘉靖皇帝在北京城的北郊又建造了专门祭祀地神的地坛，这里就成了专为祭祀上天和祈求丰收的场所，改名为"天坛"。

天坛最具特色的四大建筑是祈年殿、斋宫、皇穹宇和圜丘坛。

Square. It covers an area of 2.73 million square meters, and measures 1,700 meters from east to west and 1,600 meters from north to south. The northern part is circular, while the southern part is square, implying that "the heaven is round and the earth is square".

The Temple of Heaven is large in scale, and looks splendid and magnificent. With respect to planning, construction and environment, the Temple embodied the concept of the ancient Chinese *Yin-Yang* and the ideology of the Five Elements. That created an ideal environment of *tianren ganying* (heavenly response), bearing the reverent feelings and earnest expectations that ancient people extended towards heaven. The Temple is not only a treasure of ancient Chinese architecture, but also the world's largest architectural site used for royal offerings. In 1998, the Temple of Heaven was inscribed in the UNESCO World Heritage List.

The Temple of Heaven was originally called *Tianditan* (the Temple of Heaven and Earth). In 1530 AD, the Ming Dynasty Emperor Jiajing built a temple in the northern suburbs of Beijing specifically to offer sacrifices to the God of Earth. Thus, this place became the venue to worship heaven and pray for a good harvest, and was renamed as the Temple of Heaven.

The four most distinguished buildings of the Temple of Heaven are the Hall of Prayer for Good Harvest, the Abstinence Hall, the Imperial Vault of Heaven and the Circular Mound.

The Hall of Prayer for Good Harvest is the main building of the Temple of Heaven. According to historical data, from 1421 AD to the beginning of the 20th century, 22 emperors from the Ming and Qing dynasties held ceremonies there to worship heaven and to pray for favorable weather for crops.

TIPS | **The Son of Heaven** The son of Heaven was used to refer to the imperial emperor. Ancient Chinese regarded "Heaven" as the master of the world, and the emperor, who was the son of "Heaven", was authorized by Heaven to govern the world.

祈年殿是天坛的主体建筑。据史料记载，从公元1421年到20世纪初叶，相继有22位明清皇帝在这里举行祭天仪式，祈祷风调雨顺。

祈年殿呈圆形，直径32米，高38米，是一座有鎏金宝顶的三重檐圆形大殿。祈年殿内部为木质结构，无梁无檩，为层层相叠而环接的穹顶式，由28根楠木大柱支撑。中央4柱叫龙井柱，代表四季；中间12柱代表十二个月；外层12柱代表十二时辰；中外层相加24根，代表二十四节气；三层相加28根，代表二十八星宿，加柱顶8根短柱，代表三十六天罡。

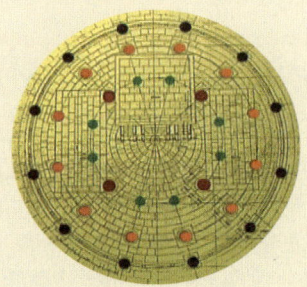

祈年殿坐落在面积达5,900多平方米的圆形汉白玉台基上。台基分3层，高6米，每层都有

雕花的汉白玉栏杆。经年累月，风雨侵蚀，栏杆上龙、凤、云的雕刻和龙形的出水口仍然给人一种呼之欲出的感觉。这些细腻饱满的浮雕与大殿相互融合，使整个祈年殿产生高耸云端的巍峨气势。

The Hall of Prayer for Good Harvest consists of a round shaped hall with three tiers of eaves under a roof of fine gold. Its total diameter is 32 meters and its height is 38 meters. The internal structure of the Hall is made of wood, without beams or ridge poles, layered and connected to the arched roof, supported by 28 wooden pillars. The four central pillars, called Dragon Well Pillars, represent the four seasons; the 12 middle pillars represent the twelve months; the 12 outer pillars represent the twelve *shichen* (traditional Chinese hours). The middle and outer pillars add up to 24, representing the 24 solar terms. Including the four Dragon Well Pillars, the pillars total to 28 pillars, representing the 28 lunar mansions. Adding the eight short columns at the top, they represent the 36 *tiangang* (heaven gods).

The Hall of Prayer for Good Harvest is located on a white round marble platform with an area of over 5,900 square meters. The platform has three levels, with a height of six meters, having carvings on the white marble railings at each level. Despite enduring years of erosion from the wind and rain, the dragon-shaped water fountains and the railing carvings of dragons, phoenixes and clouds still give people a lifelike feeling. These delicate and intricate carvings exist in perfect harmony with the great hall, creating a majestic aura as if the Hall of Prayer for Good Harvest were standing tall amongst the clouds.

Stepping out of the main door at the Hall of Prayer for Good Harvest is a straight path leading south to gateways that seem to disappear down an endless path. After a tour of the Temple of Heaven, an expert French architect was moved so much as to say that while there are many skyscrapers in the world that are much taller than the Hall of Prayer for Good Harvest, there is no other building that could match its lofty and profound ambiance.

小贴士 　天圆地方　中国古人认为，天是圆的，地是方的。这是古人对宇宙最初步的认识。天坛是专门用于祭天的地方，因此所有的宫殿、坛基都是朝南的，呈圆形，以象征天，表现出古人对"天"的崇敬之情和对上天的殷殷期盼。

天坛

跨出祈年殿的大门，就能看到笔直的甬道往南延伸，门廊重重、越远越小、极目无境。有一位法国的建筑专家，游览天坛之后感慨道，世界各国比祈年殿高得多的摩天大厦比比皆是，但却没有一座能够有祈年殿那种高大与深邃的意境。

皇穹宇是供奉皇天上帝和皇帝祖先牌位的地方。皇穹宇最令人叹为观止的就是回音壁和三音石。回音壁呈圆形，墙面光滑。人们在墙的不同

The Imperial Vault of Heaven is the place to worship the Supreme God of Heaven and the memorial tablets of the Emperors' ancestors. The most admired features at the Imperial Vault are the Echo Wall and the Three Echo Stones. The Echo Wall is circular and has a smooth surface. The voice of someone standing at one end of the wall can be heard clearly by someone standing on the opposite end, creating a divinely mysterious impression. According to expert analysis, the reasons for this echo effect include the wall was built with polished bricks,

TIPS **The heaven is round and the earth is square** Ancient Chinese believed that heaven was round and earth was square. This reflects the ancients' preliminary recognition of the universe. The Temple of Heaven is a place where the emperor offered sacrifices to Heaven. So all the palaces and foundations of the altars face the south and are in round shape to symbolize Heaven. In this way, the ancient people showed their respect for "Heaven" and expressed their wishes.

位置对着墙说话，站在远处墙边的人都能十分清晰地听到，给人造成一种天人感应的神秘气氛。据专家分析，造成回音效果的原因在于，墙壁是用磨砖对缝砌成的，墙面十分光滑整齐，墙头覆盖着蓝色琉璃瓦，而且围墙的弧度十分规则，声波不易被墙体吸收，进而产生反射，于是形成了回音。三音石就是皇穹宇殿门外御道上的第三块石板。因为三音石和皇穹宇正殿大门的角度关系，站在三音石上朝着皇穹宇正殿拍手，可以听到非常洪亮的三声回音，因而有"人间偶语，天闻若雷"的说法。

圜丘坛的主体建筑是一座露天的三层圆形

making it extremely smooth and even; it is covered with blue glazed tiles; and as the wall's radian is very regular, the sound wave cannot be easily absorbed and is reflected, creating the echo. The Three Echo Stones can be found on the third stone slab just outside the gate of the Imperial Vault of Heaven. If you stand on the third stone facing the Imperial Vault and clap your hands, you can hear three echoes very clearly due to the angle of the Three Echo Stones and the Imperial Vault. Consequently, there is a saying that "With only one whisper in this world, heaven will hear thunder."

The main building of the Circular Mound is an outdoor three-tiered circular stone altar. This is the place where the emperors would worship heaven on the Winter Solstice. The stone altar is divided into three floors: upper, middle and lower; the balustrades, pillars and the steps of each floor all use the *yang* number of nine or multiples of nine. In ancient China, odd numbers were referred to as *yang* numbers, and "9" is the largest *yang* number. As the Circular Mound is the place for worshiping heaven, the *yang* number 9 was naturally used to symbolize *tian* (heaven). In the middle of the stone altar is a round stone slab called the Heavenly Center Stone. Surrounding the Heavenly Center Stone are fan-shaped stones. The inner circle has nine pieces, the second circle has 18, and every circle

小贴士　阳数　中国古代阴阳学说认为，在天地间，天为阳，地为阴；在数字中奇数为阳，偶数为阴；在方向上南为阳，北为阴。据此，单数一、三、五、七、九属"阳数"，双数二、四、六、八、十属"阴数"。

石坛——圜丘台。这里是皇帝冬至日祭天的地方。石坛分上、中、下三层，各层栏板、望柱及台阶数目均用阳数九或九的倍数。中国古代把单数称作阳数，"九"是最大的阳数。圜丘台是祭天之地，自然就用阳数"九"来象征天。位于石坛中心的圆形石板叫天心石。围绕着天心石铺着扇形的石板，最内一圈是9块，再往外一圈为18块，依次往外每圈递增9块，直至九九八十一块，寓意为九重天。在圜丘坛的东南角还有一个绿色琉璃瓦砌成的焚炉，是冬至祭天时焚烧供物用的。

斋宫是皇帝来天坛祭天、祈谷前斋戒沐浴的地方。斋宫外围有两重"御沟"，四周以回廊163间环绕。东北角的钟楼内高悬着明成祖永乐帝在位时制造的一口太和钟，皇帝祭天时使用。

如今，天坛专供皇帝祭天的功能早已淡出了人们的生活，游客们轻松地踏进天坛，用玩味的心态完成着人与上天感应的朴素遐想。

extended outward increases by nine, up to 81 pieces (9 x 9), implying *jiuchongtian* (the ninth heaven). At the southeast corner of the Circular Mound is a burning furnace built with layers of green glazed tiles. It was used for the burning of offerings to worship heaven during the Winter Solstice.

The Abstinence Hall is the place where emperors would come to the Temple of Heaven to offer sacrifices and observe abstinence (fasting and bathing) before rituals. At the outside of the Hall are two heavy *yugou* (imperial channels), that are surrounded by 163 sections of cloister on all sides. Hanging high in the Bell Tower at the northeast corner of the Hall is the Taihe Bell that was made during the reign of Emperor Yongle of the Ming Dynasty, for use during worship.

Nowadays, use of the Temple of Heaven exclusively for emperors to worship heaven has faded out of people's lives. Tourists can now relax while taking a leisurely journey through the Temple and contemplate the amalgamation of heaven and man.

TIPS | **The *Yang* number** In Chinese philosophy of *Yin* and *Yang*, Heaven is *Yang* while Earth is *Yin*; when referring to numbers, an odd number is *Yang* and an even number is *Yin*; in light of direction, the south is *Yang* while the north is *Yin*. Thus the odd numbers like 1, 3, 5, 7 and 9 are classified as *Yang* numbers, while those even numbers like 2, 4, 6, 8 and 10 are *Yin* numbers.

武夷山
Mount Wuyi

  武夷山脉是中国东南部最负盛名的生物保护区，也是许多古代孑遗植物的避难所，其中许多生物为中国所特有。九曲溪两岸峡谷秀美，寺院庙宇众多，但其中也有不少早已成为废墟。该地区为唐宋理学的发展和传播提供了良好的地理环境。自11世纪以来，礼教对中国东部地区的文化产生了相当深刻的影响。公元前1世纪时，汉朝统治者在城村附近建立了一处较大的行政首府，厚重坚实的围墙环绕四周，极具考古价值。

世界遗产委员会评价

  武夷山位于中国东南部福建省西北的武夷山市，总面积512平方公里。武夷山的自然风光独树一帜，尤以"丹霞地貌"著称于世。这里保存着一系列优秀的考古遗址和遗迹，也是中国古代朱子理学的摇篮。

  Mount Wuyi is the most outstanding area for biodiversity conservation in southeast China and a refuge for a large number of ancient, relict species, many of them are endemic to China. The serene beauty of the dramatic gorges of the Nine Bend River, with its numerous temples and monasteries, many now in ruins, provided the setting for the development and spread of neo-Confucianism, which has been influential in the cultures of East Asia since the 11th century. In the 1st century BC, a large administrative capital was built at nearby Chengcun by the Han Dynasty rulers. Its massive walls enclose an archaeological site of great significance.

  Mount Wuyi is a mountain range located in northwestern Fujian Province's Wuyishan City, in the southeast of China. The mountains cover a total area of 512 square kilometers. Mount Wuyi boasts unique natural scenery and is especially well-known for its rosy topographical features. A series of excellent archaeological sites and historical remains are well-preserved here. In addition, Mount Wuyi is the cradle of Neo-Confucianism, founded in ancient China by Zhu Xi.

  In 1999, Mount Wuyi was inscribed by the UNESCO World Heritage Committee as a World Cultural and Natural Heritage Site.

  The glacial period that struck some three million years ago caused the earth to experience a

小贴士   丹霞地貌最主要的特点是赤壁丹崖。形成丹霞地貌的是一种沉积在内陆盆地的红色岩层，在千百万年的地质变化过程中，被水切割侵蚀，形成红色山块。武夷山是丹霞地貌的典型代表。

| 收录时间 Date of inscription：1999
| 遗产类别 Heritage category：双重遗产 CN
| 收录理由 Criteria: C(III)(VI); N(III)(IV)

　　1999年，联合国教科文组织世界遗产委员会通过武夷山为世界文化与自然双重遗产。

　　距今300万年前的冰川期让全球经历了一场生物大灾难，但是武夷山却不可思议地躲过了这次毁灭性的打击，并由此成为众多古老生物的避难所。武夷山分布的植物种类是整个欧洲大陆的七倍。在这里首次发现的新物种多达一千多种，世界生物学界评价它是物种研究的一块圣地。

　　今天，游客们到武夷山，坐竹筏漂流九曲溪，似乎已经成为不可或缺的一个项目。长度不到十公里的九曲溪，浓缩了武夷山最独特的山水风貌，是自然献给人类视觉的盛宴。九曲溪发源于武夷山森林茂密的西部，水量充沛，水质清澈。两岸是典型的丹霞地貌，分布着三十六奇峰、九十九岩，曲折萦回的九曲溪将峰岩连为一

major biological disaster. Mount Wuyi, however, unbelievably escaped this destructive attack and thus became a refuge for many ancient creatures. The number of different plant species on Mount Wuyi is seven times that of the entire European continent. With over 1,000 species having been discovered at Mount Wuyi, the world biology community views it as a holy land for the study of species.

Today, taking a bamboo raft and flowing along Jiuqu River has become a routine for tourists coming to Mount Wuyi. Spanning a length of less than 10 kilometers, Jiuqu River concentrates the most unique landscape features of Mount Wuyi; it is a great visual feast provided by nature to humankind. Jiuqu River originates at the western part of Mount Wuyi, which boasts lush forests, an abundant water supply and crystal-clear water. The banks on either side of the river boast the typical rosy topographical features,

TIPS The main characteristics of rosy topographical features is the red rocks and cliffs. In the millions of years of geological changes on the earth, a kind of red rocks sedimented in the basins of the inland was eroded by water and turned the mountains into red. Wuyi Mountain has the typical rosy topographical features.

小贴士 相传远古时期，长寿老翁彭祖隐居此山，彭祖有两个儿子，长子叫"武"，次子叫"夷"，二人开山挖河，疏浚洪水，后人为纪念他们，就把此山称为"武夷山"。

体，沿岸比肩并列的奇峰和光滑的峭壁，映衬着清澈深邃的溪水，溪光山色中溶铸了中国传统的诗情画意和美学意境。

武夷山独特的地理环境，不仅使它成为"世界生物之窗"，同时也造就了独特的武夷岩茶。早在公元14世纪初，元朝的皇帝就在武夷山开辟了一片御茶园，武夷岩茶从此正式成为献给皇家的贡品。武夷岩茶被视为品位的象征，它的饮用器具、泡沏方法都有着特别的讲究。千余年的演变，围绕着饮茶而进行的一系列仪式，已经沉淀为一种独特的茶文化。

武夷山最负盛名的茶树——大红袍，被誉为"茶中之王"。它们生长在岩壁上，岩缝中渗出的泉水滋养着它们的根茎。大红袍目前仅存4株，被视为稀世珍宝。

从明朝以来，武夷山就成为重要的茶叶贸易集散地。在今天的下梅古村，树立着一块巨大的石碑，上面记录着当年茶叶贸易的漫长路线。这条万里茶路，以武夷山下梅村为起点，北到俄罗斯，南至英伦三岛。当年，下梅古村是一片喧闹繁忙的景象，当街穿流的梅溪，便是商船启运的码头。梅溪两岸的老宅院，如今依然透露着当年的繁华和富庶。

with 36 amazing summits and 99 cliffs. The winding river connects the surrounding mountains and cliffs into a whole. The strange peaks and slick precipices lining the banks set off the clear and deep waters of the river below. The mountain hues and river's luster combine to create a poetic charm and aesthetic mood which are traditionally Chinese.

Mount Wuyi's unique geographical conditions not only make it "the world's window of biology" but also enable the production of the unique Wuyi rock tea. As early as the beginning of the 14th century, a Yuan Dynasty emperor developed a piece of land as an imperial tea garden. Thereafter, Wuyi rock tea formally became an article of tribute offered to the imperial family. Wuyi rock tea is regarded as a symbol of great taste and has many special requirements, including its method of preparation and the drinking vessels used to consume it. Over the course of more than one thousand years of evolvement, a series of ceremonies related to drinking Wuyi rock tea have forged a unique tea culture.

Mount Wuyi's most famous tea tree, Dahongpao ("Big Red Gown"), is reputed as the "king of the teas." These trees grow on cliffs, with spring waters seeping from gaps in the cliff nourishing their roots. With only four Dahongpao trees currently remaining, they are considered rare treasures.

Since the Ming Dynasty, Mount Wuyi has become an important tea trading center. In today's Xiamei Village, there is a huge stele recording the long tea trading route of former days. Starting at Xiamei Village, located at the foot of Mount Wuyi, this long tea route reaches up to Russia in the north and Great Britain in the south. Back in those days, Xiamei Village was a busy and bustling place. Mei River passed through the main street and served as a shipping port. These old houses remaining on both banks of the Mei

小贴士 在中国文化史、传统思想史、教育史和礼教史上，影响最大的，前有孔子，后有朱熹。有人曾写诗云："东周出孔子，南宋有朱熹。中国古文化，泰山与武夷。"

TIPS | It is said that in ancient times, an old man named Peng Zu, who was longevous, led a hermetic life in this mountain. He had two sons. The elder one was named "Wu" and the younger "Yi". The two sons excavated the mountain and dredged the river to control and dredge floods. Later generations named the mountain Wuyi in order to commemorate Wu and Yi.

武夷山

千百年来，人们对武夷山高耸岩壁上的悬棺有过各种各样的猜测。人们不知道在那个已经逝去的久远年代，是什么人、出于什么原因，一定要把同族死去的人送往高崖之上。面对几十米甚至数百米的悬崖绝壁，几百公斤重的悬棺如何才能安放到山洞里呢？专家们作过各种各样的猜想并且进行了实地的尝试，但最终还是没能给出一个合理的解释。如今高崖之上的悬棺依然带着永远让人猜测不尽的神秘，它独自面对着空茫的天空，传承着对久远文明的永恒表述。

1980年在武夷山的一座古村落，人们意外发现了古代的建筑遗址。这些历尽沧桑的断壁残垣，拼接出了汉帝国时期闽南地区一个最强大的地方王国——闽越古国。发掘的建筑遗址显示这是一座建制完备的古代王城，城内不仅有大型的

River still reveal the village's flourishing and affluent past.

Over the course of thousands of years, people have made all kinds of guesses about the coffins hanging on the cliff of Mount Wuyi. It remains unknown who, in this distant age, felt compelled to send their dead countrymen up this precipice and their reasons for doing so. And how did they successfully hang coffins weighing hundreds of kilograms onto rock cliffs dozens or even hundreds of meters above ground? Although experts have made all sorts of guesses and even carried out on-site experiments, they have still been unable to produce a reasonable explanation. Today, these coffins hanging on the rock cliffs are still draped in a veil of mystery, solitarily facing the empty sky in silence and expressing timeless messages from an ancient civilization.

In 1980, an archaeological site of ancient buildings was discovered in an ancient village located at Mount Wuyi. These architectural ruins, which were beset by thousands of years of disaster, tell the story of the strongest kingdom of the Han Dynasty—the ancient Minyue kingdom. Excavations at the site of these ruins indicate that it was a well-furnished and structurally sophisticated royal city; there was not only a large bathhouse but also a complex heating system inside the city. A large amount of ironware was excavated in this ancient village; many of the iron articles have unique shapes not found in other sites dated to the same era. In this ancient village, iron anchor heads measuring up to 82 centimeters in length and ploughshares weighing up to 15 kilograms were also unearthed. The discovery of these cultural relics filled a missing gap in Han Dynasty archeological studies.

Over 1,000 years have passed since the decline

TIPS | When it comes to the most influential and prominent figures in the histories of Chinese culture, traditional ideology, education and ethics, Confucius is no doubt a candidate, and Zhu Xi also enjoys an equal fame. There used to be a poem going like this, "In the East Zhou Dynasty Confucius emerged, and in the South Song Dynasty Zhu Xi appeared. When talking about Chinese ancient civilization, Mount Tai and Wuyi should be mentioned".

浴池，而且还铺设了结构复杂的取暖设施。古城还出土了大量的铁器，很多器形是同时代其他地区所没有的。这里出土的铁锚头长达82厘米，铁犁铧则重达15公斤。它们的出土填补了汉代考古学上的空白。

在闽越古国尘封一千多年后，一位智者的思想却从这里出发，源远流传。这里有一段被精心保护的房屋残墙，是中国古代最早的一所民办大学——武夷书院的遗址。它的创建者——朱熹被誉为继孔子之后中国最伟大的思想家。公元14世纪，皇帝诏令以朱熹的著作为国家科举考试的主要内容。朱熹著作对于儒学的批注成为官方认定的唯一正确解释。从此，朱熹的理学思想成为人们一切行为的规范准则，影响了中国及周边国家七百余年。

今天，在丹山碧水的怀抱中，武夷山的居民们依然过着平静的生活。但对于好奇的旅游者来说，这里奇特秀丽的自然山水是四亿年地壳演变的结果。这里丰富厚重的闽越文化，是几千年来历史沉淀的产物，它们是武夷山带给人们最宝贵的财富。

of the ancient Minyue kingdom. It was in this very kingdom, however, that a scholar named Zhu Xi founded a philosophy that spread far and wide. These well-preserved architectural ruins belong to the earliest non-government funded university, Wuyi Academy. Its founder, Zhu Xi, is regarded as the greatest ideologist in China after Confucius. In the 14th century AD, the emperor decreed that ZhuXi's literary works would constitute the main content of the civil service examination. Zhu Xi's comments on Confucianism were held by officials to be the only correct explanation. Thereafter, Zhu Xi's ideology formed a set of behavioral norms applicable to all people, influencing China and neighboring countries for over 700 years.

Today, surrounded by rosy mountains and crystal waters, the residents of Mount Wuyi still enjoy a peaceful life. In the eyes of curious tourists, the gorgeous natural scenery is the result of earth crust changes lasting over 400 million years. The rich and profound Minyue culture is not only the fruit of thousands of years of history, but also the most precious treasure that Mount Wuyi has given us.

| 收录时间 Date of inscription：1999
| 遗产类别 Heritage category：文化遗产 C
| 收录理由 Criteria：C(I)(II)(III)

大足石刻
Dazu Rock Carvings

大足地区的险峻山崖上保存着绝无仅有的系列石刻，时间跨度从公元9世纪到13世纪。这些石刻以其艺术品质极高、题材丰富多变而闻名遐迩，从世俗到宗教，鲜明地反映了中国这一时期的日常社会生活，并充分证明了这一时期佛教、道教和儒家思想和谐相处的局面。

世界遗产委员会评价

名为"千手观音"的舞蹈表演，其设计变幻莫测，造型美妙多姿，让人叫绝，曾在世界各地引起轰动。这场舞蹈的创作灵感来源于一尊佛像。

这尊佛像至今仍端坐在中国南方的一座山峰上，她的名字叫千手观音。在这个群山环绕的地方，不只拥有千手观音一个奇迹，险峻的山崖上排布着七十多处石刻，造像达到数万余尊，犹如一座石窟造像的博物馆，令人目不暇接。

The steep hillsides of the Dazu area contain an exceptional series of rock carvings dating from the 9th to the 13th century. They are remarkable for their aesthetic quality, their rich diversity of subject matters, both secular and religious, and the light that they shed on everyday life in China during this period. They provide outstanding evidence of the harmonious synthesis of Buddhism, Taoism and Confucianism.

This dance performance, entitled *Thousand-Handed Guanyin*, once caused a sensation all across the world with its phantasmagoric choreography as well as its beautiful and variegated postures. The inspiration of this dance can be traced back to a Buddha statue.

This Buddha statue still stands on a mountain peak in southern China. Its name is the "Thousand-Handed Guanyin." At this site surrounded by mountains, the Thousand-Handed Guanyin is not the only miracle; on the precipitous cliffs there are over 70 sites of stone carvings with more than tens of thousands statues. It is like a museum of stone

小贴士 "千手观音" "千手观音"是佛教六观音之一。一般千手观音的造型是两眼两手下，左右各具二十只手、眼。宝顶山大佛湾的千手观音有一千零七只手，一千零七只眼，所以被认为是中国佛教艺术中唯一名符其实的石刻千手千眼观音像。

这里叫大足，素有"石刻之乡"的美誉，位于中国重庆市西南。

大足石刻最初开凿于初唐永徽年间，历经晚唐、五代，盛于两宋，在明清时期又有所增刻，最终形成了一处规模庞大、集中国石刻艺术精华之大成的石刻群，堪称中国晚期石窟艺术的代表，与云冈石窟、龙门石窟和莫高窟齐名。

大足石刻群共包括石刻造像七十多处，总计十万余尊，其中以北山、宝顶山、南山、石篆山、石门山五处最为著名和集中。

我们看到，北山上的龛窟密密麻麻，大部分佛像和山形融为一体，气势浑厚。这些造像是大足石刻早期的作品，雕刻于公元9世纪末期。这一时期的佛像外表端庄丰满，气质浑厚，薄薄的衣服紧贴着肌肤，立体感十足。这种雕刻风格是中国北方石窟艺术的一种延续。

到10世纪时，大足石刻的佛像显现出了不同的形象。和之前的宽厚相比，佛像显得小巧玲

carvings which dazzle tourists' eyes.

This location, situated in the southwest of China's Chongqing City, is called Dazu. It is reputed as "the Homeland of Stone Carvings."

The Dazu Rock Carvings were firstly excavated during the Yonghui Reign of the early Tang Dynasty, and became prosperous in the Song Dynasty after surviving the late Tang Dynasty and the Five Dynasties. With some carvings added to the original ones during the Ming and Qing Dynasties, it developed into a large-scale cluster of carvings capturing the essence of the Chinese art of rock carving. Considered representative of late rock carvings in China, it enjoys a reputation equal to that of the Yungang Grottoes, the Longmen Grottoes and the Mogao Caves.

The Dazu Rock Carvings consist of more than 70 sites of rock carvings comprising over 100,000 statues, of which the most famous and concentrated are Beishan Mountain, Mount Baoding, Nanshan Mountain, Mount Shizhuan and Mount Shimen.

We can see that there are numerous grottoes on Beishan Mountain; most of the Buddha statues are seamlessly integrated with the mountain landscape, embodying simplicity and grandeur. These statues, carved at the end of the 9th century AD, are the early works of the Dazu Rock Carvings. The Buddha statues of this period are elegant and plump in appearance, simple and grand in disposition, and have a thin layer

小贴士 宝顶石刻 宝顶石刻距大足县城东北15公里，开凿于南宋年间。明清以来四川民间就有"上朝峨眉，下朝宝顶"的谚语，说的就是峨眉山和宝顶山这两大佛教圣地。

TIPS **Thousand-Handed Guanyin** It is one of the six Guanyins in Buddhism. The usual image of Thousand-Handed Guanyin has 20 extra eyes and 20 extra hands on the left and right sides respectively below its two eyes and two arms. The sculpture of Guanyin on the Buddha Bay of Mount Baoding has 1,007 hands and 1,007 eyes. So it is regarded as the only stone sculpture that is worthy of the name the "Thousand-Handed and Thousand-Eyed Guanyin" in Chinese Buddhist art.

大足石刻

珑，体态更加丰富，表情轻松洒脱，纹饰也越来越繁复华丽。在之后的两个多世纪里，大足的石刻雕像表现出更鲜明的个性，造像大多具有饱满的人物个性，通过丰富多变的组合，制造出层出不穷的意境。

大足石刻被誉为"中国观音造像的陈列馆"。在所有的观音造像中，最著名的莫过于千手观音了。每一个第一眼看到这尊千手观音佛像的人，都会产生这样一个疑问：她究竟有多少只手？从来没有人数清过，直到清代有一个和尚，利用给千手观音贴金箔的机会，每贴一只手就编一个号，终于数清楚共是1,007只。这尊千手观音充分利用了岩石空间，突出了观音的气势，一手一态，千手千姿，看上去犹如孔雀开屏，复杂而和谐。

千手观音位于大足的宝顶山上，宝顶山是中国佛教圣地之一。山上的石窟造像是公元12世纪一位叫赵智凤的僧人开创的。这位僧人5岁便踏入佛门，15年的苦行生活使他成为一代宗师。赵智

of skin-tight clothing, giving off a strong feeling of three-dimensionality. This carving style is a kind of continuation of the grotto arts of northern China.

By the 10th century, the Buddha statues of the Dazu Rock Carvings began to take on a different appearance—one that was more exquisite, more varied in posture and form, lighter and more relaxed in expression, and more complex and luxuriant in ornamentation compared with earlier carvings. For over two centuries thereafter, the statues of the Dazu Rock Carvings demonstrated more distinct features; most of the figures possessed rich human characteristics, which, through rich and variegated combinations, rendered countless artistic moods.

The Dazu Rock Carvings are reputed as "China's museum of Guanyin statues". Among all the statues of Guanyin, the most famous is the Thousand-Handed Guanyin statue. The first question that jumps into the minds of those witnessing this statue for the first time is: How many hands does she have? No one had ever determined the exact number until the Qing Dynasty, when a Buddhist monk took the opportunity to count the number of hands while gilding them. As he gilded a hand, he assigned it a number, and ultimately determined that the statue had 1,007 hands in total. This statue makes optimal use of the grotto space to highlight the Guanyin's vigor and prestige. Each of the thousand hands has its own unique form and gesture, giving the complex but harmonious appearance of a peacock spreading its fine plumage.

The Thousand-Handed Guanyin sits atop Mount Baoding, one of China's Buddhist holy lands. The grottoes on the mountain were created in the 12th century AD by a monk named Zhao Zhifeng, who converted to Buddhism at the age of five and became a great master after 15 years of ascetic practices. He

TIPS **Baoding Rock Carvings** Baoding Rock Carvings, 15 kilometers northeast of Dazu County were carved in the Southern Song Dynasty. A popular proverb among Sichuan folks since the Ming and Qing dynasties goes like this, "Going north to Emei Mountain and going south to Mount Baoding". Mount Emei and Mount Baoding are two prominent sacred places of Buddhism.

小贴士 摩崖 在山崖上刻的文字、佛像等。

凤四处募捐，聚集了一大批石刻高手，在宝顶山开窟造像，成就了大足石刻最辉煌的时刻。

宝顶山有上万座造像，其中大佛湾造像长达500米，给人造成了极大的视觉冲击。这里的每一尊佛像都有自己的个性，破了"千佛一面"之说。

除了北山和宝顶山，在另外三座山——南山、石篆山和石门山上，摩崖造像也十分精致。虽是佛教圣地，但这里的雕像中，既有释、道、儒"三教"分别造像者，也有佛、道合一和"三教"合一造像者。这种三教融合的特点，是当时中国思想界的写照。源于印度的石窟艺术，经过长期的发展至此完成了中国化的进程。

大足石刻在排水、采光和力学等方面都有极高的造诣，表现出中国工匠们在建筑和工艺方面的智慧与技巧。大足所在的四川盆地潮湿多雨，而水是崖舍的一大天敌，但是大足石刻

went around raising money and assembled a large team of rock-carving masters to cut grottoes and carve statues on Mount Baoding. This was the most glorious time for the Dazu Rock Carvings.

The tens of thousands of statues on Mount Baoding—among which the carvings at Dafowan (the Great Buddha Bay) stretch out for 500 meters—create a tremendous visual impact. Each statue here has its own distinctive personality, negating the belief that all Buddhas look alike.

Besides those on Beishan Mountain and Mount Baoding, the cliff-side statues on the other three mountains—Nanshan Mountain, Mount Shizhuan and Mount Shimen—are also highly exquisite. Although located in the Buddhist holy place, the statues here include those of Buddhism, Taoism and Confucianism, as well as some that integrate both Buddhism and Taoism or all three of these belief systems. The feature of combining these three faiths is a reflection of then prominent ideological views. By this time, the grotto art originating from India had completed its lengthy process of Sinicization.

The Dazu Rock Carvings reflect

小贴士 大足县 大足县始建于唐肃宗乾元元年（公元758年），取"大丰大足"之意而得名。又因"有海棠而独香"的传说，所以有"海棠香国"的美名。

TIPS | **Moya** It refers to engravings such as characters and Buddha sculptures on a cliff.

extraordinary achievements in drainage, lighting and mechanics, demonstrating the wisdom and skills of Chinese artisans in architecture and craftsmanship. The Sichuan basin, in which Dazu is located, is damp and rainy—and water is the natural enemy of grottoes. Considering that most of the Dazu Rock Carvings have been well-preserved to this day, we cannot help but admire the ancient people's ingenuity in water drainage.

Since the grotto art was introduced into China in the 3rd century AD, statue building in northern China reached two peaks—in the 5th and 7th centuries AD, respectively—with numerous majestic grotto clusters coming into being. However, the grotto art of the north began to decline around the middle of the 8th century. At this time, artisans at Dazu along the Yangtze River were thriving with new creativity, leaving behind countless rock carvings with distinct features. In fact, the rock carvings at Dazu extended the history of China's grotto art for another 400 years. As we view and admire the Dazu Rock Carvings of different periods, we may feel as if we are lingering in the corridors of time, witnessing the different aesthetic preferences of different ages.

The splendor of the Dazu Rock Carvings, however, was interrupted in the 13th century AD by wars and failed to continue since then. The grotto art of China thus reached its finale. The Dazu Rock Carvings became the last monument in the history of China's grotto art and an unsurpassable summit.

In 1999, the cliff statues at Beishan Mountain, Mount Baoding, Nanshan Mountain, Mount Shizhuan and Mount Shimen were officially listed as a UNESCO World Heritage Site; and the Dazu Rock Carvings at Chongqing was inscribed to the World Heritage List.

的大部分完好地保留到今天，让人不得不佩服古人在排水方面的匠心独运。

自石窟艺术于公元3世纪传入中国后，公元5世纪和7世纪前后，在中国的北方形成了两次造像高峰，形成了许多雄伟的石窟群。但到公元8世纪中叶，北方的石窟艺术开始走向衰落。这时，在南方长江流域的大足，工匠们却又勃发出新的创造力，留下了无数富有个性的石刻作品。正是大足石刻，把中国石窟艺术史向后延续了四百多年。观赏大足石刻不同时期的石刻，我们似乎徜徉在时光的走廊上，能清晰地看到不同时代的人们不同的审美取向。

然而，到公元13世纪，大足石刻的辉煌因为战乱而中断，从此再也没能继续，中国的石窟艺术就此落下了帷幕。大足石刻因此成为中国石窟艺术史上最后一座丰碑，一个无法超越的高峰。

1999年，北山、宝顶山、南山、石篆山、石门山五处的摩崖造像，被正式列入世界文化遗产，重庆大足石刻进入《世界遗产名录》的行列。

TIPS | **Dazu County** Dazu County was first built in 758 A.D., with the name meaning "plentiful and abundant". It is also famous for the blooming and fragrance of haitang, Chinese flowering crabapples, and enjoys the fame of the "Fragrant Kingdom of Haitang".

明清皇家陵寝
Imperial Tombs of the Ming and Qing Dynasties

明清皇家陵寝依照风水理论，精心选址，将数量众多的建筑物巧妙地安置于地下。它是人类改变自然的产物，体现了传统的建筑和装饰思想，阐释了封建中国持续五百余年的世界观与权力观。

世界遗产委员会评价

铺盖着黄色琉璃瓦的建筑，掩映在青山绿树中，仿佛一座座精巧的小宫殿，它们外形各异，大小不等，按照某种特定的要求排列和展开，这里就是中国明清两代皇帝家族的陵寝。

自2000年11月开始至2004年7月，中国共有六处明清皇家陵寝被联合国教科文组织列入《世界文化遗产名录》。明孝陵，位于南京，是明朝开国皇帝朱元璋的陵墓；明显陵，位于

It represents the addition of three Imperial Tombs of the Qing Dynasty in Liaoning to the Ming tombs inscribed in 2000 and 2003. The Three Imperial Tombs of the Qing Dynasty in Liaoning Province include the Yongling Tomb, the Fuling Tomb, and the Zhaoling Tomb, all built in the 17th century. Constructed for the founding emperors of the Qing Dynasty and their ancestors, the tombs follow the precepts of traditional Chinese geomancy and *fengshui* theory. They feature rich decoration of stone statues and carvings and tiles with dragon motifs, illustrating the development of the funerary architecture of the Qing Dynasty. The three tomb complexes, and their numerous edifices, combine traditions inherited from previous dynasties and new features of Manchu civilization.

Like a collection of small exquisite palaces, these buildings are covered in yellow glazed tiles and set off by verdant hills and trees. They come in various shapes and sizes and are arranged and spread out in accordance with specific requirements. These are the tombs for the royal families of the Ming and Qing dynasties.

From November 2000 to July 2004, a total of six imperial tombs from the Ming and Qing dynasties were inscribed to the UNESCO World Heritage List. The Ming Xiaoling Mausoleum, located in Nanjing, is the tomb of Zhu Yuanzhang, Ming Dynasty's founding emperor. In the Ming Xianling Tomb, located in Hubei Province,

---

小贴士　**风水**　风水指住宅基地、坟地等的地理形势，如山脉、山水的方向等。中国古人认为，风水的好坏可以影响其家族、子孙的盛衰吉凶。古时候很多人笃信风水，追求人与自然环境的融合。

收录时间 Date of inscription：2000；2003；2004
遗产类别 Heritage category：文化遗产 C
收录理由 Criteria：C(I)(II)(III)(IV)(VI)

湖北，里面埋葬的是一位死后才被追认的明朝皇帝；盛京三陵（永陵、福陵和昭陵），位于辽宁，埋葬着三位清朝的君主，他们生前还只是东北地区的统治者；明十三陵、清东陵和清西陵是明清皇家陵寝的精华所在，都集中在两代的首都北京附近。

明十三陵位于北京西北部，共有13座帝王陵墓，是世界上最大、保留最完整的皇帝陵墓群。从选址到规划设计，十三陵都十分注重建筑与大自然的和谐统一。虽然每座陵墓分别建在一座山前，各自独立，但是所有陵墓都是以尊卑有序的方式分列于长陵左右，像扇子一样铺展开来。

长陵是十三陵中建设最早、规模最大的一座陵寝，是明朝第三位皇帝朱棣的陵墓。长陵前的石牌坊既是长陵的入口也是整个陵墓区的入口，是中国现存石牌坊中最大的一座。从石牌坊往前有一座通体红色的大门，是陵墓区的总大门，被称为"大红门"。穿过大红门就踏上了宽阔的

is buried a Ming Dynasty emperor who was only confirmed after his death. At the Three Shengjing Mausoleums (the Yongling Mausoleum, the Fuling Mausoleum and the Zhaoling Mausoleum), located in Liaoning, are buried three Qing Dynasty monarchs—who were merely rulers of northeastern China. The Ming Dynasty Tombs (abbreviated " the Ming Tombs"), the Eastern Qing Tombs and the Western Qing Tombs—the essence of the imperial tombs—are located near Beijing, the capital of the Ming and Qing dynasties.

The Ming Tombs, which contain a total of 13 imperial tombs, are located in the northwestern suburbs of Beijing. They form the world's largest and best-preserved cluster of imperial tombs. From site selection to planning and design, the Ming Tombs demonstrate an emphasis on the harmonious unity between architecture and nature. Although each of the tombs was built independently at the foot of a mountain, they are arranged in order from most the honorable to the most humble, spreading out like a fan on either side of Changling ("the Long Mausoleum").

Changling is the earliest and largest mausoleum of the Ming Tombs. It is the mausoleum of the Yongle Emperor Zhu Di, the third emperor of the Ming Dynasty. The stone memorial arch in front of it is not only the entrance to the Changling Mausoleum but also the entrance to the whole tomb area. It is the largest existing stone memorial arch in China. In front of the stone memorial arch is a large, completely red gate, known as the Dahongmen (the Great Red Gate), used as the main access gate to the tomb area. Walking through the Great Red Gate, you will first step into Shendao (the "Sacred Way"), a 7-kilometer long passage leading to the 13 tombs. The first structure you will meet on the Sacred Way is this pavilion, in which the merits of Zhu Di are recorded

TIPS *Fengshui* It refers to the geographical location of a house or tomb, or the direction of a mountain or river, etc. Ancient Chinese believed that *fengshui* would influence the fortune of a family. Many ancient Chinese believed in *fengshui* and pursued the harmony of man and natural environment.

神道。神道全长7公里，不仅是长陵的神道还是13座陵墓的总神道。神道上的第一座建筑是一座碑亭，亭内的石碑上记载着墓主人朱棣的功绩。碑亭后面是由24座石兽和12座石人组成的石雕群，象征帝王生前的仪仗队。皇帝死后宫殿是一个由围墙封闭的大院子，前方后圆。在第二个院子矗立着十三陵最显赫的建筑——棱恩殿。殿中永乐皇帝铜像供于九龙宝座之上，形象逼真。长陵的第三重院落里才是皇帝死后真

on a stele. Behind the pavilion, there is a group of 24 stone-carved statues of beasts and another group of 12 stone-carved human statues, symbolizing the emperor's guard of honor during his lifetime. The emperor's underground palace is a closed courtyard surrounded by walls; the front section is square-shaped and the rear section is round. In the second courtyard stands the Ming Tombs' most prominent structure—Ling'en Hall. The vivid bronze statue of Emperor Yongle was placed above the "nine-dragon throne" in the hall. The third courtyard of Changling is where the emperor himself is buried. The end of the courtyard is the mausoleum's round section, known as Baocheng (the Treasure City). The emperor's grave mound looks like a small hill, named Treasure Hill, under which is the emperor's underground palace. In front of the Treasure City is Minglou (the Bright Tower), which functioned as an entrance to the Treasure City. As the symbol of the underground palace, the Bright Tower is also the highest structure that sits on the central axis.

If you want to discover the secrets hidden beneath

小贴士　赑屃驮碑的石兽叫赑屃（bì xì），传说是龙的第六个儿子，样子似龟，力大无穷，喜欢负重，是长寿和吉祥的象征。传说赑屃曾在海上背过仙山，用它来驮碑表示碑的内在分量十分重大。

正的归宿。院落的尽头是陵寝的圆形部分，被称为"宝城"。皇帝的坟丘像一座小山，叫宝山，宝山下就是皇帝的地下宫殿。宝城的前面建有明楼，相当于进出宝城的城门洞。明楼是每座陵墓的标志，也是每座陵墓中轴线上的最高建筑。

如果想看看地下宫殿的奥秘，可以去定陵。定陵是明朝万历皇帝的陵墓。定陵地宫由前、中、后、左、右五座高大宽敞的石头殿堂连结组成。中殿象征皇帝的客厅，后殿是地宫的主要部分，象征皇帝的卧室。定陵地宫中出土的文物多达三千多件，其中大多数是帝后生前的生活用品，包括各种金银器皿、漂亮的衣服和帽子。这顶皇后的凤冠镶嵌着3,500颗珍珠和195块宝石。

清朝是中国的最后一个封建王朝，由少数民族满族统治，基本沿袭旧制。皇家陵寝从规划建制到建筑造型等都是仿照明十三陵设计的。

清东陵位于河北省遵化市，共有15座陵寝。第一座陵墓是安葬清朝首位皇帝顺治的孝陵。

the underground palaces, you may wish to visit the Dingling Mausoleum, the burial place of the Ming Dynasty Emperor Wanli. The underground palace of the Dingling Mausoleum consists of five tall and spacious stone halls—the front, middle, rear, left and right halls. The middle hall symbolizes the emperor's living room, while the rear hall is the main part of the underground palace and symbolizes the emperor's bedroom. At the Dingling underground palace, over 3,000 cultural relics were unearthed, including gold and silver utensils as well as beautiful clothes and hats, most of which belonged to the emperor and empress. The *fengguan* (a phoenix-shaped crown which was worn by the empress) is inlaid with 3,500 pearls and 195 precious stones.

China's Qing Dynasty was the last feudal dynasty. It was ruled by the Manchu ethnic minority and basically followed the old political system. From planning to construction, the Qing imperial tombs are modeled on the design of the Ming Tombs.

Located in Zunhua, Hebei Province, the Eastern Qing Tombs consists of 15 tombs in total. The first tomb, called Xiaoling, is where Qing Emperor Shunzhi is interred. Of the Eastern Qing Tombs, the tomb containing Empress Dowager Cixi—*Pu*

TIPS *Bixi* Bixi is a legendary turtle used as a motif for the base of a heavy stone tablet. Legend has it that Bixi is the sixth son of the dragon and looks like a turtle. It is very strong and fond of bearing heavy load. It symbolizes longevity and good luck. Another legend is that Bixi used to bear mountains where immortals inhabited on the sea. That is why people use it as the base of the stone tablet. This indicates that the stone tablet is very heavy and important.

在清东陵中，慈禧太后的陵墓——菩陀峪定东陵三殿装修极为豪华。隆恩殿及其东西配殿全部采用名贵的黄花梨木，很多地方都用金粉画上腾飞的龙，据说有两千多条。殿前丹陛石是用高浮雕加透雕的技法雕刻而成，丹凤凌空，蛟龙出水，神态毕现。贴金的彩画、扫金的墙壁、镀金的蟠龙、精雕细刻的石栏杆，这样的豪华装修，不仅在皇陵中独一无二，就是在皇宫里也很罕见。更引人注目的是，很多石雕图案都是龙在下凤在上，或者是凤凰在前面飞、龙在后面追。在中国古代，凤凰代表皇后，龙代表皇帝，一般都是龙为主，凤为辅，而慈禧陵的石雕显然是女人掌握实权的暗示。

清西陵是由雍正帝开辟的，是清朝第二座皇家陵区，位于河北省易县，共有14座陵寝和两座附属建筑。雍正的坟墓被称作泰陵，是清西陵的第一座坟墓。泰陵最大的特色在于大红门前的三架石牌坊，坐落在宽阔的广场上，与北面的大红门组成一个宽敞的四合院。这种形制

Tuo Yu Ding Dong Ling (literally "Tomb East of the Ding Ling Tomb in the Vale of Putuo")—is among the most luxurious in its adornment. Long'en Hall and its east and west wings use valuable yellow rosewood. Many places are decorated with flying dragons, reportedly totaling over 2,000 in number, painted using golden powder. In front of the hall, the Danbi Stone adopts high relief (alto-relievo) and openwork carving techniques, vividly revealing on its surface a phoenix soaring in the air and a dragon rising out of the water. Such luxurious decorations as sparkling paintings and shining walls coverd with gold foil, gilded dragons, and exquisite stone railings are rare not only in the underground palace but also rare in real imperial palaces. Moreover, on the stone, the dragon is always carved below the phoenix; or the phoenix is depicted flying in front of the dragon, with the dragon following in pursuit. In ancient China, the phoenix represented the empress and the dragon symbolized the emperor. In most cases, the dragon is the master, followed by the phoenix. The stone carving at Empress Dowager Cixi's tomb, however, provides a clear hint of power being wielded by a female.

小贴士 松柏 在各处皇陵陵宫内外及神道两旁都栽植大量的苍松翠柏，长势茂盛，遮天蔽日。深绿颜色在中国古代表示崇敬、追念和祈求的意思，所以在坛、庙、陵寝等地都会栽种大量的松柏以增添这些地方的庄严肃穆之感。

The Western Qing Tombs, the second imperial mausoleum of the Qing Oynasty, was pioneered by Emperor Yongzheng. Located in Yi County, Hebei Province, it contains 14 tombs and two auxiliary buildings. The tomb of Emperor Yongzheng, the earliest of the Western Qing Tombs, is called Tailing. The most special feature of Tailing is that there are three stone memorial arches located in a spacious square, forming a roomy courtyard with the northern Red Gate. This form is not found in any of the other imperial tombs. Each stone memorial arch is extremely large and tall, with delicate and complex carvings. Starting from Emperor Yongzheng, the emperors of the Qing Dynasty were interred in the Eastern and Western Qing Tombs respectively, and the grandson was buried with his grandfather as a general rule.

在别的皇陵中是没有的，每架石牌坊都非常地高大，雕刻繁复细腻。清朝皇帝自雍正以后分别葬在东陵和西陵，一般来说是孙子跟随祖父埋葬。

清朝第八位的皇帝道光帝的陵墓——慕陵，外表朴实拘谨，三座大殿全部用名贵的金丝楠木建成。在天花板、群板等高处装饰着一千多个立体的龙头，雕刻手法极其精致。

夕阳西下，这些沉默的皇家陵寝显得格外庄严和肃穆。

This is the tomb of the Daoguang Emperor, the eighth emperor of the Qing Dynasty. The tomb, known as Muling, is simple and reserved in appearance, with the three main halls decorated using luxurious gold-wire *nanmu* wood. The ceiling is adorned with over 1,000 three-dimensional carved dragon heads, revealing extremely fine craftsmanship.

Under the setting sun, these silent imperial tombs appear especially venerable and solemn.

TIPS **Pines and cypress** Green pines and cypresses were planted densely alongside the passages in the imperial mausoleums. In ancient China, the color of dark green stood for respect, commemoration and pray. So in the places of temples, altars and imperial mausoleums, large amount of pine trees and cypresses would be planted to stress the air of solemnity and gravity.

龙门石窟
Longmen Grottoes

龙门地区的石窟和佛龛展现了中国北魏晚期至唐代（公元493～907年）期间最具规模和最为优秀的造型艺术。这些详实描述佛教中宗教题材的艺术作品，代表了中国石刻艺术的高峰。

世界遗产委员会评价

位于中国河南省西部的洛阳，是一座有着两千多年历史的古老城市，曾有13个朝代在这里建立都城。公元493年，北魏孝文帝决定迁都洛阳。这位笃信佛教的皇帝下令在首都附近开凿石窟，人们开始寻找合适的地点，最终发现了龙门。

龙门位于洛阳市南郊，伊水从南向北流淌，东西两面耸立着两座相对的山脉，仿佛一道天然的阙门。所以又被称为"伊阙"。唐代以后，多称其为"龙门"。这里的石头质地坚硬，结构紧密，不容易风化和脱落，很适合开凿石窟。

The grottoes and niches of Longmen contain the largest and most impressive collection of Chinese art of the late Northern Wei and Tang dynasties (316-907). These works, entirely devoted to the Buddhist religion, represent the high point of Chinese stone carving.

Luoyang, situated in the west of Henan Province of China, is an ancient city with a history spanning over 2,000 years. It served as the capital city of 13 dynasties of China. In 493 AD, Emperor Xiaowen of the Northern Wei Dynasty decided to move the capital to Luoyang. The emperor, who was a devout Buddhist, commanded his people to excavate grottoes near the capital. The people thus began searching for a proper site for the grottoes and, in the end, they discovered Longmen.

Longmen is located in the southern suburb of Luoyang City, where the Yi River flows through from south to north and two mountains sit in the east and

收录时间 Date of inscription：2000
遗产类别 Heritage category：文化遗产 C
收录理由 Criteria：C(I)(IV)(VI)

石窟南北绵延1,000米，窟龛2,100多个，造像数十万身，还有众多的碑刻题记和佛塔。龙门石窟与敦煌莫高窟、大同云冈石窟并称为中国三大石窟艺术的宝库，是最能体现古代皇家风范的石窟艺术。浓厚的历史气息和宗教韵味，是龙门石窟的魅力所在，十万余尊佛像是中国历代弘扬佛法和宗教文化的见证。

2000年11月，洛阳龙门石窟被联合国教科文组织世界遗产委员会列入《世界遗产名录》。

古阳洞是龙门石窟中开凿最早的一个洞窟，也是石窟群中内容最丰富的一座。古阳洞是孝文帝的一批大臣为其开凿的。石窟中端坐着释迦牟尼像，虽然右脸遭到了破坏，但仍能看出他面目清秀、神态安详。这里的造像无论是面貌还是穿着，都带有当时中国人的痕迹。从中亚地区传来的佛像雕刻艺术，正是从公元5世纪开始，逐步本土化的。

古阳洞中有很多佛龛造像，这些佛龛造像多有题记，记录了当时造像者的姓名，造像年月及缘由，这些都是研究北魏书法和雕刻艺术的珍贵资料。中国书法史上的里程碑"龙门二十品"，大部分集中在这里。"龙门二十品"字体端正大

the west, respectively, like a natural gate. Therefore, Longmen has also been called *Yi Que* (literally, "Gate of the Yi River") and received its current name after the Tang Dynasty. Because the stones here are rigid in texture, tight in structure, and do not weather or fall off easily, they were well-suited for building grottoes.

The Longmen Grottoes, extending 1,000 meters, contain more than 2,100 niches, hundreds of thousands of Buddhist sculptures and many inscriptions and pagodas. The Longmen Grottoes, the Dunhuang Mogao Caves and the Datong Yungang Grottoes are collectively known as the "three famous grotto art treasures of China", best representing the grotto art's ancient royal style. The great historic atmosphere and religious charm are at the root of the Longmen Grottoes' appeal. The more than 100,000 Buddhist statues and carvings provide evidence that, over the course of successive dynasties, China carried forward and promoted Buddhism and religious culture.

In November 2000, the Longmen Grottoes were inscribed to the World Heritage List by the UNESCO World Heritage Committee.

Guyang Cave is the earliest cave of the Longmen Grottoes and also the one with the richest content. This cave was dug by a group of ministers for Emperor Xiaowen. A statue of Sakyamuni Buddha sits in the middle of the grotto. Although the right side of the face is destroyed, the Buddha still looks comely and serene. The statues here, in terms of appearance and apparel, bear some resemblance to the Chinese people of that epoch. Since the 5th century AD, Buddhist carving art, which spread to China from the Central Asian region, has been gradually localized.

In Guyang Cave, there are a lot of Buddhist

小贴士 卢舍那大佛 据佛经说，卢舍那就是智慧广大、光明普照的意思。有人推测，此造像为仿武则天面目而塑，以应其本非凡人，而是神明之说。

方，气势刚健有力，仿佛刀刻出来的一般，是龙门石窟碑刻书法艺术的精华，历来为世人所推崇。

宾阳中洞是石窟群中开凿时间最长的一个洞窟，前后用了23年才建成。公元6世纪时，一位孝顺的皇帝决定为父母开凿洞窟，原计划开凿三座石窟，最后耗时23年、动工80多万人次才完成了中洞。洞窟里一共有三组大像，分别代表佛教的过去佛、现在佛和未来佛。主像释迦牟尼像，面部清秀，神情自然，堪称北魏中期石雕艺术的杰作。这组佛像的中国本土化特点更明显了，不过希腊式的鼻子和衣服的褶子，仍旧让我们看到希腊化时代的影子。

在龙门石窟成千上万的造像中，艺术价值最高的还要数奉先寺的摩崖造像。这是武则天的丈夫唐高宗为父亲营造的。奉先寺是龙门石窟中最大的一个窟，代表了唐代石刻艺术的风格。石窟的气势非同一般，它把山体劈成一个门型的平面，九尊佛像沿着崖壁排开，与山岩融为一体，所有造像都围着正中的主佛像，布局严谨

niches and images on which there are many inscriptions that record the name of the maker, the date and the purpose. All of these are precious materials for researching the calligraphy and carving art of the Northern Wei Dynasty. The "Twenty Products of Longmen", a milestone in Chinese calligraphic history, are mostly located here. They boast a natural, upright script and a vigorous, forceful look, as if they had been carved with a knife. Being the finest of the Longmen Grottoes' inscription calligraphy art, they have been praised by later generations.

The Middle Binyang Cave, the earliest excavated cave of the Longmen Grottoes, required a total of 23 years to build. In the 6th century AD, a filial-pious emperor decided to construct grottoes for his parents. The original plan was to build three grottoes; finally it took 23 years and more than 800,000 people to finish the Middle Binyang Cave. In the cave, there are three groups of sculptures, respectively representing the Buddhas of the past, the present and the future. The main statue, which depicts a comely and natural looking Sakyamuni, is a masterpiece of stone carving art from the middle period of the Northern Wei Dynasty. This group of Buddhist sculptures has obvious Chinese features; however, the Hellenic-style noses and wrinkled clothing still allow us to look back to the period of Ancient Greece.

Among the tens of thousands of sculptures in the Longmen Grottoes, the cliff sculptures in the Fengxian Temple have the highest artistic value. It was made by Tang Emperor Gaozong, the husband of Empress Wu Zetian, for his father. The Fengxian Temple, the largest grotto of the Longmen Grottoes, reveals exceptional vigor and represents the style of stone carving art of the Tang Dynasty. After the mountain was cut into a door-shaped plane, the nine Buddhist images were carved in the cliff, blending harmoniously with the

小贴士 莲花洞 莲花洞又名伊阙洞，在龙门西山奉先寺北边。因石窟的顶部雕刻着一朵精美的大莲花而得名。莲花在佛教世界中是圣洁的象征，莲花洞的这朵莲花堪称石刻浮雕中的极品。

TIPS | **Vairocana Buddha** According to the Buddhist scripture, "Vairocana" means wise and bright. It is assumed that the statue took after Empress Wu Zetian in order to echo with the legend that she was an immortal.

而协调。奉先寺长宽各30余米,整个雕塑群是一个完美的艺术整体。这尊主佛叫卢舍那大佛,是佛身的一种,象征着功德和智慧的圆满。卢舍那佛像总高17.14米,头高4米,耳长1.9米。佛像丰腴典雅,栩栩如生。他那智慧的双眼,稍稍向下俯视,目光正好与朝拜者仰视的目光交汇,令人产生心灵上的震撼,具有无穷的艺术魅力。卢舍那大佛被誉为"中国佛教艺术登峰造极之作"。

whole mountain. All other images surround the main image in the very middle, creating a precise and harmonious layout. The Fengxian Temple, which measures over 30 meters in length and width, can be considered a flawless collection of sculptures. The main image depicts Vairocana Buddha, which, as one of Buddhas, represents the completion of morality and wisdom. Vairocana Buddha is 17.14 meters high, with a four-meter high head and 1.9-meter long ears. It is plump, elegant and vivid. Its wise eyes, looking down slightly and meeting the sightline of the worshippers, are spiritually moving and full of unlimited artistic charm. Vairocana Buddha is reputed as the "masterpiece representing the zenith of Buddhist art in China".

The only Empress Regnant in Chinese history, Wu Zetian, was a devout Buddhist. The grottoes carved during her reign took up a large share of the Tang Dynasty grottoes. The Vairocana Buddha was carved under the command of Wu Zetian. According to the sculpture's inscription, in order to carve this sculpture, Wu Zetian spent 20,000 *guan* (a unit of currency in ancient China), her funds for cosmetics, and in person led ministers to attend the consecration ceremony of the sculpture.

中国历史上唯一的女皇帝——武则天,是一个虔诚的佛教徒。武则天执政时期开凿的石窟占据了唐代石窟的多数。卢舍那大佛,就是由武则天钦命雕凿的。据造像铭载,武则天为建造此寺及佛像,曾"助脂粉钱两万贯",并亲自率领朝臣参加了卢舍那大佛的"开光"仪式。

唐代不仅开凿新窟,还完成了北魏时期的残留洞窟。宾阳三洞中的南北两洞窟就是在唐代开凿的,它们和中洞有着明显的风格差异,从前的

In the Tang Dynasty, people not only carved new grottoes but also completed the grottoes left unfinished from the Northern Wei Dynasty. Among the three caves of Binyang, the South Binyang Cave and the North Binyang Cave were carved in the Tang Dynasty and are rather different from the Middle Binyang Cave in style. They are lively and natural rather than grand and rigid, have smooth lines rather than plain lines, and feature clothing that is more elegant and flowing.

Even wonderful scenery must ultimately meet with decline. After Wu Zetian died, the resplendent

TIPS | **Lotus Cave** Another name of the Lotus Cave is Yi Que Cave. It is located to the north of Fengxian Temple on the West Mountain in Longmen. It got the name from the exquisitely carved lotus on the top of the cave. The lotus symbolizes purity in Buddhism. The relief of the lotus at the Lotus Cave is considered one of the best works of stone relief.

刚毅雄伟变得活泼自然了，平实的线条趋向圆润，衣纹更加流动飘逸。

　　胜景总有衰退的时候，武则天死后，龙门石窟的辉煌时代落幕了，甚至留下了一些未完成的作品。没有了皇家的参与和鼓励，石窟的开凿渐渐失去了往日的声势。

　　一千多年过去了，卢舍那大佛始终俯视着芸芸众生，用神秘睿智的微笑观看着人间的风云变迁。

era of the Longmen Grottoes rang down its curtain and even left behind some unfinished works. With the loss of royal participation and encouragement, the grotto carvings gradually bade farewell to their prestige and influence of yore.

　　Although more than 1,000 years has elapsed, the Vairocana Buddha still looks down at the living, observing the world of humans with a wise and mysterious smile.

收录时间 Date of inscription：	2000
遗产类别 Heritage category：	文化遗产 C
收录理由 Criteria：	C(II)(IV)(VI)

青城山—都江堰
Mount Qingcheng and the Dujiangyan Irrigation System

都江堰水利工程始建于公元前3世纪，至今仍调控着岷江水系，灌溉着成都平原的千里沃野。青城山是中国道教发源地之一，以一系列古代宫观建筑而著称。

世界遗产委员会评价

都江堰，世界上最古老的水利工程之一。它与自然浑然天成，融为一体，完美地解决了目前仍困扰着人类水利工程的泥沙和水量控制问题，至今仍发挥着重要作用。

位于中国西南的四川，被称为天府之国，因为这里的生活实在是太富庶、太安逸了。然而，两千多年前，这里却是饱受水患灾害的地方。秦朝时，一位叫李冰的地方官，修建了都江堰，从此沃野千里，丰衣足食。

今天，当我们俯视经历了两千多年岁月冲刷的都江堰时，不能不惊叹创建者的智慧和胆识。从选址、设计到施工，都显示了李冰天才般的治水理念。从地图上看，被都江堰浇灌的成都平原和川中丘陵，就像一把巨大的扇子，整个扇面自西向东顺势倾斜，最高处的扇柄就是都江堰，而千百条引水渠就是那扇骨。江水顺着引水渠自然地流向广阔的平原，浇灌这片富饶的土地。

Construction of the Dujiangyan Irrigation System began in the 3rd century B.C. This system still controls the waters of the Minjiang River and distributes it to the fertile farmland of the Chengdu Plain. Mount Qingcheng was the birthplace of Taoism, which is celebrated in a series of ancient temples.

The Dujiangyan Irrigation System is one of the world's oldest water conservancy projects. Flawlessly integrated with nature, it offers a perfect solution to problems faced in irrigation works related to water sediment control which continues to perplex mankind. To this day, Dujiangyan still plays an important role in this respect.

Dujiangyan is located in the southwestern Chinese province of Sichuan, which has been dubbed the "Land of Abundance" for its prosperous and leisurely life. However, over 2,000 years ago, this was an area that was frequently beset by flooding

面对从山口奔涌而来的岷江水，没有想象中宏伟的大坝，也没有看见任何独立于山水之外、彰显人力的工程，一切似乎都是天作之合，显得那么自然和谐。

处于江心、形似鱼嘴的分水堤，将奔流而来的岷江一分为二。地势相对较低的内江用于灌溉，地势相对较高的外江用于泄洪。当江水充沛时，因为被一分为二，所以不再泛滥成灾；当枯水季节来临时，江水自然流向处于地势较低的内江，确保都江堰有充足的水源。而且，因为流入内江的是表层水，这也使得泥沙含量大为降低，只有原来的1/3。

内江水顺着堤岸一路向下，来到飞沙堰。这时，河道不再笔直，形成一个弯道，湍急的水流有所减缓。在不同水流的作用下，泥沙在这里再次

disasters. During the Qin Dynasty, a local governor named Li Bing constructed Dujiangyan. After the system was finished, fertile soil appeared and the local people were blessed with ample food and clothing.

Nowadays, as we look at the Dujiangyan Irrigation System, which has undergone a history of 2,000 years, we cannot help but be amazed at the courage, wisdom and insight of its constructor. From area selection and design to construction and implementation, it is clear that Li Bing was a genius in flood control. When looking at a map, the Chengdu Plain and Central Sichuan Hills irrigated by Dujiangyan assume the shape of a huge folding fan; the face of the fan slants outward from west to east. The highest point, Dujiangyan, represents the fan's handle, while the thousands of waterways represent the fan's ribbed framework. The river runs along the feed canal and flows naturally toward the vast plains, irrigating this fertile land.

小贴士　二王庙　建在都江堰渠首，是老百姓对李冰父子治水伟业的纪念。其中的碑刻多是对灌区水利工程维护的技术要领。每年清明时节，当地的居民都会在二王庙举行祭祀活动和开水（岁修完工后放水）典礼。

沉积。同样,当水流充沛时,飞沙堰外层的泄洪道又能把洪水分流到外江。

通过鱼嘴的分沙和飞沙堰的排沙,这时内江水含沙量不足原来的1/10。江水没有了浑浊的泥沙,变成一条多动的玉带。最后,它通过宝瓶口,奔向千万亩需要浇灌的良田。

都江堰的整个设计蕴涵着师法自然、天人合一的道家精神。这种思想的发源地就在不远处的青城山。

青城山,山峰排列的形状宛如城郭,山上林木茂盛,终年青翠。"青城天下幽"的美誉把青城山的精粹一语道破。

Facing the water of the Min River as it surges from the mountain gap, you will not find a grand dam as you might have imagined; nor will you see a conspicuous man-made construction nestled on the landscape. Everything appears so natural and harmonious, like a "union made by heaven."

The Fish Mouth(Yuzui) Levee, which is in the middle of the river and resembles the mouth of a fish, divides the surging water of the Min River into two streams. The relatively low-lying inner stream is used for irrigation, while the relatively high-elevated outer stream is used to release floodwater. Even when the river's water swells, its division into two streams ensures that no flooding occurs; when the dry season arrives, the water naturally flows into the low-lying stream, ensuring that Dujiangyan has an adequate water source. In addition, since the water flowing into the inner stream is surface water, silt and sediment is flushed out in large quantities, leaving behind only one third of the original amount.

The inner stream rushes along the embankment all the way down and joins with the Flying Sand Weir (Feishayan). At this point, it is no longer a straight river, instead forming into a curved waterway, and the rushing waters are slowed. Again, several different streams cause sediment deposits to form. Similarly, when the water flow is abundant, the Flying Sand Weir spillway on the outer layer of the Flying Sand Weir can divert floodwater into the outer stream.

Due to the outflow of sand from Fish Mouth Levee and the Flying Sand Weir, the sediment in the inner stream is reduced to less than 10 percent of its original amount. Without the turbid mud and sand, the river becomes a moving "jade belt." Finally, it passes through the Bottle-Neck Channel (Baopingkou), rushing toward thousands of acres of

TIPS | **Erwang Temple** It was built at the head of Dujiangyan by local people to commemorate Li Bing and his son for their contribution to control the floods. The inscriptions on the stone tablets in the temple record the technical essentials for the maintenance of the irrigation works. During the Qingming Festival of every year, local people would offer sacrifices in the temple and hold a ceremony for drawing off water from the reservoir.

公元143年，一位名叫张陵的人来到青城山。他被这座仙山的清幽所吸引，从此在这里悟道布道，创立了中国本土宗教——道教。传说，天师张陵最终在此领悟到宇宙和世界的奥秘，羽化登仙。从此，青城山成为道观建筑最为集中的道教名山。直到现在，历代天师都要来到青城山朝拜祖亭。

青城山分前后两个部分，前山道观密布，弥漫着浓厚的宗教气息。青城山的道教宫观以天师洞为核心，四周有建福宫、上清宫、祖师殿、老君阁、朝阳洞等十余座建筑。道观亭阁取材自然，与山林岩泉融为一体，体现道家追求天人和一、崇尚朴素自然的风格，也与以清幽著称的青城山完美结合。

植被丰富的青城山，不仅是道教圣山，还拥有30多种木本植物和大量药材。唐太宗时期，道

fertile land in need of irrigation.

The spirit of Taoism—the notion of following the rules of nature and the idea that we are one with nature—are reflected in the entire design of Dujiangyan. This philosophy originated in the nearby Mount Qingcheng.

Mount Qingcheng boasts lush forests that are verdant year-round, and the layout of the mountain's peaks resembles a city wall. With a reputation as the "Secret Green Garden", Mount Qingcheng is truly an exquisite and beautiful place.

In 143 AD, a man named Zhang Ling visited Mount Qingcheng. Attracted to the mountain by its profound serenity, he clarified his understanding and created an indigenous Chinese religion—Taoism. Legend has it that Zhang Ling, at this very mountain, ultimately grasped the mysteries of the universe and the world; he then ascended to heaven and became an immortal. Since then, Mount Qingcheng has become a famous mountain with the highest concentration of Taoist temples. To this day, Taoist masters continue to come to pay homage to the pavilion on Mount Qingcheng.

Mount Qingcheng is comprised of two parts, the Front Mountain and the Rear Mountain. The Front Mountain is filled with Taoist temples and permeated by a strong religious atmosphere. The Tianshi Cave is the core of Mount Qingcheng's Taoist temples, and is surrounded by over 10 buildings, including Jianfu Palace, Shangqing Palace, Zushi Palace, Laojun Pavilion, and Chaoyang Cave. The Taoist pavilions were built using

小贴士 ｜ 古代巴蜀原有"五斗米道"，奉行非常朴素的自我修行。公元143年，道教创始人张道陵来到青城，运用黄帝、老子的学说把这种教派改造并发扬，正式创立了"天师道"。天师道的建立，标志着中国道教体系的正式建立。

士孙思邈来到这里采集了大量药材，研究了解各种药性，撰写了医学著作《千金方》，至今仍是中医必修的典籍。孙思邈也被后人尊称为药王。

如果说前山是人们对于仙境的向往，那后山完全就是一派悠闲的人间画卷。这里景色秀美宜人，仿佛世外桃源。

一座著名的水利工程和一座道教名山，为成都人留下了千年的富足和享用不尽的思想与文化遗产。

2000年，联合国教科文组织世界遗产委员会第24届会议，通过青城山—都江堰为世界文化遗产。

materials from nature, and are seamlessly integrated with forests and clear springs, embodying Taoism's spirit of unity of man and nature. Unadorned and natural style—and the pursuit thereof—are also flawlessly combined with the deep and tranquil Mount Qingcheng.

Mount Qingcheng is not only a sacred Taoist mountain but is also rich in vegetation, with over 30 kinds of woody plants and extensive medicinal materials. During the reign of Emperor Taizong of Tang, the Taoist priest Sun Simiao collected a large volume of medicinal materials here and investigated each one's properties. He later wrote a medical book called *Qianjinfang* ("The Thousand Golden Remedies"), which is still a compulsory reading for Chinese medicine practitioners. Sun Simiao became known by later generations as the "King of Chinese Medicine."

If it is said that Mount Qingcheng's Front Mountain is the wonderland to which people aspire, then Rear Mountain can be likened to a painted scroll painting of a leisurely and carefree land. With beautiful and delightful scenery, it can truly be called a paradise on earth.

A well-known water conservancy project and a famous Taoist mountain have left Chengdu with thousands of years of abundant wealth and an endless spiritual and cultural heritage.

In 2000, at the 24th meeting of UNESCO's World Heritage Committee, Mount Qingcheng and the Dujiangyan Irrigation System were listed as a UNESCO World Heritage Site.

TIPS There used to be a popular religious sect "Five Dou Grain Sect" in Sichuan in ancient times. It advocated plain self-cultivation. In 143 A.D., the founder of Taoism, Zhang Daoling, arrived in Qingcheng city and established "Tianshi Dao" by reforming and developing the original "Five Dou Grain Sect" and applied the theories of Huangdi and Laozi. This signalized the formal establishment of the Taoist system in China.

皖南古村落——西递、宏村
Ancient Villages in Southern Anhui-Xidi and Hongcun

　　西递、宏村这两个传统的古村落在很大程度上仍然保持着那些在上个世纪已经消失或改变了的乡村的面貌。其街道的风格、古建筑和装饰物,以及供水系统完备的民居都是非常独特的文化遗存。

世界遗产委员会评价

　　皖南山区的黟县是一个人口仅十来万的小县,西递、宏村就坐落在这里。唐朝大诗人李白曾赞美道:"黟县小桃源,烟霞百里间。地多灵草木,人尚古衣冠。"道出了皖南乡村的独特意境:山水风物幽美,古老文化酝酿出淳厚从容的民风人情。

The two traditional villages of Xidi and Hongcun preserve to a remarkable extent the appearance of non-urban settlements of a type that largely disappeared or was transformed during the last century. Their street plan, their architecture and decoration, and the integration of houses with comprehensive water systems are unique surviving examples.

Yi County, located in the mountainous area of southern Anhui Province, is a small county with a population of only about 100,000 people. Xidi and Hongcun are located here. The great Tang Dynasty poet Li Bai once offered the following praise: "In the Peach Garden of Yi County, the mist and clouds drift for hundreds of miles. In this land, there are many mystic plants and the people esteem ancient attire". This line of poetry depicts the southern Anhui villages' distinct atmosphere: mountains and rivers which embody tranquility and beauty, and an ancient culture which has fostered customs and traditions typified by honesty, simplicity and leisure.

Xidi, also known as the "Family in the Peach Garden", is an ancient village linked to the blood ties of the Hu clan. Because water flows west (*xi* means "west" in Chinese) through the village and there was a relay station to send mail (*di* means "to send"), the village thus acquired the name "Xidi".

The people of Xidi surnamed "Hu" were originally

小贴士　据说西递原名为西川,之所以改称为西递有两种说法。①以前这里是交通要道,政府在此处设有驿站,驿站在古代又称为"递铺",所以西川又称为"西递铺"。②中国大地上的河流都是向东去的,而西递周围的河水却是往西流的,"东水西递",所以西川也就被称为西递了。

Date of inscription: 2000
Heritage category: 文化遗产 C
Criteria: C(III)(IV)(V)

西递是一处以胡姓宗族血缘关系为纽带的古村落，因村边有水西流，又因古有递送邮件的驿站，故而得名"西递"，素有"桃花源里人家"之称。

这里的胡姓原为唐朝李氏皇帝的后裔，为躲避追杀到此避难，并世代繁衍生息于此。故自古文风昌盛，到明清年间，一部分读书人弃儒从商，成功后大兴土木，将故里建设得非常气派、堂皇。

这座高大雄伟的牌楼屹立在村口，据说已经有近450年历史了。是明朝时候皇帝为大丞胡文光修建的，堪称明代徽派石坊的代表作。巨大的牌坊诉说着该村主人曾经的辉煌和荣耀，是胡氏家族显赫地位的象征。

the descendants of Tang Dynasty emperors. To avoid being killed, they fled to Xidi, where they continued to live and procreate. Since ancient times, therefore, Xidi had a flourishing culture. By the Ming and Qing dynasties, some intellectuals abandoned their scholarly pursuits to become businessmen. After attaining success, they set to work erecting many new buildings, and built Xidi into a stylish and magnificent village.

This large and majestic looking *pailou* (decorated archway) stands at the village entrance. It is said to have a history spanning almost 450 years. Built by a Ming Dynasty emperor to commemorate prefectural governor Hu Wenguang, it can be considered the masterpiece of Ming Dynasty Anhui-style archways. This colossal *pailou* recounts the former glory and splendor of Hu Wenguang and represents the Hu family's eminent status.

Zhuimu Hall(the memorial Hall) is the ancestral temple for the Hu family in Xidi and Jing'ai Hall(the Hall of Reverence) is a subordinate ancestral temple for the Hu family. A calligraphic scroll with the Chinese character *xiao* (meaning "filial piety") is hung in Jing'ai Hall. This scroll effectively brought into play the pictographic characteristic of Chinese characters. The top of the character, when examined from the right side, looks like the image of a deferential young man bowing with his head raised; when examined from the left side, it looks exactly like an ugly monkey. The character thus has the allegoric meaning of "those who demonstrate filial piety are human; those who do not are beasts".

Lingyun Pavilion, also known as Paoma (literally "Racehorse") Tower, was funded and built by the famous salt merchant Hu Guansan during the Qing Dynasty. "In exhilarating spring wind, the hooves sound urgently." Riding on the crest of success, the

TIPS It is said that Xidi used to be called Xichuan. There are two explanations for the change of the name. One is that Xichuan was a vital line of communication and the government set up post houses here. In ancient times, another name of the post house was "*Dipu*", so Xichuan was also called "Xidipu". The other explanation is that most rivers in China flowed eastward, while rivers around Xichuan went westward. There was a saying that "*dong shui xidi*", meaning the water from the east flows westward, thus came the name of "Xidi".

小贴士 马头墙 在中国众多的动物中，马可以称得上是一种吉祥物，中国古代有"一马当先、马到成功、汗马功劳"等成语，显现出人们对马的崇拜与喜爱。从高处往下看，聚族而居的村落中，高低起伏的马头墙，给人的视觉产生一种"万马奔腾"的动感。

追慕堂是西递村的胡氏家祠，而敬爱堂是胡氏家族的支祠，敬爱堂中挂了一幅"孝"字。字画充分发挥了汉字的象形特色。字的上半部，从右侧看，酷似一躬身仰首作揖敬奉的后生形象，而从左侧看，却活现一只尖嘴猴子，包含了"孝为人，不孝为畜生"的寓意。

"凌云阁"又名"跑马楼"，为清朝年间著名盐商胡贯三出资修建。春风得意马蹄疾，当年春风得意的胡家，骑在岁月的马上，伴着那一片马蹄声远去了，而跑马楼还在。如今，每天上演的"小姐招亲"，既重温了古村落旧时的喜

self-satisfied Hu family "rode on the horses of time", accompanying the clip-clop of the horse's hoofs and riding far away. Paoma Tower still stands to this day. The play "The Young Lady Seeks a Husband", performed daily, revives the felicity of the ancient village's former days and enables people to experience the zealous and fervent life of Xidi's old folk houses.

The *matou* ("horse head") wall is an important characteristic of Anhui-style architecture. Also known as the *fenghuo* ("seal off fire") wall, the *matou* wall has the function of cutting off the fire source during fire emergencies. *Matou* walls vary in height but are usually two or three storeys high; the *matou* walls of relatively large folk houses may have as many as five storeys, hence the expression "five mountains facing heaven." Corresponding to the *matou* wall is the *tianjing* (courtyard—literally "heaven well") in these old houses. The word *tianjing* contains the implicit meaning of "four waters returning to the house", i.e., wealth coming from all directions. The rainwater falling off the rooftop is thus collected in the owner's courtyard rather than flowing outward to the homes of others.

As you enter inside these folk houses, you will notice that almost every house has the same furnishings. During traditional sacrificial activities,

小贴士 徽商 中国古代商人集团。是中国古代势力最大的两个地方商帮之一，以居于徽州(今安徽歙县、黟县、婺源一带)而得名。徽商有"徽骆驼"和"绩溪牛"之称。以骆驼和牛来形容，一方面说明徽商创业的艰辛，另一方面指的是徽商具有忍辱负重、坚忍不拔的精神。

TIPS **Matou Wall** The horse is regarded as an auspicious animal in China. People's adoration of the horse can be shown in many idiomatic expressions with "horse", such as "一马当先(take the lead)", "马到成功(gain an immediate victory)", and "汗马功劳(contributions in work)" etc. When looking down from a high position, the undulating in the village walls are just like thousands of horses galloping.

皖南古村落——西递、宏村

庆，也让人们感受着民居里的火热生活。

马头墙，是徽派建筑的重要特色。马头墙又称为封火墙，在发生火灾的时候起着隔断火源的作用。马头墙高低错落，一般为两叠式或三叠式，较大的民居可多至五叠，俗称"五岳朝天"。与之相应的便是这老宅里的"天井"，这叫做"四水归堂"，即四方之财如房顶上的雨水，汇集于天井内，不致于外流他家。

踱步进门，几乎家家摆设都一样。传统祭祀活动时，照壁上就挂上祖宗的画像，下方中间摆着自鸣钟，两边摆放架礼帽用的高瓷筒，左右分别是古瓷瓶和镜子，整个摆设取谐音"终生平静"，祈求生活平平静静。看似平常的摆件，寄寓着徽州人几多希望几多深情。

历经数百年社会的动荡、风雨的侵袭，西递村仍留存了数百幢古民居，保留了明清村落的基本面貌和特征，被誉为"中国传统文化的缩影""中国明清民居博物馆"。

ancestors' portraits would be hung on the *zhaobi* (a screen wall facing the gate of a house). A chime clock was placed at the bottom and long porcelain tubes, used for hanging top hats, were erected on either side. An ancient ceramic bottle and a mirror were positioned to the left and right, respectively. When arranged in a certain way, the furnishings of the *zhaobi* sound like the Chinese phrase "lifelong tranquility", reflecting people's hopes of having a placid life. These seemingly simple furnishings thus carry the countless hopes and feelings of the Huizhou people.

Despite witnessing hundreds of years of social turbulence as well as the onslaught of nature, the villages of Xidi still retain several hundred ancient folk houses and preserve the basic appearance and features of the Ming-Qing villages. Xidi is reputed as the "epitome of Chinese traditional culture" and "China's Ming-Qing Folk House Museum."

Hongcun is an extremely beautiful village, with distant mountains, nearby rivers, and architecture featuring red walls and green tiles. People refer to it as the "village in Chinese paintings". Hongcun is probably a fairly close match to the rural scenes depicted by poets or the earthly paradise of people's dreams.

"Water flows into thousands of homes; thousands of homes have flowing water." An endless current of water flows past the gate of every house. Without barely having to set foot outdoors, Hongcun villagers can thus enjoy clear spring water; similarly, they do not have to worry about fire outbreaks. When it rains heavily, accumulated rainwater in the courtyard can enter a closed conduit and be discharged through a water canal.

TIPS **Merchants of Hui** It refers to a group of ancient businessmen from Huizhou, which includes present Shexian, Yixian and Wuyuan in Anhui Province. It was one of the two biggest groups of merchants in ancient China. Merchants of Hui were described as "camel of Hui" or "cattle of Jixi" to imply that they had experienced tough time when starting their businesses. Another implication is that merchants of Hui showed great fortitude and perseverance when confronted with difficulties.

小贴士 宏村 "宏村",是取宏广发达之意。徽州素有"四门三面水,十姓九汪家"的说法,可见汪氏在当地可谓人多势众,是个大户人家。

宏村是个非常美丽的村庄,远山近水、粉墙黛瓦,人们说她是中国画里的乡村。诗人笔下的田园风光,人们梦中的世外桃源,大概就是这样子的。

"水流千家,千家流水",源源不断的水,从家家户户门前流过,使宏村人足不出户就可以享用清泉,也使他们不再为火灾担忧。下大雨时,院中的积水还可以通过暗沟经水渠排出去。

从高处俯瞰,宏村宛若一头斜卧山前溪边的青牛。山是牛头,古树是牛角,民居是牛身,村西溪水上架起的四座石桥为牛腿,村中的小水塘是牛胃,村口的大水塘是牛肚。一条四百余米长的溪水盘绕在"牛腹"内,弯弯曲曲的,被称做牛肠。

这种别出心裁的村落水系设计,一水绕村、户户清泉,使得宏村历经几百年,仍然充

From a bird's-eye view, Hongcun looks uncannily like an ox lying by a brook in front of a mountain. The mountain is the ox's head, the old trees are the horns, and the folk houses are the ox's body. The four stone bridges that stretch across the brook in the west of the village represent the ox's legs; the small pond in the village is the ox's stomach; and the large pond at the village entrance is the abdomen. A brook over 400 meters long weaves and winds through the "ox's belly"; it is known as the "ox's intestine".

This unique kind of water system design, with a brook flowing around the village, has allowed each family to have access to clear spring water and enabled Hongcun to maintain its full vitality, even after hundreds of years. People visiting Hongcun today cannot help but admire the wisdom of those who designed this ancient water system.

The mystic quality of Hongcun is also found in luxurious residences concealed within these high walls. Among them, Chengzhi Hall, reputed as the "Imperial

小贴士 徽州三雕 古代徽州地区流传的木雕、砖雕和石雕三种工艺的统称,它们均为古代徽州地区明清建筑的装饰性雕刻,具有浓厚的地方文化色彩。

TIPS **Hongcun** The word "hong" in "Hongcun" means broad and flourishing. An old saying in Huizhou goes like this, "Of four houses, the gates of three face the river, and of ten families, the family names of nine are Wang". This shows that the clan of Wang family is rather big and flourishing.

皖南古村落——西递、宏村

满了生命感。今天来到宏村的人，无不惊叹古水系设计者的智慧。

宏村的神奇还在于隐藏在这高墙里的豪宅。承志堂是其中最为宏大、最为精美的代表作，被誉为"民间故宫"。精美绝伦的木雕，几乎布满了整座宅子所有的空间，层次丰富，繁复生动，经过百余年时光的消磨，至今仍金碧辉煌。承志堂是黟县境内保护最完美的古民居，到此参观的国内外游客，无不为之倾倒。

徽派民居，外形都是这样简单的青瓦白墙，在青山绿水中，一切显得那么简约而和谐。世外桃源般的田园风光，保存完好的村落形态，工艺精湛的徽派民居和丰富多彩的历史文化内涵，使得西递、宏村闻名天下。

2000年11月，在澳大利亚凯恩斯召开的第24届世界遗产委员会会议作出决定，将中国安徽古村落——西递、宏村列入《世界遗产名录》。

Palace for the Populace", is the finest and grandest. These multilayered, intricate and vivid wood carvings, which practically fill up the entire residence, are exquisite beyond compare. Over one hundred years later, they are as resplendent and magnificent as ever. Chengzhi Hall is the best-preserved ancient folk house in Yi County. Whether coming from near or far, visitors who behold this sight are bound to be filled with wonder and awe.

The exterior of Anhui-style folk houses is characterized by harmony and simplicity—green tiles and white walls against a backdrop of verdant mountains and clear blue rivers. Heavenly rural scenes, perfectly preserved villages, masterfully artistic Anhui-style houses, and rich historic and cultural meaning have combined to make Xidi and Hongcun famous all over the world.

In November 2000, at the 24th session of the UNESCO World Heritage Committee held in Cairns, Australia, the Ancient Villages in Southern Anhui—Xidi and Hongcun—were inscribed as a World Heritage Site.

TIPS **The Three Carvings in Huizhou** "The Three Carvings in Huizhou" refers to the three well-known crafts in ancient Huizhou, the wood carving, brick carving and stone carving. They were decorative sculptures in Huizhou areas during the Ming and Qing dynasties and embodied typical flavor of the local culture.

云冈石窟
Yungang Grottoes

位于山西省大同市的云冈石窟，有窟龛252个，造像51,000余尊，代表了公元5世纪和6世纪时中国杰出的佛教石窟艺术。其中的昙曜五窟，布局设计严谨统一，是中国佛教艺术第一个巅峰时期的经典杰作。

世界遗产委员会评价

在山西大同市以西16公里武周山南麓，一个琉璃飞金、朱墙抹红的崭新云冈藏在万绿丛中。这就是被法国总统蓬皮杜誉为"世界的艺术高峰之一"的云冈石窟。石窟依山而凿，东西绵延约一公里，共有大小石窟53个，佛雕51,000多尊，因为武周山的最高峰叫云冈，云冈石窟因此得名。

The Yungang Grottoes, in Datong City, Shanxi Province, with their 252 caves and 51,000 statues, represent the outstanding achievement of Buddhist cave art in China in the 5th and 6th centuries. The Five Caves created by Tanyao, with their strict unity of layout and design, constitute a classical masterpiece of the first peak of Chinese Buddhist art.

Located 16 kilometers west of Shanxi Province's Datong City, at the south foot of Wuzhou Mountain, the brand-new "Yungang", with golden colored glaze and ruby red walls, is hidden within the lush greenery. These are the Yungang Grottoes, once praised by former French president Georges Pompidou as "One of the Peaks of World Art". The grottoes, which are carved on the mountain and span about one kilometer from east to west, contain a total of 53 caves of varying sizes

小贴士 云冈石窟与敦煌莫高窟不同，传说莫高窟是僧人乐尊和尚云游到此，发现一道佛光，自己开凿石窟，由少到多，形成规模；云冈石窟则是皇帝信佛，官方推行佛教，凿石而成。

| | Date of inscription：2001 |
| Heritage category：文化遗产 C |
| Criteria：C(I)(II)(III)(IV) |

云冈石窟是中国最大的石窟之一，以宏伟而精美的雕刻和彩绘佛像闻名天下，与敦煌千佛洞、洛阳龙门石窟并称为"中国三大石窟艺术宝库"。

2001年12月，云冈石窟被列入《世界遗产名录》。

1,600多年前，游牧民族鲜卑族建立北魏政权，定都在平城，也就是今天的大同。公元460年，第五代君王文成皇帝下令开凿云冈石窟，以祈求国家的繁荣昌盛。

云冈石窟的开凿大约经历了70年，长度达一公里，有编号的洞窟有200多个，主要洞窟有45个，是中国规模最大、艺术成就最高的古代石窟群之一。按照开凿时间的前后和艺术风格的不同，云冈石窟分为早期、中期和晚期三个部分。

编号第十六至二十的五个石窟属于早期作品，开凿于公元460年至公元464年，因为是著名高僧昙曜主持修建的，也称为"昙曜五窟"。五个石窟的主要佛像都高达10米以上，气势宏伟。最为奇特的是，五个主佛的形象分别融入了北魏

and over 51,000 Buddha sculptures. The highest peak of Wuzhou Mountain is called "Yungang", and the Yungang Grottoes are named accordingly.

Constituting one of the largest grotto clusters in China, the Yungang Grottoes feature sculptures and colored paintings are famous in the world for their grandeur and delicacy. The Yungang Grottoes, together with Dunhuang's Mogao Caves (also known as the "Caves of the Thousand Buddhas") and Luoyang's Longmen Grottoes are renowned as the "Three Grotto Art Treasures of China".

In December 2001, the Yungang Grottoes were inscribed to the World Heritage List.

More than 1,600 years ago, the nomadic Xianbei people established the Northern Wei Dynasty, and made the city of Pingcheng, known today as Datong, as its capital. In 460 AD, the fifth generation of King Wencheng made his order to start carving the Yungang Grottoes, as a way to pray for affluence and prosperity throughout his nation.

Carving of the kilometer-long Yungang Grottoes lasted for about 70 years. There are over 200 numbered caves, of which there are 45 main caves. The Yungang Grottoes are one of the largest and most artistically supreme clusters of ancient grottoes in China. Based on carving periods and differences in art style, the Yungang Grottoes are divided into three periods: early, middle and late.

The five grottoes numbered 16 to 20, carved between 460 AD and 464 AD, belong to the early period. Since construction of these grottoes was led by the eminent monk Tanyao, they are also known as the "Five Grottoes of Tanyao". The main Buddha statue in each of the five grottoes measures over 10 meters in height and is both grand and magnificent. Most peculiar of all, the five main Buddhas were made according to

TIPS Yungang Grottoes are different from Mogao Caves. Legend has it that an ancient monk named Le Zun once visited Mogao and saw a flash of Buddha's halo. He was inspired by the magic light and began to carve grottoes here by himself. More and more grottoes were carved after years and eventually became grand in scale. However, Yungang Grottoes were ordered to be built by the emperor, who believed in Buddhism and officially advocated and sponsored Buddhism.

最早的五个皇帝的面貌，达到了既建造了佛像又建造了皇帝（纪念）像的目的。

云冈石窟的早期造像在端庄细腻的中国文化表现手法中，继承了浑厚淳朴的西域情调。许多佛像有着宽宽的额头、高高的鼻梁、大大的眼睛和薄薄的嘴唇，具有异域人种的面貌特点，展现出佛教作为外来文化的特征。

在云冈石窟这个恢弘绚烂的佛国世界，第二十窟的露天大佛，是最具代表性的作品。一位学者曾说，假如只能给你一刻钟时间来观看云冈石窟，那你只需要看第二十窟就可以了。

这座气势雄伟的释迦牟尼佛像，高达14米，面部丰满慈祥，双耳垂肩，两肩宽厚有力。他是为了纪念北魏的开国皇帝拓跋珪而建造的，佛像简约的形式，表现了极为生动的精神世界。

第一至十五窟开凿于公元465年至494年，是云冈石窟的中期作品，以精雕细琢、装饰华丽著称于世，显示出复杂多变富丽堂皇的北魏时期的艺术风格。

第五窟与第六窟是云冈石窟中期的代表作。第五窟的释迦牟尼坐像高达17米，是云冈石窟中最高的佛像，大佛的膝上可容纳120人。

the appearances of the five earliest emperors of the Northern Wei Dynasty. The statues thus not only were representations of Buddha, but also served as a commemoration of the past emperors.

In the early-period statues of the Yungang Grottoes, the artistic expression was that of a typical Chinese style of dignity and exquisiteness, carrying forward the air of simplicity and honesty characteristic of the Western Regions. Many of the Buddha statues possess features of foreign peoples, including a wide forehead, high nose bridge, big eyes and thin lips, revealing that the religion and culture of Buddhism originated beyond China's borders.

In the vast and splendid Buddhist land of the Yungang Grottoes, the open-air Buddha at Grotto No. 20 is the most typical sculpture. A scholar once said, "Assuming you had just 15 minutes to see the Yungang Grottoes, you need only see Grotto No. 20."

This is the majestic statue of Sakyamuni, with a height of 14 meters. His face is chubby and kind with long, auspicious earlobes and broad and strong shoulders. The statue was built to commemorate Tuoba Gui, founder of the Northern Wei Dynasty. The statue's simple form manifests an extremely colorful spiritual world.

小贴士 昙曜五窟 据说按照"皇帝即如来"的旨意，昙曜带领工匠把北魏太祖以来的五位帝王形象搬到山崖的释迦牟尼佛身上。第十六窟的佛像最年轻，是模拟当时在位的20多岁的文成帝，佛像高13.5米。

代表了北魏石窟艺术最高境界的是第六窟，这一石窟规模宏伟，以精巧著称，被称为云冈第一伟窟。整个洞窟富丽堂皇，塔柱和四面墙壁上雕满了佛像、菩萨、罗汉、飞天和瑞鸟、神兽、花卉等佛教形象，真是一个热闹拥挤、琳琅满目的佛国世界。

公元494年，北魏孝文帝把都城从大同迁到了南面的洛阳，云冈石窟大规模的开凿活动就结束

Grottoes No. 1 to 15, constructed between 465 AD and 494 AD, belong to the middle period. Famous for their delicate carving and luxurious ornamentation, they reveal the complex variation and magnificent splendor of the Northern Wei Dynasty's artistic style.

Grottoes No. 5 and 6 are masterpieces of the middle period. The Sakyamuni sitting sculpture at Grotto No. 5 reaches a height of 17 meters, making it the highest Buddha in the Yungang Grottoes. The knee of the sitting Buddha is big enough to accommodate 120 people. Grotto No. 6 represents the artistic pinnacle of the Northern Wei Dynasty grotto arts. Famous for its large scale and delicacy, it has been dubbed the "Grandest Grotto of Yungang". The grotto is thoroughly magnificent and beautiful, with the columns and walls carved full of Buddhas, Bodhisattvas, Arhats (spiritual practitioners who had realized the goal of nirvana) and Flying Apsaras (a female spirit of the clouds and waters), as well as Chinese phoenixes, spiritual beasts, flowers and plants. It is indeed a lively and bustling Buddhist world as well as a feast for the eyes.

In 494 AD, Emperor Xiaowen of the Northern Wei Dynasty moved the capital south from Datong to Luoyang. Although this meant the end of large-scale construction at the Yungang Grottoes, carving on a smaller scale continued for another 30 years. During this time, Grottoes No. 21 to 45, the late-period grottoes, were built.

Datong City was a famous summer resort. After moving the capital, Emperor Xiaowen learned that many aristocrats missed the old capital. He thus gave them special permission to go back and spend their summers at Datong. As a result, the aristocrats frequently traveled back and forth between the cities of Luoyang and Datong, and brought the culture of

TIPS **Five Grottoes of Tanyao** Following the order that "the emperor is Buddha", Tanyao led craftsmen and made five statues of Buddha grottoes on the mountain cliff. Those statues of Sakyamuni took after five emperors of the Northern Wei Dynasty. The Buddha statue in Grotto No.16 looks the youngest, and it took after Emperor Wencheng, who was only at his twenties then. The statue is about 13.5 meters in height.

了，但小规模的零散开凿仍然持续了30年，这就是第二十一窟到四十五窟，为石窟的晚期造像。

大同是著名的避暑胜地，迁都后的孝文帝看到许多贵族都非常留恋故都，特地准许他们夏天回到大同避暑。这样，北魏的贵族们频繁地往来于洛阳与大同之间，中原的文化也被他们带到了云冈石窟。

晚期石窟的规模虽小，但逐渐脱离了异域文化的影响，具有了浓厚的中国化风格和人性化气息，成为中国北方石窟艺术的范本和后期石刻秀古倾向的起源。

纵观群佛，在这绵延一公里的石雕群中，雕像大至十几米，小至几公分，巨石横亘，石雕满目，蔚为大观。他们的形态，神采动人，栩栩如生：或击鼓或敲钟，或手捧短笛或载歌载舞，或怀抱琵琶，面向游人。这些佛像、飞天、供养人的面目、身上、衣纹上，都留有古代劳动人民的智慧与艰辛。这些佛像与乐伎刻像，还明显地流露着波斯色彩。这是中国古代人民与其他国家友好往来的历史见证。开凿石窟的北魏鲜卑民族，被一些史学家称为来无影去无踪的民族。值得庆幸的是，这个早已消失的民族通过山崖上的巨石，在历史的长河中为自己留下了永恒的足迹。

central China with them to the Yungang Grottoes.

Although the late-period grottoes were smaller in scale, they gradually broke away from the influence of foreign culture. Increasingly, they embody a rich Sinicized style and humanized features. The grottoes of this period thus became the model for northern Chinese grotto art as well as the basis for later revival of ancient stone carving arts.

Comprehensively surveying the Buddhas within the kilometer-long Yungang Grottoes, statues can be found ranging from up to 10-20 meters to as small as several centimeters. Carved out of huge stones, the myriad carvings are a spectacular sight to behold. Their expressions and postures are vividly crafted. Some are depicted hitting drums or bells, or playing the Chinese flute; some of them are singing and dancing; and others are shown holding *pipas* (a plucked Chinese string instrument), facing captivated visitors. On the faces, bodies and clothes of these statues of Buddhas, Apsaras and sacrifice providers, the wisdom and painstaking efforts of the ancient Chinese people are revealed. These Buddha and Gandharva statues distinctly reveal Persian features, providing historical evidence of amicable relationships between China and other nations during ancient times. Some historians have referred to the Yungang Grottoes' creators, the Xianbei people of the Northern Wei Dynasty, as a people who came in silence and disappeared without a trace. Fortunately, this long-vanished people—through giant rocks on the cliffs of mountains—left behind an eternal footprint in the long river of history.

| Date of inscription: 2003
| Heritage category: 自然遗产 N
| Criteria: N(I)(II)(III)(IV)

云南"三江并流"保护区
Three Parallel Rivers of Yunnan Protected Areas

　　三江并流国家公园在云南省西北部的多山地带，占地170万公顷，是具有八种地理学特征组合的保护区。亚洲三条大江长江、湄公河、萨尔温江的上游金沙江、澜沧江、怒江在此并行。它们由北向南，下穿3,000米深的峡谷，上接6,000米高的雪山。这里是中国生物多样化的中心，也是全球同具多样化生态条件区域中最富饶、温和的地区之一。

世界遗产委员会评价

　　4,000万年前，印度次大陆板块与欧亚大陆板块大碰撞，引发了横断山脉的急剧挤压、隆升、切割，高山与大江交替展布。金沙江、澜沧江和怒江这三条发源于唐古拉山的大江在云南省境内自北向南并行奔流于横断山脉的高黎贡山、怒山和云岭等崇山峻岭之间，形成三江并流170多公里而不交汇的奇特景观。其中怒江与澜沧江最短直线距离仅18.6公里，而澜沧江与金沙江最短直线距离仅66.3公里。

Consisting of eight geographical clusters of protected areas within the boundaries of the Three Parallel Rivers National Park, in the mountainous northwest of Yunnan Province, the 1.7 million hectare site features sections of the upper reaches of three of the great rivers of Asia: the Yangtze (Jinsha), Mekong and Salween run roughly parallel, from north to south, through steep gorges which, in places, are 3,000 m deep and are bordered by glaciated peaks more than 6,000 m high. The site is an epicenter of Chinese biodiversity. It is also one of the richest temperate regions of the world in terms of biodiversity.

Some forty million years ago, large collisions between the Indian subcontinental plate and Eurasian continental plate resulted in fierce extrusion, uplift and cutting in the Hengduan Mountains. Large mountains and great rivers were formed in staggered distribution. Three large rivers—the Jinsha, Lancang, and Nujiang rivers—originate from the Tanggula Mountains. Near the boundary of Yunnan Province, these rivers flow southbound in

金沙江由北东去，汇集雅砻江、大渡河、嘉陵江，于是中国便有了长江。澜沧江由北南下缓缓而流，穿越国界便成了邻国湄公河的上游。怒江由北南下奔腾急流闯进缅甸便成了萨尔温江的上游。三条发源于同一山路的大江在云南境内画出三条平行线之后，分头注入太平洋和印度洋，河口东西达3,000公里之遥，实属举世罕见。

"三江并流"地区是世界上蕴藏最丰富的地质地貌博物馆。景区内高山雪峰横亘，海拔变化呈垂直分布，从760米的怒江干热河谷到6,740米的卡瓦格博峰，汇集了高山峡谷、雪峰冰川、高原湿地、森林草甸、淡水湖泊、稀有动物、珍贵植物等奇观异景。景区有118座海拔5,000米以上造型迥异的雪山。与雪山相伴的是静立的原始森林和星罗棋布的数百个冰蚀湖泊。梅里雪山主峰卡瓦格博峰上覆盖着万年冰川，晶莹剔透的冰川从峰顶一直延伸至海拔2,700米的明永村森林地带，这是目前世界上最为壮观且稀有的低纬度低海拔季风海洋性现代冰川。千百年来，藏族人民把梅里雪山视为

parallel among the lofty and precipitous peaks of the Gaoligong, Nushan, and Yunling mountain regions of the Hengduan Mountains. The resulting spectacular sight is that of three parallel rivers flowing over 170 kilometers without intersecting. The minimum straight-line distance between the Lancang and Jinsha rivers is only 66.3 kilometers, while the minimum between the Nujiang and Lancang rivers is mere 18.6 kilometers.

The Jinsha River, which flows southwardly and eastwardly, forms a confluence with the Yalong, Dadu and Jialing rivers, thus resulting in China's Yangtze River. The Lancang River flows down southward, traverses the Chinese border, and becomes the upstream of the Mekong River in neighboring countries. The Nujiang River also flows down southward and becomes the upstream of the Salween River in Myanmar. After the three rivers, which all originate from the same piedmont in Yunnan Province, form a picture of three parallel lines, they separately enter the Pacific and Indian Oceans. The east-west distance between the river mouths reaches up to 3,000 kilometers, which is a rare phenomenon in the world.

This "Three Parallel Rivers" region is the world biggest natural museum of geology and topography. Inside the scenic area, the huge mountains and snow peaks are vertically distributed with changes in altitude; from the 760-meter Ganre Valley of the Nujiang River to the 6,740-meter Kawagebo Peak, there are high mountain canyons, mountain peak glaciations, plateau wetlands, forest meadows, fresh water lakes, rare animals, and precious plant species. The scenic area contains 118 variously shaped snow mountains over 5,000 meters in altitude. Accompanying them are virgin forests and hundreds of ice erosion lakes quietly existing in the exceptional beauty of nature. Kawagebo Peak, the main peak of Meri Snow Mountain, is

小贴士 **长江第一湾** 金沙江是中国第一大河、世界第三大河长江的上游段，金沙江从"世界屋脊"青藏高原奔腾而下，到老君山、玉龙雪山交汇处冲破两座雪山的阻挡，形成100多度的"V"字形急转弯，人们称这一天下奇观为"长江第一湾"。

云南"三江并流"保护区

神山,恪守着登山者不得擅入的禁忌。

"三江并流"地区被誉为"世界生物基因库"。由于"三江并流"地区未受第四纪冰期大陆冰川的覆盖,加之区域内山脉为南北走向,因此这里成为欧亚大陆生物物种南来北往的主要通道和避难所,是欧亚大陆生物群落最富集的地区。这一地区占中国国土面积不到0.4%,却拥有中国20%以上的高等植物和25%的动物种数。目前,这一区域内栖息着珍稀濒危动物滇金丝猴、羚羊、雪豹、孟加拉虎、黑颈鹤等77种中国国家级保护动物和秃杉、桫椤、红豆杉等34种国家级保护植物。

covered with a bright and lucent 10,000-year-old glacier, which extends all the way to the Mingyong Village forest area at an altitude of 2,700 meters. This is a rare and the world's grandest sight of a low-latitude, low-altitude monsoon oceanic modern glacier. For thousands of years, the Tibetan people have regarded the Meri Snow Mountain as a holy place and strictly prohibited mountaineers from arbitrarily climbing there.

The Three Parallel Rivers area is reputed as the "world's biological gene archive". Since the area had not been covered by Quaternary continental glaciers and the mountain range runs in a north-south orientation, it became the major passage and asylum for all kinds of passing species living on the Eurasian continent and the continent's richest biotic community. The area occupies less than 0.4% of the Chinese national territorial acreage, while nurturing more than 20% of the vascular plants and 25% of animal species. Currently, the Three Parallel Rivers area contains 77 endangered animals under Chinese national protection (including the Yunnan snub-nosed monkey, antelope, snow leopard, Bengal tiger, and black neck crane) and 34 plants (including Taiwaniaflousiana, Gymnosphaera, and Taxus chinensis), also under national protection.

Every spring, on the green carpet of the meadows, in the tranquility of the forests, and

TIPS **The First Bend in Yangtze River** It refers to Jinsha River, which is located in the upper reaches of Yangtze River. Yangtze River ranks the first river in China and the third in the world. Running down from the Qinghai-Tibet Plateau, Jinsha River hits the meeting point of Laojun Mountain and Yulong Snow Mountain and advances against the block, forming a V-shape bend of more than 100 degrees. People call this marvelous scene "the First Bend in Yangtze River".

每年春暖花开的时候，这里绿毯般的草甸上、幽静的林中、湛蓝的湖边，到处是花的海洋，可以观赏到两百多种杜鹃、近百种龙胆、报春及绿绒蒿、杓兰、百合等野生花卉。因此，植物学界将"三江并流"地区称为"天然高山花园"。

传说中世界上有一处人与自然和谐相处，充满和平、安宁和幸福的世外桃源——香格里拉。其实美丽的香格里拉就在云南"三江并流"地区。早在上世纪20年代，奥籍美国人洛克在这一地区为美国《国家地理》杂志撰稿、摄影、收集物种二十多年。英国人希尔顿创作的《消失的地平线》让香格里拉影响了整个世界。香格里拉是中国著名的国际古商道——茶马古道的发祥地。香格里拉在藏语中有"心中

beside the blue lakes, the area blossoms into an ocean of flowers. Visitors can admire and enjoy over 200 types of rhododendrons, almost 100 types of Chinese gentians and primroses, as well as wild flowers like meconopsis, pedicularis, cypripedium flavum, and lilies. Botanists thus refer to the Three Parallel Rivers area as a "natural garden of high mountains".

According to legend, there is a heaven of peace and happiness on earth called Shangri-La. In fact, the beautiful Shangri-La is found in the Three Parallel Rivers area. As early as the 1920s, an Austrian American called Joseph Rock wrote essays, shot photos and collected species for almost 20 years in this region for US *National Geographic* magazine. The novel *Lost Horizon*, written by British writer James Hilton, caused Shangri-La to create a sensation around the world. Shangri-La is also the primary land of China's famous Ancient Tea-Horse Road for international trade. In

小贴士　香格里拉 在藏语里，"香格里拉"意为"心中的日月"，是藏民心目中的理想生活环境和至高至尚的境界。"香"字藏语意思为"心"，"格"相当于汉语中的"的"，"里拉"是"日月"的意思。

的日月"之意，它代表了藏民所神往的至善至美的生活境界。

"三江并流"地区还是少数民族聚居地，16个少数民族千百年来在这里和睦相处、生息与共。与三江腹地生物的多样性相比，在这里的各民族所创造的民族文化，同样五彩斑斓，毫不逊色。

长期以来，"三江并流"区域一直是科学家、探险家和旅游者的向往之地，他们对此区域显著的科学价值、美学意义和少数民族独特文化给予了高度评价。

2003年7月2日，联合国教科文组织第27届世界遗产大会一致决定，将中国云南省西北部的"三江并流"保护区列入《世界遗产名录》。

the Tibetan language, the word "Shangri-La" means "the sun and the moon", representing the perfect and beautiful world to which the Tibetan people aspire.

The Three Parallel River area is inhabited by several ethnic minorities. 16 different ethnic groups have lived peacefully together here for thousands of years. In comparison to the biotic variation of the three-river hinterland, the ethic culture created by the people living here is also brilliant.

For decades, the Three Parallel River area has attracted scientists, explorers, and tourists, all of whom praise it highly for its scientific value, aesthetic significance and cultural diversity.

On July 2, 2003, at the 27th session of the UNESCO World Heritage Committee, the Three Parallel Rivers of Yunnan Protected Areas was unanimously voted into the World Heritage List.

TIPS **Shangri-la** In Tibetan language, "Shangri-la" means "the sun and the moon in heart". It is an ideal place to live and an ultimate and supreme realm in Tibetan people's mind. "Shang" in Tibetan language means "heart", "g" is equal to "of", "ri-la" refers to "the sun and the moon".

高句丽王城、王陵及贵族墓葬

Capital Cities and Tombs of the Ancient Koguryo Kingdom

这个遗址包括3座古城和40座墓葬的考古遗存：五女山城、国内城和丸都山城，14座王陵，26座贵族墓葬。这些遗存都属于高句丽文化，以高句丽王朝命名。这个政权在公元前37年～公元668年统治了中国北部的部分地区和朝鲜半岛的北部。

世界遗产委员会评价

The site includes archaeological remains of three cities and 40 tombs: Wunu Mountain City, Guonei City and Wandu Mountain City, 14 tombs are imperial, 26 of nobles. All belong to the Koguryo culture, named after the dynasty that ruled over parts of northern China and the northern half of the Korean Peninsula from 37 BC to AD 668.

中国高句丽王城、王陵及贵族墓葬距今已有2,000多年的历史，主要分布在吉林省集安市境内以及辽宁省桓仁县境内，它们是被历史长河湮没的高句丽古代文明的经典。

"高句丽"，简称"句丽"或"句骊"。桓仁与集安是高句丽政权早中期的政治、文化、经济中心所在，累计共465年，是高句丽文化遗产分布最集中的地区。

Located primarily in Ji'an City of Jilin Province and Huanren County of Liaoning Province, the Capital Cities and Tombs of the Ancient Koguryo Kingdom are the classic remnants of the long-vanished civilization of Koguryo with a history of over 2000 years.

"Koguryo" is abbreviated as "Guryo." Huanren and Ji'an served as the political, cultural and economic centers of the Koguryo Kingdom for a total of 465 years during the regime's early and middle periods. As a result, the richest cultural relics of the Koguryo Kingdom are found here.

In 37 BC, Prince Zhumeng of the Fuyu Kingdom in northeastern China fled southward to escape the persecution of his brothers and established the Koguryo Kingdom with Huanren County's Wunu Mountain City at its center. As the city had the mountain's precipices as a natural fort, it was easy for people in Wunu Mountain City to defend and difficult for enemies to conquer. As the early capital and the cradle of the Koguryo Kingdom, Wunu Mountain City

收录时间 Date of inscription：2004
遗产类别 Heritage category：文化遗产 N
收录理由 Criteria：C(I)(II)(III)(IV)(V)

公元前37年，中国东北的夫余国王子朱蒙为避免兄弟迫害，逃离夫余国南下，以辽宁省桓仁县的五女山城为中心建立了高句丽王国。五女山城利用山体的天然悬崖为壁垒，易守难攻。作为高句丽的早期王城和发祥之地，此后数百年，五女山城一直是高句丽的重镇和交通要冲，不断得以续建。在高句丽时期，这座山城从未被敌人攻占。

公元3年，高句丽将都城从五女山城迁至国内城，同时筑丸都山城。在公元427年向南迁往朝鲜平壤前，高句丽建都在集安境内的历史达424年之久。

国内城和丸都山城分别坐落于平原与附近山上，形成了高句丽的一对"附和式都城"。高句丽国王平时居住在平原城，战时则退守到深山中的卫城。这对"附和式王城"，开创了中世纪都城建筑模式的一个先河，显示了高句丽时代的军事智慧。

served as the kingdom's strategic post and transport hub. It was rebuilt several times over the following several hundred years and was never occupied by enemies during the Koguryo period.

In 3 AD, Koguryo moved its capital from Wunü Mountain City to Guonei City and, concurrently, built Wandu Mountain City. The kingdom had its capital in Ji'an for 424 years before moving it to the present Pyongyang, North Korea, in 427 AD.

Guonei City and Wandu Mountain City were situated in the plains and the neighboring mountains, respectively, forming the shape of a pair of "echoing capitals" of the Koguryo Kingdom. The Koguryo kings usually lived in the city on the plains, and retreated to the defensive city in the lush mountains when wars broke out. The pair of "echoing capitals" served as a model for other capital cities during the Middle Ages, revealing the military wisdom of the Koguryo era.

　　国内城位于鸭绿江中游右岸通沟盆地西部，背靠禹山，前傍鸭绿江。整座城略呈方形，东墙长554.7米，西墙长702米，南墙长751.5米，北墙长730米，总周长达2,738.2米。城墙内外两面全部以长方形石条垒砌而成，中间为土石混筑。由于年代久远，除了北墙保存较好外，城墙大部分已失去原状。

　　国内城以北2.5公里的丸都山城，修建在起伏险峻的丸都山上，海拔最高处为676米，是高句丽时代最为典型的早期山城之一。丸都山城依山势而建，以环山为屏障，以山谷出口为城门，外临陡峭的绝壁，内抱较为平缓的坡地，北高南低，形如簸箕状，平面呈不规则的四边形。城墙防御坚固，城内却又宽敞自如、环境优美，将军事、生产、生活巧妙地融于一体。瞭望台是丸都山城保存最完好的一处建筑，它地处南门以北200米的高冈上，由石块垒筑，高11.75米，登上瞭望台可清晰看见国内城。

　　高句丽王城外，在群山环抱的通沟平原上，现存有近7,000座高句丽时代的墓葬——洞沟古墓群，堪称东北亚地区古墓群之冠。

With Yushan Mountain at its back and Yalu River in its front, Guonei City was situated in the west of Tonggou Basin on the right bank of the middle reaches of Yalu River. The city had a square-like configuration; the length of the north, east, south and west walls measured 730 meters, 554.7 meters, 751.5 meters and 702 meters, respectively. The circumference of the city measured 2,738.2 meters. The internal and external walls were all built with rectangular stone stripes, and the middle wall was built with a mixture of soil and stone. As a result of the passage of time, most of the walls have been deteriorated. The northern wall, however, is fairly well-preserved.

Wandu Mountain City, located 2.5 kilometers north of Guonei City, was built on the meandering and precipitous Wandu Mountain and is one of the most typical mountain cities of the early Koguryo period. The city's summit rose 676 meters above sea level. Built to follow the mountain's natural contours, Wandu Mountain City used surrounding mountains as its screen and the exit of the valley as its city gate. Facing the precipitous cliff and embracing the relatively smooth land on the slopes, its north part was higher than the south part, presenting an irregular quadrangle like a winnowing pan. While the city wall was defensive and sturdy, the city had a beautiful and

小贴士　好太王碑　碑体重约37吨，整座石碑未借助任何外力，直接矗立在一块不规则的花岗岩石板上。据考察，好太王在位的22年间是高句丽历史上的空前繁荣发展时期。

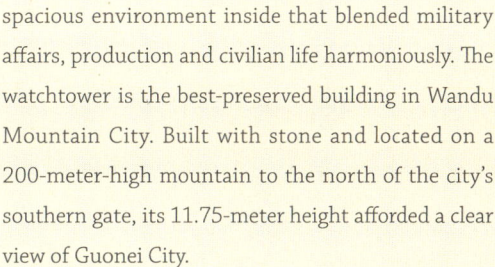

高句丽王城、王陵及贵族墓葬

spacious environment inside that blended military affairs, production and civilian life harmoniously. The watchtower is the best-preserved building in Wandu Mountain City. Built with stone and located on a 200-meter-high mountain to the north of the city's southern gate, its 11.75-meter height afforded a clear view of Guonei City.

Located away from the Koguryo Kingdom on the mountain-surrounded Tonggou Plain are nearly 7,000 tombs built during the Koguryo era. These are the Donggou Ancient Tomb Complex—the finest one amongst ancient tomb complex found anywhere in Northeast Asia.

The Tomb of the General, also known as the "Pyramid of the East," was the mausoleum of King Jangsu, the 20th monarch of Goguryeo. The tomb's base measures 31 meters in length and 12 meters in height. The body of the tomb is tapered and has seven steps altogether, similar to the tombs of the ancient Egyptian pharaohs. The tomb of the General sits at the foot of Longshan Mountain, by Yushan Mountain on the north. It represents over ten thousands of other ancient Koguryo tombs at Ji'an, and is one of the most magnificent ancient tombs of China still in existence today.

具有"东方金字塔"之称的将军坟是高句丽第20代王"长寿王"的陵寝。墓基长31米，高12米，墓体呈方锥形，共有7级阶梯，造型颇似古埃及法老的陵墓。将军坟巍然屹立于龙山脚下，北依禹山。将军坟是集安上万座高句丽古墓中方坛阶梯墓的代表，也是中国现存最为宏伟的古墓之一。

这座价值连城的石碑，被荒烟蔓草整整湮没了十个世纪之久。它便是被誉为"东方第一碑"

This priceless stone monument of nearly 1,600 years old once fell into oblivion for an entire millennium. Praised as the "Best Monument of the East," the Gwanggaeto Stele (or the stele of King Gwanggaeto of Goguryeo) was erected by King Jangsu (of Goguryeo) to commemorate his father's merits. Carved on a huge column-shaped stone, it measures over six meters in height and has 1,775 Chinese characters inscribed

TIPS Gwanggaeto Stele (or the stele of King Gwanggaeto of Goguryeo) Weighing about 37 tons, the whole stele stands on a slab of granite in irregular shape without being supported by any external force. According to records, the 22-year reign of Gwanggaeto was an unprecedented period of prosperity and development in Koguryo history.

的好太王碑，距今已有近1,600年的历史。好太王碑是长寿王为纪念其父的功业而树立的，碑石由一块方柱形巨石修琢而成，高6米多，四面环刻文字共1,775个，记述了好太王一生的功绩和有关高句丽起源及建立政权的传说。据记载，高句丽历史上目前已知有文字的文物仅存三件，好太王碑是其中记述内容最为丰富的。

高句丽壁画墓记载了中国古代东北少数民族的特殊文化，是五千年中华文明中的一朵奇葩，被誉为"东北亚艺术宝库"。许多墓室中的壁画线条飘逸流畅，内容颇具传奇色彩。由于高句丽留下的文字资料很少，这些内容丰富的高句丽古墓壁画就成为专家学者研究高句丽历史、文化、风俗等的重要考古资料。

2004年7月，世界遗产委员会将中国高句丽王城、王陵和包括部分壁画墓在内的贵族墓葬列入《世界文化遗产名录》。

on its four sides. The inscriptions recorded the merits of King Gwanggaeto the Great (the 19th monarch of Goguryeo) as well as legends about the origins of the Koguryo Kingdom and the establishment of its political power. Of the three existing cultural relics discovered to date, the Gwanggaeto Stele provides the richest and most detailed account.

As a piece amongst the treasures of China's 5,000-year-old civilization, the Koguryo fresco tombs have recorded the distinctive culture of ancient northeastern China's ethnic minorities and are acclaimed as a "repository of art treasures." Many of the frescos reveal a flowing elegance and grace, while others take on a legendary flavor. Since few written records remain from the Koguryo Kingdom, these richly detailed tomb paintings have become an important source of archaeological data for experts researching the history, culture and customs of Koguryo.

In July 2004, UNESCO's World Heritage Committee added the Capital Cities and Tombs of the Ancient Koguryo Kingdom (including some of the fresco in the tombs) to the World Heritage List.

收录时间 Date of inscription：2005
遗产类别 Heritage category：文化遗产 C
收录理由 Criteria：C(II)(III)(IV)(VI)

澳门历史城区
Historic Center of Macao

  澳门历史城区，是中国现存最古老的西式建筑遗产，是东西方建筑艺术的综合体现；见证了西方宗教文化在中国以至远东地区的发展，也见证了向西方传播中国民间宗教的历史渊源；是中西方文化多元共存的独特反映，是中国城市中极具特色的组合；是中西生活社区有序的组合，从历史到今天，都与居民的生活习俗、文化传统密不可分。

世界遗产委员会评价

  时光流转，拥有四百多年历史的澳门历史城区正散发着一种独特的艺术魅力和历史风韵。街道、欧式住宅、中式庙宇、教堂，和谐地交织在一起，形成一种中西文化交融的特殊景象。

  Macao, a lucrative port of strategic importance in the development of international trade, was under Portuguese administration from the mid-16th century until 1999, when it came under Chinese sovereignty. With its historic street, residential, religious and public Portuguese and Chinese buildings, the historic center of Macao provides a unique testimony to the meeting of aesthetic, cultural, architectural and technological influences from East and West. The site also contains a fortress and a lighthouse, the oldest in China. It bears witness to one of the earliest and longest-lasting encounters between China and the West, based on the vibrancy of international trade.

  Time is always in perpetual motion. Macao, as a city owning 400 years of history, emits its own unique artistic glamour and historical charm. It has created a special blend of "East meets West" scenery through a harmoniously interwoven fusion found in the streets, continental residences, Chinese temples and churches of this evolving city.

  The Historic Center of Macao is located in the Macao Peninsula. Although the area is less than nine square kilometers, it has still retained its ancient architecture carried by several hundred years of history behind it. This has made it China's longest lasting, largest, most fully preserved and most concentrated ensemble of architecture which simultaneously combines Eastern and Western

小贴士 澳门历史建筑群 澳门历史城区的旧称。澳门历史城区由22座位于澳门半岛的建筑物和相邻的8块前地所组成，以旧城区为核心。

澳门历史城区位于澳门半岛上，虽然面积不足九平方公里，却保存着一群有数百年历史的古老建筑，成为中国境内现存年代最久远、规模最大、保存最完整、最集中的东西方风格共存的建筑群。2005年被联合国教科文组织列入《世界文化遗产名录》。

澳门位于中国东南部的沿海，由澳门半岛、凼仔岛和路环岛组成。16世纪中期，第一批葡萄牙人在澳门登陆。当时的澳门还只是一个小渔村，叫濠镜。葡萄牙人询问当地名称时，居民误以为指的是妈祖阁，答称"妈阁"，葡萄牙人音译为"MACAO"，"澳门"的名称由此而来。妈祖阁是澳门最古老的寺庙，供奉的是渔民的保护神——妈祖。寺庙体现了中式庙宇的布局和审美观。历代的画家和诗人在此留下了无数的题词和石刻，为这座古庙平添了几分

styles. In 2005, it was inscribed on UNESCO's World Cultural Heritage List.

Macao, located along China's southeast coast, is formed from the Macao Peninsula and the islands of Taipa and Coloane. During the mid-16th century, the first group of Portuguese landed in Macao. At that time, Macao was only a very small fishing village called *Haojing*. When the Portuguese inquired about its name from the locals, the residents mistakenly thought they were referring to the Temple *Mazu Ge*, and replied "Ma Ge." The Portuguese transcribed it linguistically to "Macao", resulting in its current name. *Mazu Ge* (A-Ma Temple) is the oldest temple in Macao, where the fishermen's protective god Mazu is consecrated. The temple exemplifies the aesthetics and layout of the conventional Chinese temples. Generations of painters and poets have left numerous verses and stone inscriptions here, adding to the elegance of the temple. In front of the A-Ma Temple, visitors around the world

小贴士 妈祖 "妈祖"在福建话里是"母亲"的意思。"妈祖"姓林名默，宋朝福建莆田人，自幼聪颖，传说得老道秘传法术，能通神，经常在海上搭救遇难船只，"升天"后仍屡次在海上显灵，救助遇难的人。

> **TIPS** | **The historic architectures in Macao** The historic city proper of Macao consists of 22 buildings on the Macao Peninsula and 8 neighboring "Qiandi", with the old city proper as the core part.

雅致。妈祖阁门前还可以看到富有当地特色的舞狮活动，人们用这种方式迎接来自世界各地的客人。

are greeted with a lion dance rich in local flavor.

This was the city center planned by the Portuguese in those days—Senado Square (or Senate Square), which is still Macao's city center today.

这是葡萄牙人当年规划的城市中心——议事亭前地，现在仍然是澳门的市中心。广场占地3,700平方米，路面由碎石子铺就，组成波浪形的图案，中间是一个喷泉，两侧是建于19世纪末20世纪初的西式建筑，具有浓郁的南欧风情。

这座大炮台始建于1617年，是中国最古老的炮台，上面可以架设32门大炮，是当时整个澳门防御系统的中心。葡萄牙人进驻澳门后，为了保护商船和城市免受海盗和其他威胁，一心想把澳门修筑成为一个堡垒，于是建造

The public square occupies an area of 3,700 square meters, and the road surface is paved with small broken stones, forming a wave-shaped design. In the middle is a fountain sandwiched between Western-style buildings on either side that were built at the late-19th to early-20th centuries, and have a strong southern European flavor.

Mount Fortress, built in 1617, is China's oldest fortress—on top of which 32 cannons can be positioned—and was the center of the entire defence system for Macao at that time. After the Portuguese were stationed

> **TIPS** | **Mazu** Mazu means "mother" in Fujian dialect. The worldly name of Mazu is Lin Mo, and she lived in Putian, Fujian Province in the Song Dynasty. Legend has it that she was a clever girl and had been instructed by some secret Taoist priest and acquired immense capabilities. She frequently saved ships in storm and made her appearance at sea to rescue people in danger several times even after she had gone to heaven.

小贴士 | 前地 "前地"称呼译自葡萄牙文,是指建筑前面比较开阔的空地,即小广场。澳门有二十余处"前地"。

了大量的炮台。这座灯塔同样具有海防功能,白墙红顶,高达13.5米,有"远东第一灯塔"之称。夜间,在25海里以外的地方都可以看到塔上的灯光。

对于远行在外的葡萄牙人来说,教堂是不可缺少的。圣母玫瑰堂供奉的是葡萄牙人最崇拜的圣母。黄色的墙壁、白色的装饰、浅绿色的门窗、简洁的色彩搭配使教堂显得端庄而柔和。圣老楞佐教堂是澳门规模最大的一座教堂,依山而建。底层有近一层高的高台,这使

in Macao, they wanted to build the city into a fortress to protect their merchant ships and cities from pirates and other threats. They thus constructed a large number of forts. Another security measure they devised to protect their city was to build a lighthouse. Standing at a height of 13.5 meters with white walls and a red roof, the lighthouse in Macao has earned the reputation of being "the First Beacon of the Far East." At night, you can see the tower's light from as far away as 25 nautical miles.

To the Portuguese who were far away from home, a church was indispensable. The Church of Holy Rosary consecrated the most revered the Holy Mother of the Portuguese. It was made up of mostly simple colors, including yellow walls, white decorations, and light green doors and windows; the combination made the church appear both dignified and gentle. St. Lawrence's Church is Macao's largest church, built close to the mountains. The lowest level has a terrace almost one storey high, endowing the church with a unique style and making it look particularly tall, straight, prominent and strong. Passing through St. Joseph's Seminary at the end of the road, one does not have the slightest feeling of noise; there is only a peaceful quiet, like the Holy Mother herself. This was once known as the "Cradle of the missionaries in the Far East."

Out of Macao's collection of Western style architectures, the most famous is Dasanba Memorial Arch (the Ruins of St. Paul's). In fact, Dasanba is a relic of St. Paul's Church which used to be the first Western college in the Far East. After experiencing three big fires, only the remnants of its walls remained. Due to its likeness to Chinese memorial arches, people are accustomed to calling it Dasanba Memorial Archway. Reaching a height of 27 meters and five storeys tall, the archway remains straight and erect, majestic and lofty with a variety of complex and delicate decorations

小贴士 | 圣老楞佐教堂 通称风顺堂。在很多年前,风顺堂在华人口中是称做风信堂的,意谓顺风顺水。当年居澳的葡萄牙人大多为出海营商为生,他们的家人为求亲人能平安归来,多于此教堂祈祷。

> **TIPS**   *Qiandi* "*Qiandi*" is translated from Portuguese, which refers to the open and wide area in front of a building, namely the small square. In Macao, there are more than 20 so-called "Qiandi".

得教堂显得格外地挺拔、显眼、阳刚、气派。圣若瑟修院虽然位于马路的尽头,却没有丝毫的喧嚣之感,像圣母一样沉静,这里曾经是"远东传教士的摇篮"。

在澳门的西式建筑中,最有名的是大三巴牌坊。实际上,大三巴牌坊是圣保罗大教堂的遗迹。圣保罗教堂曾经是远东第一所西式大学,历经三次大火后,只剩下这些残留的墙壁。因其酷似中国的纪念式建筑牌坊,所以人们习惯称之为大三巴牌坊。牌坊挺拔巍峨,高达27米,上下五层,装饰复杂而细腻,各种类型的雕塑布满周身。牌坊主要采用意大利文艺复兴时期流行的样式,不过在细节上也可以看到东方的艺术特征。牡丹代表的是中国,菊花代表的是日本。大三巴牌坊历尽沧桑,这种残缺的美一直在吸引着游客的目光。

在大三巴牌坊后面的小山坡上有一座风格迥

and sculptures all over its body. Although it mostly uses popular styles from the Italian Renaissance Period, by looking at the details, one can see distinct artistic features from the Orient as well. The peony represents China while the chrysanthemum represents Japan. Even though Dasanba Memorial Archway has experienced all the difficulties of life, this maimed beauty still attracts the attention of tourists from around the world.

On the hillside behind Dasanba Memorial Archway is a different style of temple named Na Tcha Temple. It is said that before this temple was built, there was a plague in Macao and, in order to expel the evil spirits and end the disaster, the local residents built this

temple. Lin Fung Miu (Temple of Lotus), which has 400 years of history, is a place of worship where many gods—such as A-Ma and Guanyin Bodhisattva—were consecrated. *Pujichanyuan* mainly worships the Buddhist gods. *Chanyuan* the (Meditation Courtyard) is open and bright, and the buildings are decorated

> **TIPS**   St. Lawrence's Church St. Lawrence's Church is called "Fengshuntang." Many years ago, it was also called "Fengxintang" among Chinese people, which means "everything goes smoothly." Most Portuguese in Macao at that time were doing sea business and their folks would go to the church to pray for the safety of their family members.

异的庙宇，那就是哪吒庙。据说建庙前澳门瘟疫流行，当地居民为了驱邪息灾，于是兴建此庙。莲峰庙已有四百年的历史了，里面供奉着很多神灵，如妈祖、观音菩萨等。普济禅院里面供奉的主要是佛教的神灵。禅院舒朗开阔，殿宇陈设富丽，琉璃瓦的装饰令人惊叹。琉璃瓦上的人物、吉祥动物等雕刻得非常精巧细致！

城区里有一座公园，是19世纪一个叫卢廉若的富商修建的。精致的院门、曲折的小路、小巧的亭子、人工开凿的池塘、造型奇特的假山、幽静的竹林，让人似乎徜徉在中国江南的经典园林当中。池塘边的建筑是典型的中西结合：既有西式的廊柱，又有中式的琉璃瓦屋顶，而飞翘起来的屋檐很难说是中式的还是西式的。

中西文化的碰撞和融合形成了澳门的历史城区，多彩的文化以及各异的生活习惯在这里得到同样的尊重，并且互相映衬和借鉴。今天的澳门正以更加博大、更加包容的胸怀吸引着来自世界各地的游客。

richly and beautifully while their sparkling glazed tile decorations are astounding. The human and auspicious animal engravings are elaborate and meticulous.

Lou Lim Ieoc Garden was built by Lou Kau, a wealthy merchant, in the 19th century. Delicate courtyards, winding pathways, small and skilful pavilions, manually excavated ponds, peculiar shaped man-made hills, and secluded bamboo forests allow people to feel like they are in the midst of the classical gardens south of Yangtze River. The building beside the pond is a typical example of an integration of East and West: not only does it have Westernized corridors and pillars but it also has Chinese-style glazed tile roofs. With these types of upturned eaves, it is difficult to tell whether they reflect an Eastern-style or Western-style design.

Chinese and Western cultures collide and intermingle to form the Historic Center of Macao. Through a colorful culture and diverse living habits that are equally respected, Macao reflects a combination of Eastern and Western characteristics as well as their dynamic interactions. Today's Macao is even more extensive, with an inclusive and open attitude that perpetually attracts tourists from around the world.

殷 墟
Yin Xu

Date of inscription: 2006
Heritage category: 文化遗产 C
Criteria: C(Ⅱ)(Ⅲ)(Ⅳ)(Ⅵ)

殷墟遗址，接近安阳市，位于北京南约500公里处，是商代晚期（公元前1300-1046年）的都城，它见证了早期中国文化、工艺、科学的辉煌和青铜时代极度的繁荣。数量众多的原型建筑、王室坟墓和宫殿，以及宫廷王室祖先们的祭祀场所，大约有超过80间房屋地基和商王朝家室成员及富豪的坟墓仍原封不动地埋藏在地下。大量精美的人造陪葬品证明了殷商先进的手工业。在殷墟发现的甲骨文确切地展示了世界上最古老的文字体系、古人信仰和社会制度的发展历程。

世界遗产委员会评价

在中国华北平原的中部，有一座宁静的小城叫安阳。殷墟，是镶嵌在这座历史文化名城上的一颗璀璨明珠。

2006年7月，殷墟作为世界文化遗产列入《世界遗产名录》，安阳殷墟由此成为中国第33处世界遗产。

殷墟是商朝后朝的文化遗址，位于安阳市的西北郊。据史料记载，公元前1300年，商朝第20位国王盘庚把都城由"奄"（今山东曲阜）迁到"殷"（今安阳小屯），并在此建立都城，历经8代12王，共254年。从此，这里成为殷商王朝政治、文化、经济的中心。到公元前1046年，商王朝被一个叫做周的王朝打败，这片土地逐渐荒

The archaeological site of Yin Xu, close to Anyang City, some 500 kilometers south of Beijing, is an ancient capital city of the late Shang Dynasty (1300-1046 BC). It testifies to the golden age of early Chinese culture, crafts and sciences, a time of great prosperity of the Chinese Bronze Age. A number of royal tombs and palaces, prototypes of later Chinese architecture, have been unearthed on the site, including the Palace and Royal Ancestral Shrines Area, with more than 80 house foundations, and the only tomb of members of the royal family of the Shang Dynasty to have remained intact. The large number and superb craftsmanship of the burial accessories found there bear testimony to the advanced level of Shang crafts industry. Inscriptions on oracle bones found in Yin Xu bear invaluable testimony to the development of one of the world's oldest writing systems, ancient beliefs and social systems.

At the center of the North China Plain, there is a small and quiet city called Anyang. Yin Xu is the gleaming pearl that lies in this famous historic and cultural city.

In July 2006, Yin Xu was inscribed to the UNESCO World Heritage List, making it China's 33rd World Heritage Site.

Situated in the northwest suburbs of Anyang City, Yin Xu is the cultural remains of the last capital of the Shang Dynasty. According to historical records, Pan Geng, the 20th king of the Shang

芜，变成了一片废墟，史称"殷墟"。

殷墟是一座开放形制的古代都城，总面积约24平方公里。总体布局以宫殿宗庙遗址为中心，沿洹河两岸呈环型、放射状分布。南岸是宫殿宗庙区，北岸是埋葬死者的王陵区。

宫殿宗庙遗址位于洹河南岸的小屯村、花园庄一带，是商王居住和处理政务的场所。当年这里是都城的中心，也是全城最气派的地方。自1928年以来，这里先后发现夯土建筑基址80多座。这些宫殿宗庙建筑，多坐落于厚实高大的夯土台基上，以黄土、木料为主要建筑材料，房架用木柱支撑，四面的墙用夯土版筑，屋顶上盖着茅草，造型庄重肃穆、质朴典雅，具有浓郁的中国宫殿建筑特色，代表了中国古代早期宫殿建筑的先进水平。

Dynasty, transferred the capital from Yan (present-day Qufu, Shandong Province) to Yin (present-day Xiaotun, Anyang) in 1300 BC. Here he ordered the construction of the capital city, which served 12 kings for 254 years and eight generations. From then on, it became the political, cultural and economic center of the Shang (Yin) Dynasty. Since the Shang Dynasty was defeated by the Zhou Dynasty in 1046 BC, this city was gradually abandoned, became a place of ruins, and took on the historical name of Yin Xu (literally, "the Ruins of Yin").

Yin Xu, which covers an area of 24 square kilometers, is an ancient capital with an open structure. The remains of the palaces and temples lie at the city's center and the site's overall layout radiates outward in a circle along the Huan River. Along the south bank is the area of the palaces and temples, while along the north bank are the imperial mausoleums where the dead are buried.

小贴士 **殷墟发掘过程** 1899年，金石学家王懿荣发现，北京一家中药店所售的龙骨上刻有一些很古老的文字，他意识到这是很珍贵的文物，于是开始重金收买。后来，这些甲骨被证实来自河南安阳小屯。通过对甲骨上的文字的考证，小屯被证实为商朝中后期的殷墟。

殷墟王陵遗址与宫殿宗庙遗址隔河相对，是商王的陵地和祭祀场所。在中国目前已知完整的王陵墓葬群中，它是建立最早的。遗址面积达11.3公顷。王陵遗址共发现有13座王陵大墓和2,500多座祭祀坑。王陵大墓多为"亚"、"中"、"甲"字形大墓。

王陵区的墓葬多数都遭到了盗墓贼的破坏，但有一座例外。这是一座商王朝晚期的王后墓，墓的主人是商王的一个妻子，名字叫妇好。妇好

Located in the villages of Xiaotun and Huayuanzhuang along the south bank of the Huan River, the site of the palaces and temples was the place where the Shang kings managed government affairs and resided. It was once the center of the capital and the most magnificent spot in the city. Since 1928, more than 80 rammed-earth buildings have been discovered here. Most of the palaces and temples were based on massive rammed-earth podiums, with loess and wood used as the main construction material. With rooms supported by wood posts, rammed-earth walls, and roofs covered with thatches, the solemn, simple and elegant shape of the buildings represents the strong flavor and advanced standards of China's ancient palace architecture.

The relics of the mausoleums and the remains of the palaces and temples sit at opposite banks of the river. The mausoleums served as the tomb sites and places of sacrifice for the Shang kings. Of all the intact mausoleums discovered in China to date, the ones at Yin Xu were constructed the earliest. The whole site covers an area of 11.3 hectares, with 13

TIPS | **The discovery of Yin Xu** In 1899, Wang Yirong, an epigraphist, found some ancient characters carved on the bones sold in a Chinese drug store in Beijing. He realized that these were precious historic relics and began to buy them with huge sum of money. Later he reached a conclusion that what Yin Xu recorded is located in the area of Xiaotun Village. It is confirmed that the area near Xiaotun Village is where Yin Xu of the middle and late Shang Dynasty lied.

墓虽然墓室不大，但保存完好，随葬品极为丰富，共出土了不同材质的随葬品1,928件，有青铜器、玉器、宝石器、象牙器等，让我们看到了那个年代的一个侧影。

在所有出土文物中，最眩目的是青铜器和玉器。出土的礼器类别较全，规格很高，这说明妇好在王室拥有尊贵的地位。出土的大量兵器说明，妇好不仅是一个王妃，还是一名彪悍的女将军。

殷墟规模浩大的科学挖掘，发现了沉睡地下三千多年的古汉字——被誉为汉字"鼻祖"的甲骨文。

目前，殷墟共出土甲骨15万片，单字约4,500个，其中约1/3已被释读。在世界四大古文字体系中，唯有以殷墟甲骨文为代表的中国古汉字体系，历经数千年的演变而承续至今，书写出了一部博大精深的中华文明史。殷墟甲骨文的发现，是照亮中华文明的一盏明灯，把有记载的中华文明史向前推进了近五个世纪。

large tombs in the shape of the Chinese characters "亞" (yà), "中" (zhōng) and "甲" (jiǎ), and more than 2,500 burial pits.

Most of the tombs suffered the damage of robbers, but there is one exception—the tomb of Queen Fu Hao, who was a wife of a late Shang Dynasty king. Despite the small scale, it is well-preserved and rich in sacrificial items. Altogether, 1,928 sacrificial items made of a variety of materials—including articles made of bronze, jade, gemstones and ivory—were excavated, providing us with a profile of that epoch.

Among all the items unearthed, the most spectacular are the bronzeware and jade articles. The sacrificial vessels uncovered are comprehensive and elegant, revealing Fu Hao's respectable position in the royal family. The large number of unearthed weapons indicates that she was not merely a queen, but also a valiant female general.

Large-scale scientific excavation at Yin Xu also yielded the discovery of ancient characters on oracle bones that were buried under the earth's surface for over 3,000 years. They have been deemed "the earliest ancestor of Chinese characters."

Presently, a total of 150,000 pieces

小贴士　**甲骨文**　甲骨文因镌刻于龟甲与兽骨上而得名，是目前已知的中国最早的成熟文字，被称为"档案库"。甲骨文所记载的内容非常丰富，涉及到商代社会经济生活的各个方面，不仅包括政治、文化、军事、社会习俗等内容，同时涉及天文、历法、医药等科学技术。

除了文字外，那个时代最能代表人类文明程度的是青铜器。中国青铜文化源远流长，具有浓郁的民族特色和艺术风格。殷墟出土的大量青铜器，包括礼器、乐器、兵器、工具、生活用具、装饰品、艺术品等，形成了以青铜礼器和兵器为主的青铜文明，达到中国青铜时代发展的巅峰。

在出土的所有青铜器中，最让世人惊异的是这个大方鼎，由于在鼎的腹内找到了"司母戊"三个字，所以得名"司母戊大方鼎"。所谓"司"，是祭祀，"母"是母亲，"戊"是个人名。这个巨鼎是一位商王为纪念他的母亲而铸造的。这件高133厘米，重达875公斤的鼎，是目前世界上最大最重的青铜器，制作工艺非常精巧，

of oracle bones and 4,500 single characters have been excavated at Yin Xu, one-third of which have been interpreted. Among the four ancient writing systems of the world, the ancient Chinese writing system—epitomized by inscriptions on the Yin Xu oracle bones—is the only one that has developed over thousands of years and endured to modern times, illustrating the profound history of Chinese civilization. The discovery of oracle bones at Yin Xu is a beacon that illuminates Chinese civilization and has pushed back the beginning of China's recorded history almost five centuries.

Aside from Chinese characters, the level of human civilization reached in that epoch is best-represented by bronzeware. With a long history, China's bronze culture exudes artistic style and abundant Chinese flavor. The bronzes unearthed at Yin Xu including sacrificial vessels, musical instruments, weapons, tools, household articles, decorations, and works of art. The bronze culture that they developed, which centers around sacrificial vessels and weapons, represents the pinnacle of China's bronze era.

Among all the excavated bronzes, the most breathtaking is the Simuwu Rectangular Ding (cooking vessel), named after the Chinese characters "司" (sī), "母" (mǔ) and "戊" (wù) discovered inside. The character sī means sacrifice, mǔ means mother, and wù is a person's name. The casting of this giant vessel was ordered by one of the Shang kings to commemorate his mother. With a height of 133 centimeters and a weight of 875 kilograms, it is currently the largest and heaviest bronze in the world. The vessel exhibits delicate craftsmanship; its casting and artistic level represent the pinnacle of Shang Dynasty bronze casting technology. A symbol of royal power, the Simuwu Rectangle Ding tells silently of the splendid

TIPS **Oracle Bone Inscriptions** They were ancient Chinese characters carved on tortoise shells or animal bones. They are regarded as the earliest mature written language that has been discovered so far in China. These inscriptions are called "file archives" which recorded plentiful information on all aspects of the social and economic life in the Shang Dynasty. The content ranges from politics, culture, military affairs and social customs, to science and technology such as astronomy, calendar and medicine.

它的铸造技术和艺术水平代表了商代青铜铸造技术的最高成就。象征王权的司母戊大方鼎，无声地诉说着那个时代创造的辉煌、灿烂的古代文明。

那个遥远的时代创造了璀璨的文明，却也体现了旧社会礼制野蛮残酷的一面。在王陵遗址的东区和西区，分布着2,000余座小墓葬。这些墓葬除少数为陪葬墓外，大多是祭祀坑，是商王祭祀先祖的遗迹。坑内埋葬着数千具祭祀牺牲的遗骨。这些祭祀坑的存在成为商代残酷人祭制度的历史见证。随着历史的变迁和社会的发展，这些习俗逐渐消失湮没。

在国际上被承认的、没有争议的中国最早的文明就是商代。殷墟不是一座简单的建筑物，它是一座都城，是殷朝王国的缩影，展现了殷商王都的宏大气派。

ancient civilization created during that era.

That remote era created a brilliant civilization, but it also demonstrates the brutality and cruelty of ancient social etiquette. In the eastern and western sections of the remains of the mausoleums are scattered more than 2,000 tombs. Most of them, with the exception of a few accessory tombs, are sacrificial pits, in which human beings were sacrificed by the Shang kings in deference to their ancestors. In these sacrificial pits lie thousands of sacrificial bone remains. The existence of these pits bears historical testimony to the cruel system of sacrificing human beings during the Shang Dynasty. With the passage of time and the development of society, these customs gradually disappeared.

The Shang Dynasty is the earliest Chinese civilization that is internationally recognized without dispute. Yin Xu is not simply an architectural construction; it is a former capital and a miniature representation of the Shang Dynasty, fully demonstrating the Shang capital's splendor and magnificence.

收录时间 Date of inscription：2006
遗产类别 Heritage category：自然遗产 N
收录理由 Criteria：N(Ⅳ)

四川大熊猫栖息地
Sichuan Giant Panda Sanctuaries

　　四川大熊猫栖息地的濒危动物大熊猫占全球数量的30%，覆盖面积为924,500公顷，包括邛崃和夹金山脉内的7个自然保护区和9个风景名胜区。这个栖息地也是最大的与熊猫相关的物种的保护区，其地区环境与第三纪热带雨林相仿。这里也是物种最重要的繁殖地。这里还是红熊猫、雪豹及云豹等濒危物种栖息的地方。它是全球除热带雨林之外拥有植被种类最丰富的地区，大约有1,000多个类别包括5,000到6,000个物种。

世界遗产委员会评价

　　中国四川大熊猫栖息地地处青藏高原东部边缘的高山密林，涵盖范围为邛崃山系的卧龙、四姑娘山、夹金山，是大熊猫这一地球上生活了800万年的古老物种最后的家园。目前世界上仅存大熊猫1,000多只，而超过30%的野生大熊猫生活在这里，是中国最大最完整的大熊猫栖息地。

Sichuan Giant Panda Sanctuaries, home to more than 30% of the world's pandas which are classed as highly endangered, cover 924,500 ha with seven nature reserves and nine scenic parks in the Qionglai and Jiajin mountains. The sanctuaries constitute the largest remaining contiguous habitat of the giant panda, a relict from the paleo-tropic forests of the Tertiary Era. They are also the species' most important site for captive breeding. The sanctuaries are home to other globally endangered animals such as the red panda, the snow leopard and clouded leopard. They are among the botanically richest sites of any region in the world outside the tropical rainforests, with between 5,000 and 6,000 species of flora in over 1,000 genera.

The giant panda habitats of China's Sichuan Province are located in the dense, highly elevated jungles of the eastern edge of the Qinghai-Tibetan plateau, covering the areas of Wolong, Siguniang Mountain, and Jiajin Mountain in the Qionglai mountain range. This is the most recent homeland of the giant panda, an ancient species that has lived on this earth for eight million years. Currently, the giant panda population of the world numbers just over 1,000, and yet over 30% of wild giant pandas live in this area, making it the largest, most comprehensive giant panda habitat in China.

The giant panda, which has been dubbed a

　　大熊猫,这种被誉为"活化石"的珍稀动物,从漫长的岁月中蹒跚走来,在自然历史的巨变中神奇地幸存至今,成为全世界的宠儿,被视为中国的国宝。黑白浑然的模样、温顺可掬的憨态,使得它人见人爱,无论走到哪里都备受欢迎。

　　大自然鬼斧神工,在成都平原和青藏高原之间造就了秀色怡人的"山水盆景"雅安,也造就了大熊猫这样神奇的生命。四川雅安是世界上第一只大熊猫的发现地。1869年,法国传教士、生物学家阿曼德·戴维在雅安宝兴县邓池沟发现了世界上第一只野生大熊猫。戴维在日记中写道:"……在返回教堂途中,我看到一张展开的那种著名的黑白熊皮,这张皮非常奇特,它可能成为科学上一个有趣的新种。"戴维将这只黑白熊制成世界第一具大熊猫标本,寄给巴黎自然历

rare "living fossil", has tottered across the ages and miraculously survived the multitude of changes in the course of natural history to become the darling of the world as well as China's national treasure. Its black-and-white appearance and docile naiveté make it loved by everyone who sees it; no matter where the panda goes, it is welcomed whole-heartedly.

　　Nature's divine hand has crafted an elegant, harmonious "garden" of hills and streams at Ya'an, located between the plains of Chengdu and the Qinghai-Tibetan Plateau. It has also crafted the mysterious existence of the giant panda. Ya'an, Sichuan, is the place where the giant panda was first discovered. In 1869, French missionary and biologist Father Jean-Pierre Armand David discovered the first wild giant panda ever seen in the world at Dengchi Pond in Baoxing County, Ya'an. Father David wrote in his diary: "… on the way back to the church, I saw a laid-out piece of bearskin of the famous black-and-white kind.

小贴士　卧龙　在造山运动过程中,卧龙遭受外力的侵蚀切割,地面被雕刻成群峰绵延、翠谷纵横、景色秀丽的高山峡谷景观。在高空俯瞰,好似一条青龙盘旋在山冈上,所以称为卧龙。

史博物馆馆长米勒·爱德华兹，这位馆长鉴定这是一个新的物种，并给这只黑白熊取名叫"大熊猫"。从此，大熊猫开始走向世界，西方掀起了持续了上百年的"熊猫热"。

虽然在动物学上，大熊猫是一个新的物种，但是，从生存时间来说，大熊猫这个物种显然已经很古老了。为了适应环境，熊猫从食肉改为吃竹子，但它的消化系统对竹子的消化吸收功能很低下。为了获得足够的营养，只能采用"快吃快拉"的办法维持体能。一只体重为100公斤的大熊猫，每天要进食50公斤以上的鲜竹笋，同时再排出几乎等量的粪便。它的食品实在太单一了，每天只能获得很少的营养物质，因此大熊猫通常不做能量消耗过大的活动，这就是为什么它总是一副慢条斯理、不慌不忙的笨拙模样。大熊猫的过度偏食不仅限制了它的生活范围，而且，一旦它喜食的竹类大面积开花枯萎时，会严重威胁到它的生存。同时，独来独往的生活习惯增加了近亲繁殖的几率，这也让野生大熊猫的数量越来越少。隐居于高山深谷中的大熊猫，目前已处于极危状态。

为了保护大熊猫这种世界上珍稀的野生动物，上世纪60年代，中国政府开始设立专门的保护区。四川大熊猫栖息地内就包括了七个这样的

This piece of skin is quite strange. It may be a very interesting new discovery for science". Father David made it the world's first giant panda specimen and sent it to Dr. Henri Milar-Edwards, Director of the Paris Museum of Natural History. After appraising this specimen, Dr. Milne-Edwards gave this black-and-white bear the name "giant panda." Henceforth, the giant panda started traveling the world, and the West came down with a case of "panda fever" that

has lasted over a hundred years.

Though the giant panda is a fairly new species in zoology, it has an obviously ancient history in terms of existence. To adapt to its environment, the panda changed its diet from meat to bamboo; however, its digestive system has a very low capacity for digestion and absorption of bamboo. To get enough nutrition, it must adopt a "fast in, fast out" way of eating. A panda weighing 100 kilograms must eat at least 50 kilograms of fresh bamboo shoots per day, and at the same time, it will emit nearly the same amount of excrement. Because of its overly simplistic diet, it gets a very small amount of nutrients every day.

TIPS **Wolong** During the process of the mountain-making movement, Wolong area was eroded and cut by outer force, and undulating mountain ranges, green valleys and beautiful canyons were formed in this area. It looks like a blue dragon lying and winding over the mountains when you look down over the area, thus named "Wolong", meaning lying dragon in Chinese.

小贴士 ▎四姑娘山 四姑娘山由横断山脉中四座毗连的山峰组成，传说中为四个美丽的姑娘所化，因而得名。

国家级自然保护区,并且逐渐形成了一个熊猫的生态走廊，有效地改善了大熊猫的生存状况。

卧龙自然保护区建于1963年，1980年加入联合国教科文组织人与生物圈保护区网。卧龙以"熊猫之乡"、"宝贵的生物基因库"、"天然动植物园"享誉中外。目前拥有全国1/10的野生大熊猫、一半以上的圈养大熊猫，是世界闻名的"大熊猫之乡"。

卧龙的西面是四姑娘山，最高峰海拔6,250米，被称为"中国的阿尔卑斯"。四姑娘山由四座毗连的雪峰组成，终年冰雪覆盖，银光照人，如四个美丽的白衣仙女在群山之中，因而得名。这是一片神奇美丽的土地，气候特殊，垂直高差显著，因此动植物资源十分丰富。海

Therefore, the panda avoids energy-consumptive activities, which is why it always has a slow, unhurried, somewhat clumsy appearance. The giant panda's picky eating habits not only limit its habitat, but also threaten its existence when its favorite bamboo undergoes mass flowering and withering. Furthermore, the panda's habit of solitary wandering increases the chances of inbreeding, which contributes to the decline in the giant panda population. Presently, this hermit of the mountain canyons is in an extremely dangerous condition.

To protect this world treasure animal, the Chinese government began establishing special protected areas in the 1960s. There are seven of these national nature reserves in the panda habitats of Sichuan, which have gradually created an ecological corridor for the pandas, effectively changing their survival situation.

The Wolong Nature Reserve was established in 1963, and joined the ecosphere protection net of UNESCO in 1980. Wolong has a reputation both at home and abroad of being the "homeland of the pandas", the "gene archive of precious organisms", as well as a "natural botanical and zoological garden". With one-tenth of the country's wild pandas, as well as over half of those bred in captivity, Wolong is world-renowned as the "homeland of the pandas".

West of Wolong sits the Siguniang Mountain, which, with its highest peak at 6,250 meters above

小贴士 ▎夹金山 又名"甲金山"，藏语称为"甲几"，夹金为译音，意为很高很陡。

TIPS **Siguniang Mountain** Siguniang Mountain is composed of four joint summits. Legend has it that these four summits were turned from four beautiful girls and it was named accordingly.

四川大熊猫栖息地

拔2,500米左右的原始森林中，大片的竹林给熊猫提供了一个生活的乐园。

夹金山脉现有野生大熊猫约240只，约占全国总数的1/4。自1955年起，雅安市夹金山脉地区为国家先后提供"国礼"大熊猫，并成为国际上野生大熊猫的最大供给地。

2006年7月，联合国教科文组织第30届世界遗产大会一致决定，将中国四川大熊猫栖息地作为世界自然遗产列入《世界遗产名录》。这一中国稀有的"活化石"动物栖息地成为中国第32处世界遗产。

这是一座活的博物馆，除了大熊猫，还有金丝猴、小熊猫、雪豹、牛角羚羊等珍稀动物，是全球25个生物多样性热点地区之一。申遗的成功，意味着大熊猫栖息地内的其他珍稀濒危动植物也将受益。

sea level, has been dubbed "China's Alps." Mount Siguniang (literally "four girls") gets its name from the four adjoining peaks that comprise it, which are covered with snow in the winter and give off silver light as if there were four beautiful fairies in white clothing living in the mountains. This is a mystical and beautiful place, with a special climate and remarkable vertical elevations; thus, the botanical and zoological resources here are plentiful. In the primitive forests found at around 2,500 meters above sea level, large bamboo groves provide a living paradise for giant pandas.

There are approximately 240 giant pandas living in the Jiajin mountain range, comprising one-fourth of the country's total panda population. Starting in 1955, the Jiajin mountain range in Ya'an produced several "gift pandas" in succession, becoming the largest international supplier of wild giant pandas.

In July of 2006, UNESCO's 30th World Heritage Congress unanimously decided to add the Sichuan giant panda habitats to the World Heritage List. The habitat of this rare "living fossil" is China's 32nd World Heritage Site.

This is a living museum, which houses a number of rare species in addition to the giant panda, including the golden snub-nosed monkey, lesser panda, snow leopard, and cow-horned antelope. It is one of the 25 biodiversity "hot spots" found in the world. The designation as a heritage site also implies benefits for other rare and endangered species that live in the giant panda habitats.

TIPS **Jiajin Mountain** Jiajin Mountain is called "Jiaji" in Tibetan language. Jiajin is a translation of Tibetan language, which means very high and steep.

开平碉楼与村落
Kaiping Diaolou and Villages

　　开平碉楼与村落是开平一种用于防卫的多层村落房屋建筑，展现了中西建筑艺术和装饰形式复杂而灿烂的融合。它们表现了19世纪末及20世纪初开平侨民在南亚、澳大拉西亚及北美国家发展进程中的重要作用。……开平碉楼与周围的乡村景观和谐共生，见证了明代以来以防匪为目的的当地建筑传统的最后繁荣。

世界遗产委员会评价

　　在中国南方省份广东，有一个叫开平的小城市。开着汽车穿越开平时，你会发现沿着公路两旁经常有一些碉堡式的建筑进入你的视线。这些千姿百态、富有欧陆风情的碉楼，或两三为伴倚在村庄旁边，或四五成群立在田野上，像一颗颗珍珠散落在开平市区的竹林中，

Kaiping Diaolou and Villages feature the Diaolou, multi-storeyed defensive village houses in Kaiping, which display a complex and flamboyant fusion of Chinese and Western structural and decorative forms. They reflect the significant role of *émigré* Kaiping people in the development of several countries in South Asia, Australasia and North America, during the late 19th and early 20th centuries. Retaining a harmonious relationship with the surrounding landscape, the Diaolou testify to the final flowering of local building traditions that started in the Ming Period in response to local banditry.

Kaiping is a small city located in the southern Chinese province of Guangdong. Driving through

Date of inscription: 2007
Heritage category: 文化遗产 C
Criteria: C(II)(III)(IV)

Kaiping, your eyesight will be caught by many blockhouse-style buildings on both sides of the road. Diverse in form and endowed with European style, these buildings scattered beside the villages or in the fields form a kind of magnificent scenery, like a string of shining pearls scattered in the city's bamboo groves. Since these buildings were combined with defensive features of military watchtowers, they became known as *diaolou* ("military watchtowers").

In contrast to traditional Chinese architecture, these buildings prominently feature Western architectural style; stoae (covered walkways or porticos) of ancient Greece as well as arches and arched roofs of ancient Rome, for instance, were commonly used. Architectural elements of different styles, schools and religions—such as the Gothic, Byzantine and Islamic styles of medieval Europe as well as the Baroque style of the Renaissance and 17th century—are harmoniously and flawlessly combined. As one walks through the charming and architecturally artistic corridor, it may be difficult to believe that this is just a common southern Chinese village.

Kaiping's *diaolou*s are highly diverse in form and appearance. Based on their functions, they can be divided into three types: communal towers, residential towers and watchtowers.

In general, the funds to build the earliest *diaolou* were raised by several families or by all the villagers. In the event of a disaster, people could move into the *diaolou* for temporary refuge; every family had a room in which to seek shelter. They stayed together, shared food and fought against the danger. These multi-storey buildings—of which 473 remain—are known as *zhonglou*s ("communal towers"). Simple in appearance and bearing minimal external ornamentation, these towers were built to be tall,

美轮美奂。这些与具有防御功能的碉堡相结合的楼，又被称为"碉楼"。

与传统的中国乡村建筑不同，这些碉楼具有浓郁的西洋建筑风格，古希腊的柱廊，古罗马的拱券和穹隆，欧洲中世纪的哥特式、拜占庭式、伊斯兰风格，文艺复兴时期和17世纪的巴洛克建筑，不同风格、不同流派、不同宗教的建筑元素，和谐而又完美地聚集在一起。穿行在这独具魅力的建筑艺术长廊中，很难想象，这里竟是中国南方的一个普通乡村。

开平碉楼千姿百态、形式多样。从使用功能看，分为众楼、居楼和更楼三大类。

最早的碉楼一般是多户人家或全村人集资修建的，遇有灾难时众人一起搬上碉楼，每户分一间屋，大家同吃同住共同抵御危险，这种楼被称做"众楼"。在开平现存的碉楼中，有473座众楼。众楼造型简单，外部装饰少，楼体高大坚固，楼层较多，封闭性强。

赤坎镇三门里村的迎龙楼，不仅是开平碉楼的嫡族，也是众楼中的老大。无论从功能还是从

样式上看，它都保留着碉楼最原始的面貌：厚重的墙体上开着小小的窗户，窗内装有铁栅栏和窗扇，外部有钢板做的窗门，大门也用厚钢板做成。一旦关上窗户和大门，碉楼就成了封闭的堡垒，即使枪炮也无法穿透。碉楼上部建有"燕子窝"，燕子窝是当地人对碉楼上防御工事的俗称。除了燕子窝，有的碉楼上部各层的墙壁上也开有射击孔，这样就增加了楼内的反击点。

几百年间，正是这一座座坚固的碉楼，使开平人免遭了无数次洪

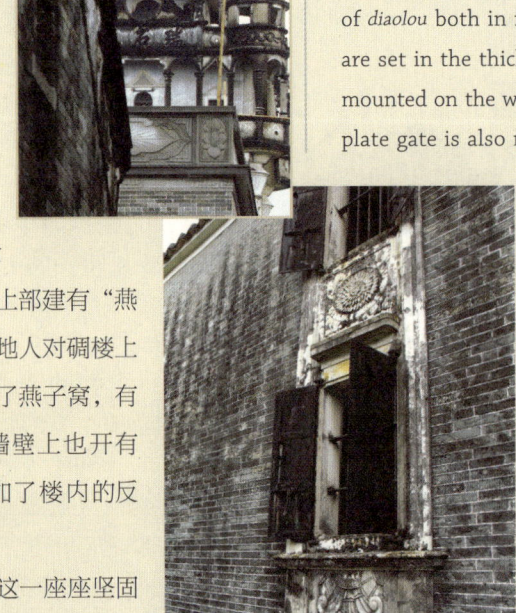

sturdy, multi-storeyed and well-enclosed.

Yinglong Tower is located in Sanmenli Village, Chikan Town. It is not only the earliest *diaolou* in Kaiping, but also the most dominant one among all the communal towers. It maintained the original features of *diaolou* both in function and style. Small windows are set in the thick walls; iron fences and sashes are mounted on the windows outside where a thick steel-plate gate is also mounted. As soon as the windows and the gate are closed, the *diaolou* becomes a sealed fortress that can even stop bullets from penetrating. "Swallow's nests", the local term for the towers' defensive fortifications, are built on the upper part of the *diaolou*. Besides the swallow's nests, shooting holes used for counterattack purposes are also cut on the walls of the upper storeys of some *diaolou*s.

For centuries, these solid *diaolou*s have successfully protected the Kaiping people from flooding and bandits' plundering, securing a prosperous and peaceful life for them.

The residential towers are the prettiest ones among the *diaolou*s. As implied by the name, residential towers demonstrate a fusion of residential and defensive use. Since they were mainly used as living quarters, the local people also referred

小贴士 **金山客** 远赴重洋的开平人创业的道路是艰辛的，最终衣锦还乡时，建起一座座中西合璧、风格迥异的碉楼，也带回了很多具有西方特色的室内陈设品。由于回乡的华侨大多家境富裕，所以被当地人称为"金山客"。

水的侵袭和盗寇的劫掠，守护了这里的富足与安宁。

开平碉楼中最美的是"居楼"。顾名思义，居楼就是用来居住的楼。居楼将防御与居住相结合，以居住为主，因此当地人

又称它们为"庐"，也有人干脆就叫"别墅"。在开平现存的碉楼中，居楼多达1,149座。这些楼一般是富有人家独资修建的，最大的特点是多姿多彩的造型和美轮美奂的装饰。走进碉楼，浓浓的中国传统文化之风迎面扑来：窗框门楣上雕着传统的吉祥图案，格栅上雕有中国字的条幅，既表达了楼主人对幸福生活的向往，也显示了他们与国际潮流和时代气息并存的文化品味。

号称"开平第一楼"的瑞石楼，建于1923年，是开平最高的碉楼。楼高九层，占地92平方米，人们坐车从公路经过，老远就可以看到它在

to them as cottages or villas. Among all the existing *diaolous* in Kaiping, there are 1,149 surviving residential towers. They were usually built by individual rich families, with their own funds, and are characterized by their diverse forms and beautiful ornamentation. The rich traditional Chinese decorations will catch your attention when you enter: traditional auspicious patterns are carved on window lintels while scrolls of Chinese calligraphy are carved on the fences, expressing the owner's wishes for a happy life and also showcasing the cultural taste of the coexistence of traditional culture with international trends and characteristics of the times.

Ruishi Tower, the highest *diaolou* in Kaiping, is claimed as the "No. 1 Tower of Kaiping." Constructed in 1923, it has nine floors and covers an area of 92 square meters. Driving by in a car or bus, passengers can witness the majestic appearance of the Ruishi Tower through the bamboo groves and woods from far away. This tower represents a perfect fusion of Chinese and Western architectural styles, and dominates the other *diaolou* not only in height but also in appearance.

Diaolou symbolized the wealth and glory of the Kaiping people but, at the same time, also brought them danger. In the early 20th century, bandit activity was rampant in Kaiping. In order to safeguard their homeland, the Kaiping people made improvements to the *diaolou*. The *genglou* ("watchtower") first appeared at this time. In contrast to the communal towers and residential towers, these watchtowers mainly served the purpose of detecting floods or bandits and were also used to sound alarms. These functions are similar to those of the Great Wall's beacon towers.

TIPS

Men from the Gold Mountain Those Kaiping folks who went abroad for a better life had experienced a hard time. When they returned to their hometown, they not only built the *diaolous* that combined Chinese and Western architectural styles, but also brought back with them furnishings of Western feature. As most of the returned overseas Chinese were very wealthy, the local people addressed them "Men from the Gold Mountain".

竹丛树林背景的衬托下高高耸立的雄姿。该楼是中西建筑风格完好结合的典型，它不仅高度上是第一，外观上也是别的碉楼难以相比的。

碉楼显示了开平人的富有和荣耀，同时也给他们带来了危险。20世纪初，开平土匪活动猖獗，开平人为了保卫家园，在碉楼的建造上又有创新，"更楼"就是这一时期出现的。更楼与众楼和居楼不同，主要用来瞭望和报警，功能与长城上的烽火台相似。

更楼一般建在村口或山外的山岗河岸，高耸挺立、视野开阔，更楼上配有探照灯和报警器，一旦发现敌情拉响报警器，周边各村都能听到。

由于更楼出现时间晚，在碉楼中所占比例不大，现仅存221座，其中坐落于塘口镇自力村

The watchtowers were mostly built in dominant positions with broad vision, either at the entrance of the village or on the hill or beside the river outside the village. They were equipped with searchlights or alarms. In case of enemy's attack, alarms could be heard by people in the surrounding villages.

Because they were not developed until relatively late, the watchtowers comprise a small proportion of the *diaolous*; only 221 remain today. Among them, the Fangshi light touer on the slope of south Zili Village in Tangkou Town is the most classic example.

Today, Fangshi light tower still stands silently under brilliant sunset glow. It is as if they were still safeguarding the *diaolous*—even if their original functions of defense, residence and warning have been lost—as well as the culture and civilization of the *diaolou*.

The marvelous and diversified architectural styles

小贴士 |《开平县志》这样记述："开平人富于冒险性质，五洲各地均有邑人足迹"。这大概可以解释碉楼的异域风情了。

南面山坡上的方氏灯楼是典范之作。

如今，方氏灯楼仍默默站立在灿烂的晚霞中，似乎还在守护着这些已经失去防御、居住和预警功能的碉楼，守护着碉楼中的文化与文明。

开平碉楼的建筑风格和装饰艺术千姿百态，让人叹为观止。它是洋为中用、中西合璧的典范。有人尊之为万国建筑的博览园。夕阳西下，远处不知名的碉楼在夕阳的掩映下显现出神秘的肃穆。

2007年6月，联合国教科文组织第31届世界遗产大会上，开平碉楼与村落顺利通过审议，成为中国第35处世界遗产。

开平，一个将时间和空间浓缩的地方，让每一个走近她的人心中都充满好奇。

and decorative arts of the Kaiping towers are classic examples of applying foreign concepts to serve China and blending Chinese and Western architectural styles. Some people refer to these towers as an exposition park of multinational architecture. As the sun sets, a group of unknown *diaolous* stand in mysterious solemnity under the sun's shadow.

In June 2007, the application for World Heritage Site of the Kaiping Diaolou and Villages was approved at the 31st session of the UNESCO World Heritage Committee, making it the 35th Chinese site inscribed on the World Heritage List.

Kaiping, a place that condenses time and space, brings curiosity to each who comes close to it.

TIPS | According to the *Annals of Kaiping County*, there were footprints of Kaiping people all over the world because they were adventurous and brave. This might explain why these *diaolous* in Kaiping exhibit exotic flavor.

中国南方喀斯特
South China Karst

中国南方喀斯特地貌绵延地表50万平方公里，大部分位于云南、贵州和广西境内。代表了世界上湿润热带到亚热带喀斯特景观最壮观的范例。石林县的石林、荔波的锥状喀斯特和武隆的塔状喀斯特被誉为自然奇观，是世界喀斯特地貌的典型代表。武隆喀斯特入选《名录》是因其巨大的石灰坑、天然桥梁和天然洞穴。

世界遗产委员会评价

The South China Karst region extends over a surface of half a million kilometers lying mainly in Yunnan, Guizhou and Guangxi provinces. It represents one of the world's most spectacular examples of humid tropical to subtropical karst landscapes. The stone forests of Shilin County, the cone and tower karsts of Shilin Libo and Wulong Karst are considered the world reference site for these types of karst, forming a distinctive and beautiful landscape and Wulong karst has been inscribed for its giant dolines (sinkholes), natural bridges and caves.

喀斯特是一种岩溶地貌，是发育在以石灰岩和白云岩为主的碳酸盐岩上的。喀斯特地貌在世界上集中分布于地中海沿岸、拉丁美洲和东亚地区，在中国主要分布在华南和西南地区。

2007年，中国南方喀斯特被联合国教科文组织列入《世界自然遗产名录》，主要包括云南石林、贵州荔波

Karst is a type of landform that evolves from carbonate rocks which mainly consist of limestone and dolomite. The world's karst landscapes are centrally distributed along the Mediterranean coast, in Latin America and in East Asia. In China, they are primarily scattered in the southern and southwestern regions.

In 2007, the South China Karst was inscribed on UNESCO's World Heritage List, mainly comprising of three karst landforms at Shilin of Yunnan, Libo of Guizhou and Wulong of Chongqing. This region

小贴士 喀斯特 可溶性岩石特别是碳酸盐类岩石（如石灰岩）受含有二氧化碳的流水溶蚀，并加上沉积作用而形成的地貌。形状奇特，有洞穴也有峭壁。由亚得里亚海岸的喀斯特（Krast）高地而得名。

收录时间 Date of inscription：2007
遗产类别 Heritage category：自然遗产 N
收录理由 Criteria：N(II)(III)

和重庆武隆三种喀斯特地貌。这一区域东西长约1,380公里，南北宽约1,010公里，覆盖面积超过50万平方公里，是中国最具代表性的喀斯特地形地貌，也是世界上湿润热带和亚热带喀斯特景观最壮观的范例。据推测，这些喀斯特地貌形成于距今50万年至3亿年间。

云南石林是世界上唯一一处位于亚热带高原地区的喀斯特石林，面积达400平方公里，被誉为"最好的自然现象和世界上该类喀斯特的最好参照"。在晚古生代，这片区域曾是一片浅海，沉积了上千米的石灰岩和白云岩。之后，这片区域随着地壳的运动逐渐抬升为陆地。到了间冰期，这里有相当长的时间都处在热带气候条件之下，丰沛的雨水和地表河流反复溶蚀着松软

is about 1,380 kilometers long from east to west and around 1,010 kilometers wide from north to south, covering an area of over half a million square kilometers. It is the most representative of China's karst landforms, and also the world's most spectacular example of humid tropical and subtropical karst landscapes. It is estimated that these karst landforms had taken shape about half a million to 300 million years ago.

Shilin of Yunnan is the world's only karst stone forest located in the subtropical plateau region, with an area reaching 400 square kilometers and a reputation of the "best natural phenomena and the world's reference site for this type of karst." In the late Paleozoic Era, this region used to be a shallow sea with over 1,000 meters of limestone and dolomite sediment. Later, due to the movement of the earth, this region was gradually uplifted as dry land. During the interglacial period, it was under tropical climate conditions for a long time, and abundant rain and river would repeatedly dissolve and erode the soft limestone and dolomite. Water would flow through the crevices to permeate the rocks, and

TIPS **Karst** Karst is a special type of landscape which is largely shaped by the dissolving action of water on the carbonate bedrock, especially limestone. Karst takes various formations such as caves and cliffs etc. It gets the name from the Karst Plateau on the coastal area of Adriatic Sea.

小贴士 **地质年代** 地质学家和古生物学家根据地层自然形成的先后顺序，将地层分为5代，即早期的太古代和元古代，以后的古生代、中生代和新生代。这5代又可细分为12纪。

的石灰岩和白云岩。水流顺着裂缝渗透到岩石当中，待其溶解后，连同地表其他物质一起带走，剩下没有被溶解的石灰岩和白云岩，便快速发育成喀斯特地貌。在不同的地质、气候和水纹条件下，多起石林相继发展，相互叠置，最终形成类型多样、层次分明的石林景观。剑状、蘑菇状和塔状，各种各样发育完美的喀斯特应有尽有，几乎世界上最典型的石林喀斯特形态在这里都可以找到，堪称"石林喀斯特地貌博物馆"。

荔波位于贵州省东南部。这里是世界上锥状喀斯特地形中发育演化过程最完整、保存相关遗迹最丰富、集中连片分布面积最大的地区。荔波喀斯特的山、水、岭、洞、瀑、石融

after dissolution, would take away other substances with it, leaving the limestone and dolomite that were not dissolved to be developed quickly into karst landscapes. Under different geologic, climatic and waterline conditions, many stone forests were formed in succession, overlaying each other, and eventually forming diverse types and heights of stone forest sceneries. Shapes of swords, mushrooms, towers, and many other varieties of karsts were perfectly formed. Almost all of the world's most typical karst landforms can be found in this region, making it worthy of the acclaim as the "Museum of Stone Forest Karsts."

Libo is situated in the southeast of Guizhou Province. This area has the world's most complete cone karst landforms, and the richest related relics' preservation, that focus on the connection of distribution to the largest area. The mountains, water, ranges, caves, waterfalls, and rocks of the Libo karsts are integrated into a magical and beautiful landscape which has the reputation of being the "emerald on the earth's belt". This is a part of the humid subtropical monsoon climate, with lush trees in the region and streams flowing effortlessly. The Forest in the Water

小贴士 **间冰期** 冰期是地质历史上出现大规模冰川的时期；间冰期是两次冰期之间气候变暖的时期。冰期时，冰川大规模扩张或前进；间冰期时，气候温暖，雪线上升，冰川消融退缩。在整个地球历史中，大部分时间（占90％以上年代）为间冰期的温暖气候，而寒冷的冰期气候只是短暂的。

> **TIPS** **Geological Era** The geologists and paleontologists classify the strata of the earth into 5 eras according to stratigraphic sequence. The 5 eras refer to Archaeozoic Era, Proterozoic Era, Paleozoic Era, Mesozoic Period and Cenozoic Era. The 5 eras are further divided into 12 periods.

为一体，地貌神奇秀美，被誉为"地球腰带上的一颗绿宝石"。这里属于中亚热带季风湿润气候，区内树木茂盛、溪流纵横。水上森林是荔波的著名景观：一株株珍奇的树木，透过水中顽石，扎根于水底的河床，呈现出极为罕见的岩溶地貌的水上森林景观。除了水上森林，荔波还有拉雅瀑布、68级瀑布、鸳鸯湖和被专家认为大自然神力所塑造的东方凯旋门——天生桥。

重庆武隆县地处四川盆地东南边缘、长江右岸支流乌江下游峡谷区。这里的喀斯特是中国深切型峡谷的重要代表，是反应地球演化历史的杰出范例。由于不同岩性的碳酸盐岩与砂页岩交叉分布，从而孕育出独具特色的喀斯特地貌，最著名的有芙蓉洞芙蓉江、天生三桥和后坪天坑。这些喀斯特景观是新近纪以来在长江三峡地区地壳大幅抬升的机制下发育形成的。芙蓉洞发育于寒武纪和奥陶纪碳酸盐岩中。洞内自生物理化学沉积物极为丰富，溶石形态多种多样，既有为数众多的纵

is a famous Libo landscape that has been created by precious trees being rooted in stubborn rocks at the bottom of the riverbed, resulting in the emergence of a very rare karst landform. In addition to the Forest in the Water landscape, Libo also has Laya Waterfall, 68-Step Waterfall, Yuanyang Lake and what experts believe could only be portrayed by the powerful gods of Nature, the "Eastern Arc de Triomphe"—*Tianshengqiao*.

The Wulong County of Chongqing is located at the southeast edge of the Sichuan Basin, at the gorge area of the Wujiang downriver which is a tributary on the right bank of the Yangtze River. These karsts are important representatives of deep-cut gorges in China, as well as outstanding models of the Earth's response to the history of evolution. The cross distribution of different lithology of carbonate and sand rocks have developed these unique karst landforms, the most famous being Furong Cave and Furong River, *Tianshengsanqiao* (Three Natural Bridges) and *Houping* Natural Pit. Since the Neogene Period, the karsts' formation was a result of the substantial uplift in the earth's crust around the area of the Three Gorges at the Yangtze River. Furongdong (Furong Cave) was formed in the carbonate rocks of the Cambrian-Ordovician Period. Inside the Cave, there are abundant biological and chemical sediments, diverse forms of melted rock, numerous vertical and grand horizontal caverns, spectacular ruins, as well as sharp stalactites and secluded ponds. This contributes to Furongdong being reputed as the "World's Number One Cave". Wulong's Three Natural Bridges are the world's largest cluster of natural bridges, distributed in a carbonate

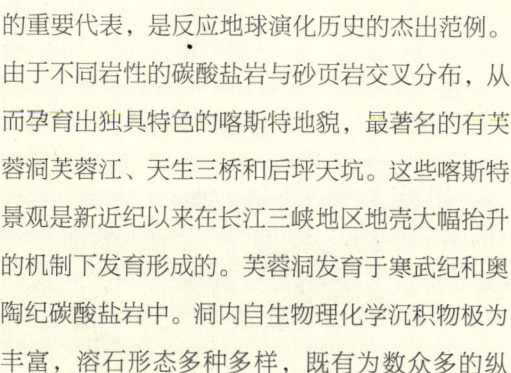

> **TIPS** **The Interglacial Period** A glacial period is an interval of time within which massive glaciers are formed. It is marked by glacier expansion and movement. An interglacial period, on the other hand, is a period of warmer climate between two glacial periods, when the snow line rises and the glacier melts away. Throughout the history of the earth, 90% of the time is in mild and warm climate of interglacials, and the cold climate in the glacial periods is just temporary.

向洞穴，也有规模宏大的横向洞穴；既有壮观的崩塌堆积，还有凌厉的钟乳石、幽密的洞内池塘，因而芙蓉洞有"天下第一洞"的美称。武隆天生桥是世界上规模最大的串珠式天生桥群，分布在十公里长的碳酸盐岩河段内。最著名的喀斯特天生桥有三座——天龙桥、青龙桥和黑龙桥，处于它们中间的是一处巨大的天坑，这种组合世上罕见。天龙桥有南北两个穿洞，形状酷似人工桥梁。每当雨后，青龙桥便有飞瀑自桥面倾泻而下，状如青龙。黑龙桥拱洞幽深，仿佛有一条黑龙在其间蜿蜒。三座天生桥的总高度、桥拱高度和桥面厚度都居于世界首位。

中国南方喀斯特地貌千姿百态，不饰雕琢，神奇俊美，仿佛大自然用其神来之笔所绘制的一幅幅长卷，令人叹为观止。

rocks river section with ten kilometers long. The three most famous natural bridge karsts are Tianlong Bridge, Qinglong Bridge and Heilong Bridge, and in their midst is a huge *tiankeng* (collapsed doline) which is a rare combination in the world. Tianlong Bridge has two *chuandong* from north to south, strongly resembling the shape of a man-made bridge. After every rainfall, Qinglong Bridge would have a "flying" waterfall pouring down over its bridge deck, similar to a robust *qinglong* (green dragon). With a deep and long arch passage at Heilong Bridge, it appears as though a black dragon is winding in its midst. The Three Natural Bridges' total height, deck height and the thickness of the bridge's surface rank first place in the world.

The South China Karst landscapes are diverse and multifaceted. Without the need for adornment, they are magnificent and beautiful, as if nature has used its supernatural pen to draw on a long scroll, leaving everyone in wonderment.

福建土楼
Fujian Tulou

收录时间 Date of inscription：2008
遗产类别 Heritage category：文化遗产 C
收录理由 Criteria：C(Ⅲ)(Ⅳ)(Ⅴ)

　　福建土楼位于福建省西南部内陆地区，由12至20世纪建造的46座房屋组成。这些土楼矗立在稻田、茶园、烟田中，由泥土搭建而成，呈环形或方形格局，有几层楼高，最多可住800人。为了达到居住和防御目的，土楼围绕一个居于中心的开放式庭院而建，只有几扇朝外的窗户和一个入口。福建土楼是将传统建筑和功能融为一体的成功典范，它以实例展示了一种特殊的群体生活和防御组织。从人与自然和谐相处的角度来看，福建土楼也是人类居住地的杰出典范。

世界遗产委员会评价

　　福建土楼主要分布在闽西南的永定、南靖一带。大多数为福建客家人所建，因此又称"客家土楼"。福建土楼历史悠久、风格奇特、构筑巧妙、规模宏大，被誉为世界民居建筑奇观。2008年7月，联合国教科文组织世界遗产委员会第32届会议通过福建土楼为世界文化遗产。

　　福建土楼产生于宋元时期，至明末、清代和民国时期逐渐成熟，并一直延续至今。客家人之所以建造土楼，聚族而居，主要是源于对中原文化的认同，土楼表现出来的向心性、匀称性和前低后高的特点，正是儒家文化的一个缩影。

　　土楼依山就势，布局合理，巧妙地利用了山间狭小的平地和当地的生土、木材、鹅卵石等建

Fujian Tulou is a property of 46 houses built between the 12th and 20th centuries over 120 kilometers in southwest of Fujian province, inland from the Taiwan Strait. Set amongst rice, tea and tobacco fields the tulou are earthen houses. Several storeys high, they are built along an inward-looking, circular or square floor plan as housing for up to 800 people each. They were built for defence purposes around a central open courtyard with few windows to the outside and only one entrance. They are inscribed as exceptional examples of a building tradition and function exemplifying a particular type of communal living and defensive organization, and, in terms of their harmonious relationship with their environment, an outstanding example of human settlement.

　　Fujian *tulous* are scattered mostly in Yongding and Nanjing counties of southeastern Fujian. Since most of them were built by the Fujian's Hakka people in Fujian, they are also known as the Hakka *tulous*. Reputed for their long history, unusual style, exquisite configuration and large scale, the Fujian *tulous* are regarded as a wonder of residential architecture. In July 2008, at the 32nd session of the UNESCO World Heritage Committee, Fujian *tulous* were inscribed to the World Heritage List.

　　Fujian *tulous* first appeared in the Song and Yuan dynasties (960–1368 AD) and reached their maturity by the time of the Ming-Qing dynasties (1368-1912 AD)

小贴士 | 五凤 原为五方配五色所引申的五行意义，以五凤命名宅院，表示四方与中央相应的寓意。

筑材料，不仅能满足聚族而居、安全防卫的要求，还具有防风抗震、冬暖夏凉等良好性能。土楼的造型多彩多姿，品类繁多，其中以圆楼、方楼、五凤楼最为常见。

五凤楼，由中原四合院式民居衍变而来，在土楼中历史最为悠久。最具代表性的五凤楼有永定的"大夫第"、湖坑的"福裕楼"等。五凤楼保持了突出中轴线，规整、内向的传统布局，讲究左右均衡对称，前后高低有序，体现出土楼与中原文化千丝万缕的联系。五凤楼重装饰艺术，画栋雕梁，十分精美，是土楼中最豪华的一种，其色彩造型之美，广受专家称道。

and that of the Republic of China (1912-1949 AD). Even today, they are still in use. The main reason that the Hakka people constructed these large rammed-earth buildings, in which they lived communally, was their appreciation of the Zhongyuan culture—the culture of China's Central Plains. Confucian culture is also reflected in several features of Fujian *tulous*, including the symmetrical design, centripetal orientation, and the fact that the rear part is higher than the front.

The *tulous* were built in accordance with the run of the mountain range and each one's layout cleverly took advantage of the narrow ground of the hill as well as that of local building materials, such as raw soil, wood and cobbles. As a result, the tulou not only provided a shelter in which the Hakka people could live together and defend themselves against enemies, but also a place where people could escape from earthquakes and fierce winds. The *tulous* tend to be warm in winter and cool in summer. They feature a variety of shapes, among which the most common ones include the *yuanlou* ("round building"), *fanglou* ("square building") and *wufenglou* ("five-phoenix building").

The wufenglou evolved from the siheyuan, a type of civilian housing popular in the Central Plains. Of the different varieties of *tulous*, the wufenglou has the longest history. It is exemplified by Dafudi in Yongding and Fuyulou in Hukeng. Several features of the wufenglou—the emphasized central axis, the regular and introverted traditional layout, the symmetry of the well-proportioned left and right sides and the well-ordered arrangement of the front and rear sections—demonstrate the tulou's innumerable ties to the culture of the Central Plains. As the most luxurious style of the tulou, the wufenglou was heavily ornamented. Its painted pillars and carved beams, as well as its beautiful colors and shape, have been widely acclaimed by experts.

小贴士 | 客家 从两宋开始，中原汉民大举南迁，经赣南、闽西到达梅州，最终形成相对成熟的、具有很强稳定性的客家民系。

TIPS **Wufeng** Matching five colors to the five directions was originally based on the ideology of Five Elements. Using Wufenglou to name the courtyard is to indicate the implication of the four directions and the center.

方楼由五凤楼衍变而来,加强了防卫性,建筑结构趋于简单,因而成了客家人广泛采用的住宅。

环形圆柱状的圆楼是福建土楼中最有代表性的一种,圆楼外观庞大巍峨,直径50~70米者比比皆是。有人形象地将其喻为"地下冒出的蘑菇,天上降下的飞碟"。

土楼一层基本不开窗,二层以上只开少量的小窗,可有效防御盗匪。虽然土楼对外极为封闭,内部却别有洞天:所有的房间通过连廊向内敞开,形成一个富有人情味的"中庭"。在建筑功能分布上,通常一层为厨房和餐厅,二层用于储物和存放粮食,三层以上为卧室。

每一座土楼都有一个名字,大都取自族谱里的祖训。号称"土楼之王"的承启楼,建于明末清初,规模巨大,充满着浓郁的乡土气息。全楼3圈4层,直径达73米,共400个房间,曾住过80户600余人。土楼墙壁下厚上薄,底层墙厚1米以上,越往高越窄,顶层仅约0.8米。与方楼相比,

The fanglou, which evolved from the wufenglou, boasted better defensive capabilitys and a simpler architectural design than its predecessor. It thus became widely adopted by the Hakka people.

The most representative of the Fujian tulou is the ring-shaped round building, yuanlou. The yuanlou with a diameter of 50-70 meters is the most prevalent. With its colossal and towering appearance, the yuanlou has been likened to a "mushroom rising from the ground" and a "UFO fallen from the sky".

For the purpose of effectively guarding against bandits, the windows on the first floor of the tulou are usually closed, while the small windows on the second and higher floors are left slightly open. Although the tulou is enclosed, it offers paradise inside. Every room opens to the adjoining corridor to form a friendly "middle courtyard." In terms of architectural functions, the rooms on the first floor are usually used as the kitchens and dining halls, those on the second as the store rooms, and those on the third and higher floors as the bedrooms.

Each tulou has a name, which is typically based on the ancestral precepts from the family record. Chengqilou ("Linkage Building"), built during the late-Ming to early-Qing dynasties and acclaimed as the "King of the Tulou", is large in scale and imbued with the local flavor. The building has four floors in three circles. With a diameter of 73 meters, it contains 400 rooms and can provide shelter for 80 families, or over 600 people. With the lower part being much thicker than the upper part, the bottom wall of the tulou is more than one meter thick and narrows to 0.8 meter on the

TIPS **Hakka people** Starting from Northern and Southern Song Dynasties (960-1279), Han people in the Central Plains began to relocate southward. After going through south of Jiangxi and west of Fujian, they arrived at Meizhou and finally formed a relatively mature and stable group—Hakka people.

圆楼取消了角间，构件尺寸统一，施工相对简单。其房间朝向好坏差别不明显，有利于宗族内部的分配。因为无角间，对大木料的需求相应减少，抗风抗震防火的性能更高。永定历史上发生过七次强烈地震，却从未发生过土楼坍塌事故。建于公元1693年的"环极楼"，300年来经历了数次地震，1918年经历7级大地震后，仅在外墙裂开一条50厘米宽的裂缝，后来这条裂缝又神奇地慢慢合拢，只留下一条细长的裂痕。

top. In contrast to the fanglou, the yuanlou contains no corner rooms, is uniform in the size of its components, and utilizes simpler construction. The distribution of the rooms in the yuanlou among the families was facilitated by inconspicuousness of difference in the favorableness of each room's orientation. With no corner rooms, the yuanlou does not require much large wood to construct, and can withstand better against earthquakes and strong winds. Despite the fact that Yongding has been the site of seven major earthquakes during its history, not a single tulou has ever caved in. Huanjilou, built in 1693, has endured several

小贴士　八卦　中国古代的一套有象征意义的符号。用"—"代表阳，用"--"代表阴，用三个这样的符号，组成八种形式，叫做八卦。每一卦形代表一定的事物。

土楼多按八卦设计，其中最为典型的当属振成楼。振成楼建于1912年，占地5,000平方米，分内外两圈，形成楼中有楼，楼外有楼的格局。外楼圈4层，每层48间，每卦6间，卦与卦之间是隔火墙，一卦失火，不会殃及全楼。内楼中间的祖堂很像一个舞台，舞台两侧上下两层30间房圈成一个内圈。楼内大厅及门楣上有永久性楹联及题词20余幅，充分展示了土楼丰富的文化内涵。

earthquakes over its 300-plus year existence. In 1918, following an earthquake measuring 7.0 on the Richter scale, the only damage that Huanjilou sustained was a 50-centimeter-wide crevice on its surface. As if by magic, the crevice gradually healed over time and became a narrow rift.

Most *tulous* were designed in accordance with the Bagua (often referred to as the "Eight Trigrams"), among which the most typical is Zhenchenglou.

田螺坑土楼群是所有福建土楼中形体组合最壮观的土楼群。居高俯瞰，田螺坑土楼群由1座方楼、3座圆楼和1座椭圆形楼组成，方楼居于中央，其余4座环绕周围，依山势错落布局，宛如一朵盛开的梅花点缀大地。站在山脚仰视，它又像一座雄居山腰的巨型宫殿，傲视人间。

而离田螺坑土楼群不远的"东倒西歪"

Built in 1912, Zhenchenglou covers 5,000 square meters and is divided into two circles, so that the outer building embraces the inner one. The four-level outer building contains six rooms in each gua, and 48 rooms in each level. Fire walls were set up between each gua, to prevent the whole building from being damaged or destroyed if any one gua caught fire. The ancestral hall, located in the middle of the inner

TIPS Bagua (often refers to as the "Eight Trigrams") It is a set of symbols used in ancient China. "—" is used to represent *yang* and "— —" is used to represent *yin*. Eight images formed by different combinations of the three symbols are called Bagua, each of which represents a certain thing.

楼——裕昌楼则是目前历史最为悠久的土楼。裕昌楼建于1308年，楼内回廊的木柱最大倾斜度达到15度，但历经700年有惊无险，依然如故，因而被誉为东方的"比萨斜塔"。

土楼在建筑上的神奇令人叹为观止，但更令人称奇的是这些历尽沧桑的土楼至今仍是当地客家人主要的生活居住地。一座土楼既是一座艺术的殿堂，也是一部活着的历史。

building, resembles a stage. Thirty rooms on the two levels on both sides of the stage form an inner circle. The never-changing couplets and over 20 inscriptions on the lintels of the hall and doors as well as on the pillars fully demonstrate the rich cultural connotations of the tulou.

The Tianluokeng tulou complex displays the most magnificent form of all the Fujian tulou. From a bird's eye view, it is revealed that the complex consists of one fanglou, three *yuanlou*s and one tuoyuanxinglou ("elliptical building") with the fanglou in the center surrounded by the other four. Conforming to the mountain's contours, the distribution of the buildings of the Tianluokeng tulou complex takes on the appearance of a plum blossom. Looking up from the foot of the mountain, it also resembles a giant palace, poising majestically on the mountainside and overlooking the world.

Not far from the Tianluokeng tulou complex lies Yuchanglou, which was built in 1308 AD and is the oldest tulou still in existence. Although the winding corridor's wooden pillars tilt at an angle of up to 15 degrees, Yuchanglou still has remained its old self since its construction 700 years ago and, not surprisingly, has earned the title of "Leaning Tower of the East".

The architectural achievement of Fujian tulou is certain to leave every visitor with a sense of wonder and awe. Even more amazing, however, is the fact that, to this day, it remains a primary form of residence for the Hakka people, even after having experienced so many vicissitudes of life. In this respect, Fujian tulou represents not only a magnificent palace of art, but also a living history as well.

收录时间 Date of inscription：2008
遗产类别 Heritage category：自然 N
收录理由 Criteria：N(Ⅲ)

三清山
Mount Sanqingshanshan National Park

这里有48座花岗岩山峰和89座花岗岩石柱，其中很多山峰和石柱形似人或动物的侧面轮廓。一排排并列的花岗岩上长有多种植被，特殊的气象条件为云朵染上了明亮的晕圈，也让彩虹看起来宛若白色，造成了变幻莫测、引人入胜的景观，为这座1,817米高的怀玉山增添了秀色。

世界遗产委员会评价

三清山位于江西上饶东北部，自古就有"天下无双福地"、"江南第一仙峰"之称。因山上玉京、玉虚、玉华三座山峰高耸入云，好似道教所尊的玉清、上清、太清三神并肩端坐其巅，三

48 granite peaks and 89 granite pillars, many of which resemble human or animal silhouettes. The natural beauty of the 1,817 meters high Mount Huaiyu is further enhanced by the juxtaposition of granite features with the vegetation and particular meteorological conditions which make for an ever-changing and arresting landscape with bright halos on clouds and white rainbows.

Located in the northeastern part of Jiangxi's Shangrao County, Mount Sanqingshan has been reputed since ancient times as a "fairyland under heaven" and the "best peak of Jiangnan inhabited

清山因而得名。主峰玉京峰海拔1,819.9米，雄踞于怀玉山脉群峰之上。

三清山地处扬子板块与华夏板块的结合带，经历了14亿年的地质演变，形成了举世无双的花岗岩峰林地貌，也因此形成了今日的奇伟景观——并称自然四绝的"奇峰怪石、古树名花、流泉飞瀑、云海雾涛"。

这里的花岗岩裂隙和节理发育最为齐全，是花岗岩节理的地质博物馆，中国和美国地质学家一致认为三清山是"西太平洋边缘最美丽的花岗岩"。

据考察，三清山有奇峰48座，怪石89处，景物、景观300来处。群山姿态万千，妙趣横

by immortals". Mount Sanqingshan gets this name because its three peaks, Yujing, Yuxi and Yuhua, reach to the clouds, as if the three highest deities of Taoism (the Jade Pure One, the Supreme Pure One, and the Grand Pure One) were seated together on the summit. The main peak, Yujing, rises 1,819.9 meters above sea level and majestically towers above the peaks of the Huaiyu mountain range.

Mount Sanqingshan is located at the junction of the Yangzi Plate and Huaxia Plate. 1.4 billion years of geological evolution led to the formation of Mount Sanqingshan's unique granite rock formation and landscape, as well as today's four marvelous natural attractions, "strange peaks and exotic rocks," "ancient trees and famous flowers", "torrential springs and waterfalls," and "seas of clouds and waves of fog".

With the best-developed granite crevices and joints, Mount Sanqingshan is acclaimed as a "geological museum of granite" and is considered by Chinese and American geologists alike to be the "most beautiful granite along the edge of the West Pacific".

According to some studies, Mount Sanqingshan contains 48 strange peaks, 89 exotic rocks and over 300 scenic spots and landscapes. Diverse in form and full of marvels, the mountain features a "perilous" east peak, "exotic" west peak, "beautiful" north peak,

小贴士 观音听琵琶 由三座高耸云霄的山峰组成，惟妙惟肖。第一个山峰，活像一把琵琶，第二个山峰，状如削发和尚，怀抱琵琶在弹奏。第三个山峰，就如一尊南海观音，高坐云霄，倾听和尚弹琵琶。

生，具有东险西奇、北秀南绝、中峰巍峨的特点，峰林地貌类型齐全，典型而完美，既集结了名山大川的精华，又展现了别具一格的风采，堪称天下峰林的橱窗，《中国国家地理》杂志推选其为"中国最美的五大峰林"之一。

在所有这些奇峰石景中，更有景中"三绝"。它们是"神女峰"、"观音听琵琶"和"巨蟒出山"。最绝的当属"神女峰"——司春女神。此峰高约80米，像一位年轻而温和的少女端坐云间，体态轻盈，秀发披肩，若有所思。与司春女神相峙而立的"巨蟒出山"，为一高达128米的瘦奇石峰，如擎天玉柱昂首屹立，耸入云

"wondrous" south peak and "towering" middle peak. The flawless and full-ranging styles of the physical contours of Mount Sanqingshan reveals the essence of various mountains and displays the unique charm of Mount Sanqingshan. For this reason, it is considered a showcase of peaks and rocks, and was selected as "one of China's five most beautiful peak landscapes" by Chinese National Geography magazine.

Among all of the fantastically shaped peaks and rocks, there are three exceptional scenic spots, Shennü Peak (literally "Goddess Peak" (also known as the "Sichun Goddess"), Guanyin Ting Pipa ("Guanyin listening to the pipa"), and Jumang Chushan ("the Gigantic Python Coming Out of the Mountain"). The best of all is Shennü Peak. With a height of about 80 meters, this peak resembles a young and gentle girl with a little and graceful bearing, perched on the clouds and deep in thought with her beautiful hair hanging down to the shoulders. Jumang Chushan, which faces Peak Shennü, is a thin and exotic towering peak measuring 128 meters in height. It pierces into the clouds with its head raising up like a jade pillar. The summit of the peak is as thick as a python's head, while the middle of the peak is as slim as a snake's waist. Among the clouds and the mists, the peak looks like a python shaking its head, swirling its body, puffing out clouds, and shaking heaven and earth.

Mount Sanqingshan also features a large number of fantastically shaped ancient pines and rare plants. The pine trees on the mountain have various shapes and postures. Some are in a standing position, while others are hanging; some lying, while others suspended; and some are clustered together, while others stand alone. Each pine tree is like a natural bonsai, unfolding a picture scroll of Mother Nature.

TIPS | Guanyin Ting Pipa It consists of three peaks reaching to the clouds. The first peak looks like a pipa and the second resembles a bald monk who is playing the pipa. The third one looks like a Guanyin Bodhisattva who is sitting on the cloud and listening to the monk playing the pipa.

端，峰端略粗形似蟒头，峰腰纤细犹如蛇身。云罩雾绕之时，如蟒头窜动，蛇身微摇，吞云吐雾，撼天动地。

三清山自然景观的另一特色是山上有许多形状奇特的古松和珍稀植物。千姿百态的三清松，或站或挂，或卧或悬，或成群结伴，或独领风骚。每一棵松树都宛如天然的艺术盆景，抒写着大自然的优美画卷。无论在悬崖峭壁，还是峰尖石隙，苍松破石而出，凌空而长，生机勃勃，赋予奇峰异石以生命之美，从而构成了许多绝妙的画面。清风送过，动静合一的松的倩影，伴随着松涛阵阵，沁人心脾，醉人于山谷之间。

不仅古松有灵性之美，三清山上众多的奇花异卉和珍稀植物也为人世罕见。华东黄杉、华东铁杉、福建白玉兰、香果树、高山黄杨、木莲等均为中国国家一类保护树种。

三清山共分为七个景区，其中南部景区的南清园集中展示了14亿年地质演化形成的花岗岩峰林地貌特征，为三清山自然景观的精华。拾级登山，一路上满目都是苍松翠柏和飞瀑流泉，使人心旷神怡。

Whether they grow out of the cliffs, peaks or crevices, all the lush pines on the mountain break through the soil and tower into the skies, endowing the bizarre peaks and marvelous rocks with the beauty of life, and providing a veritable feast for the eyes. When the cool breeze blows, the serene silhouettes of the pines sway back and forth, lending a refreshing enchantment to the mountain and valley.

In addition to the intelligent beauty of the ancient pines, Mount Sanqingshan also boasts countless exotic flowers and rare plants. The narrow-cone Chinese Douglas-fir, the Chinese hemlock, the Yulan magnolia, the *Emmenopterys henryi*, the Chinese little-leaf box

三清山还是一座经历了1,600多年人文浸润的道教名山。尤其是按先天八卦图布局的三清宫古建筑群，被认为是中国古代道教建筑的露天博物馆。

1997年8月，美国国家公园基金会主席保罗先生慕名来三清山考察后称赞道："三清山是世界上为数极少的精品之一，是全人类的瑰宝。"

2008年7月8日，在加拿大魁北克召开的第32届世界遗产大会，将三清山列入《世界遗产名录》，三清山成为中国第七个世界自然遗产地。

and the *Magnolia fordiana* are all under first-class state protection.

In total, Mount Sanqingshan has seven scenic areas. Among them Nanqing Park in the southern area showcases the distinctive typographic features of the granite landform, which is the result of the 1.4 billion years' geological evolution and is regarded as the essence of Mount Sanqingshan's natural landscape. As visitors walk up the steps, they will feel carefree and delighted while enjoying a full range of green pines and cypresses, torrential waterfalls and springs.

Mount Sanqingshan is also renowned for having been immersed in Taoism for over 1,600 years. Sanqing Palace, an ancient Architectural Complex with a configuration based on the Eight Trigrams arranged in an Octagon, is regarded as an open-air museum of ancient Chinese Taoist architecture.

Having heard so much about Mount Sanqingshan, Mr. Paul, then the chairman of the U.S. National Park Foundation, came to conduct a study of Mount Sanqingshan in August 1997. After his visit, he stated: "Mount Sanqingshan is one of the few top landscapes in the world and a treasure for the entire human race."

On July 8, 2008, at the 32nd session of the UNESCO World Heritage Committee held in Quebec, Canada, Mount Sanqingshan National Park was inscribed to the World Heritage List, becoming China's seventh World Natural Heritage Site.